HARLEY QUINN and the BIRDS OF PREY

THE HUNT FOR HARLEY

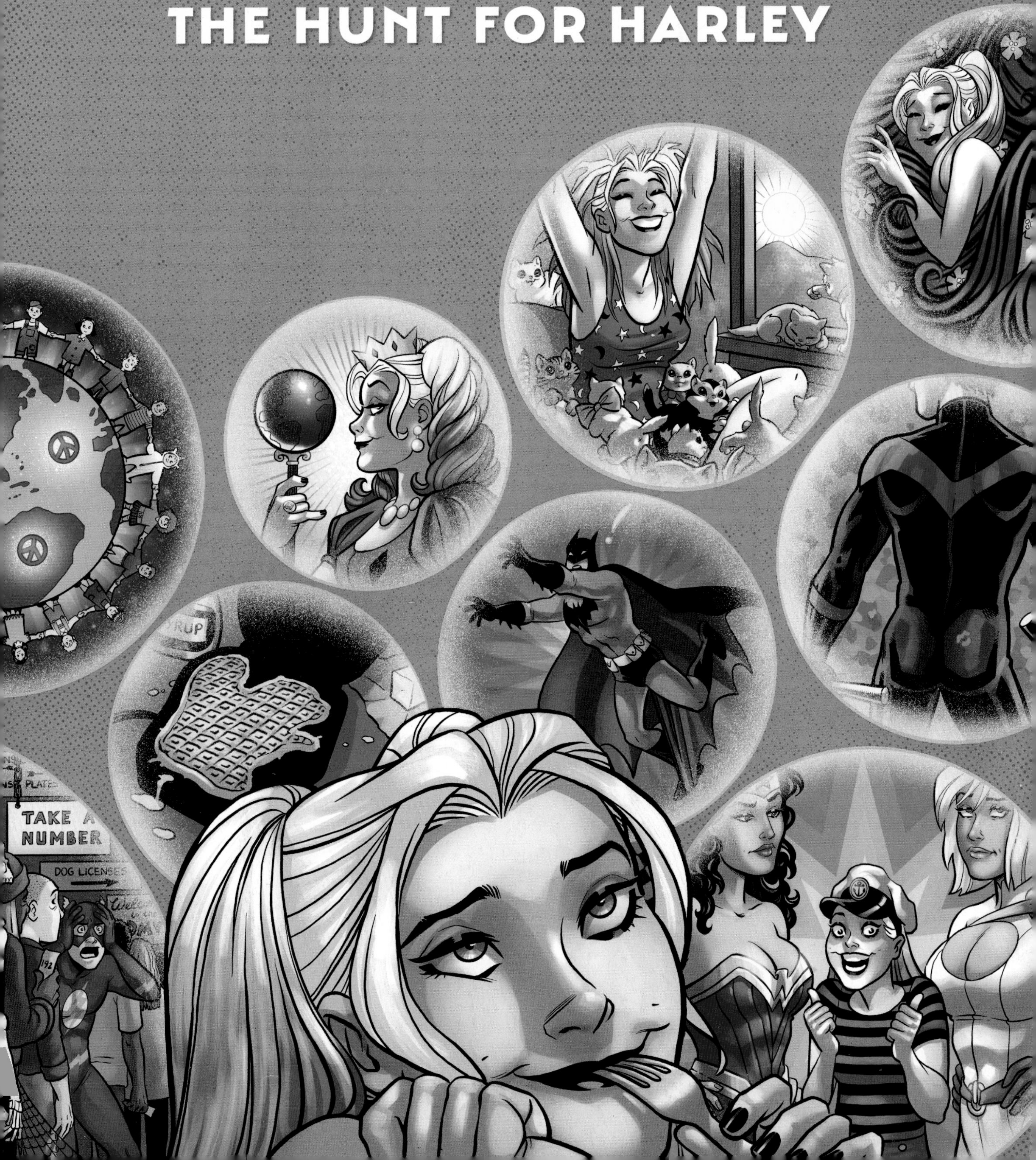
TAKE A NUMBER
DOG LICENSES

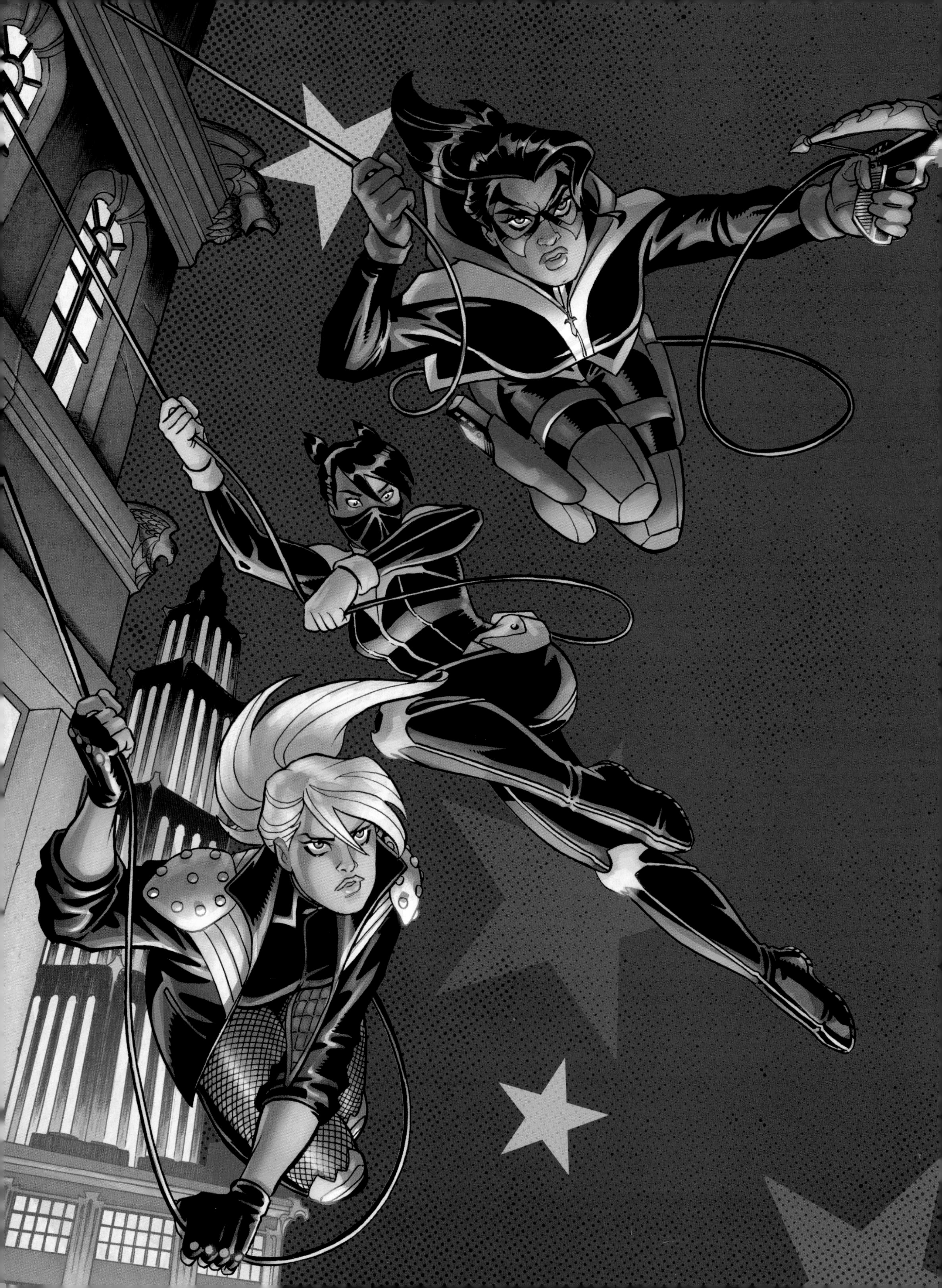

HARLEY QUINN
and the BIRDS OF PREY
THE HUNT FOR HARLEY

◆ ◆ ◆ ◆ ◆ ◆ ◆ ◆

AMANDA CONNER & JIMMY PALMIOTTI
writers

AMANDA CONNER
CHAD HARDIN
artists

ALEX SINCLAIR
PAUL MOUNTS   ENRICA EREN ANGIOLINI
colorists

JOHN J. HILL
DAVE SHARPE
letterers

AMANDA CONNER & PAUL MOUNTS
collection and issue #1 cover artists

AMANDA CONNER & ALEX SINCLAIR
issues #2-4 cover artists

HARLEY QUINN created by PAUL DINI & BRUCE TIMM

CHRIS CONROY Editor – Original Series & Collected Edition
MAGGIE HOWELL, AMEDEO TURTURRO Associate Editors – Original Series
STEVE COOK Design Director – Books
MEGEN BELLERSEN Publication Design
SUZANNAH ROWNTREE Publication Production

MARIE JAVINS Editor-in-Chief, DC Comics

DANIEL CHERRY III Senior VP – General Manager
JIM LEE Publisher & Chief Creative Officer
JOEN CHOE VP – Global Brand & Creative Services
DON FALLETTI VP – Manufacturing Operations & Workflow Management
LAWRENCE GANEM VP – Talent Services
ALISON GILL Senior VP – Manufacturing & Operations
NICK J. NAPOLITANO VP – Manufacturing Administration & Design
NANCY SPEARS VP – Revenue

HARLEY QUINN & THE BIRDS OF PREY: THE HUNT FOR HARLEY

Published by DC Comics. Compilation and all new material Copyright © 2022 DC Comics. All Rights Reserved. Originally published in single magazine form in *Harley Quinn & the Birds of Prey* 1-4 and online as *Harley Quinn Black + White + Red* 12. Copyright © 2020, 2021 DC Comics. All Rights Reserved. All characters, their distinctive likenesses, and related elements featured in this publication are trademarks of DC Comics. The stories, characters, and incidents featured in this publication are entirely fictional. DC Comics does not read or accept unsolicited submissions of ideas, stories, or artwork. DC – a WarnerMedia Company.

DC Comics, 2900 West Alameda Ave., Burbank, CA 91505
Printed by Transcontinental Interglobe, Beauceville, QC, Canada. 1/21/22. First Printing.
ISBN: 978-1-77951-504-9

Library of Congress Cataloging-in-Publication Data is available.

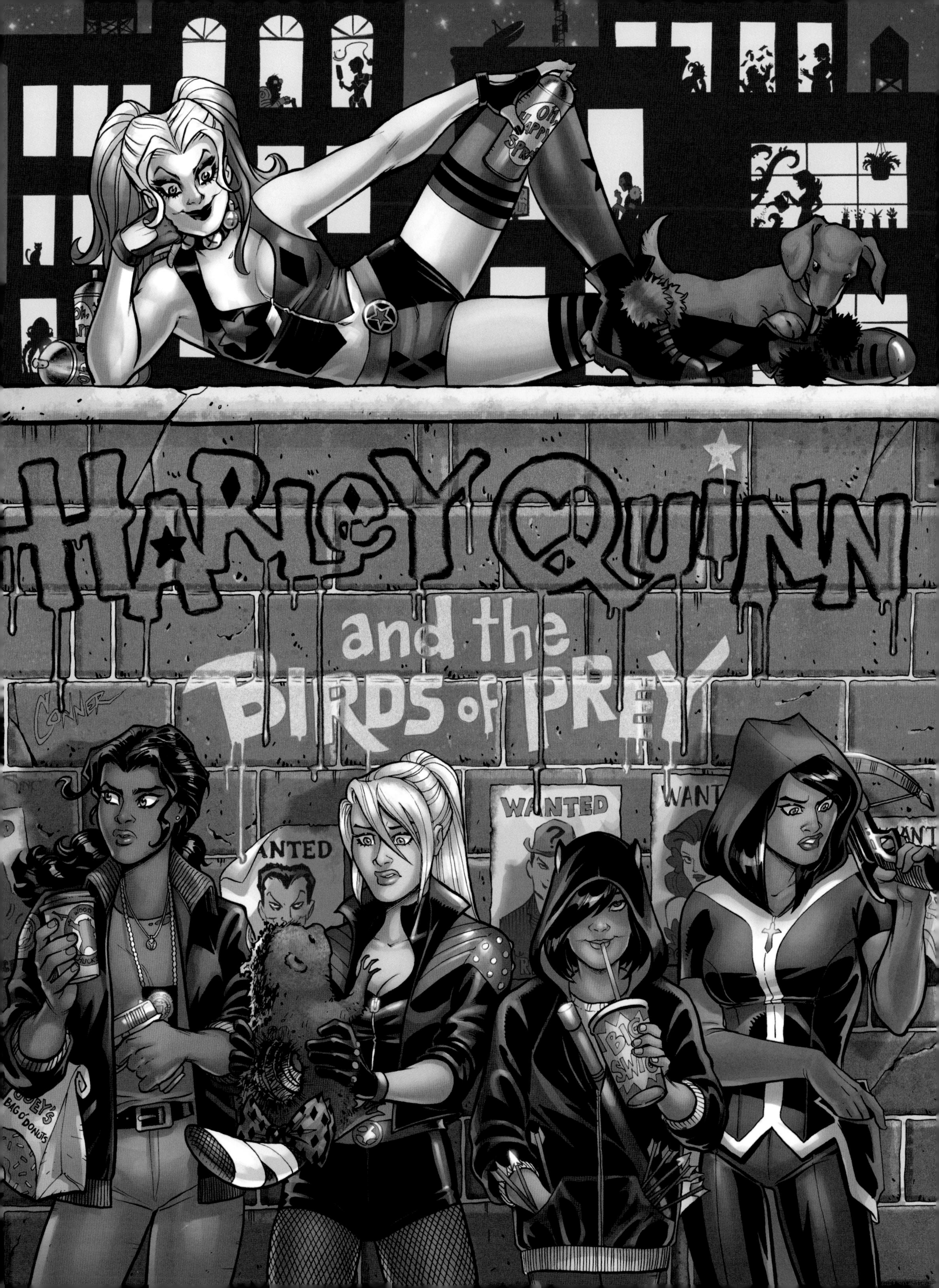
HARLEY QUINN
and the
BIRDS of PREY
CONNER
WANTED
BIG SWIG

BOOK ONE
NO SLEEP TILL...GOTHAM!

"I got some PERSONAL BUSINESS that needs my attention..."

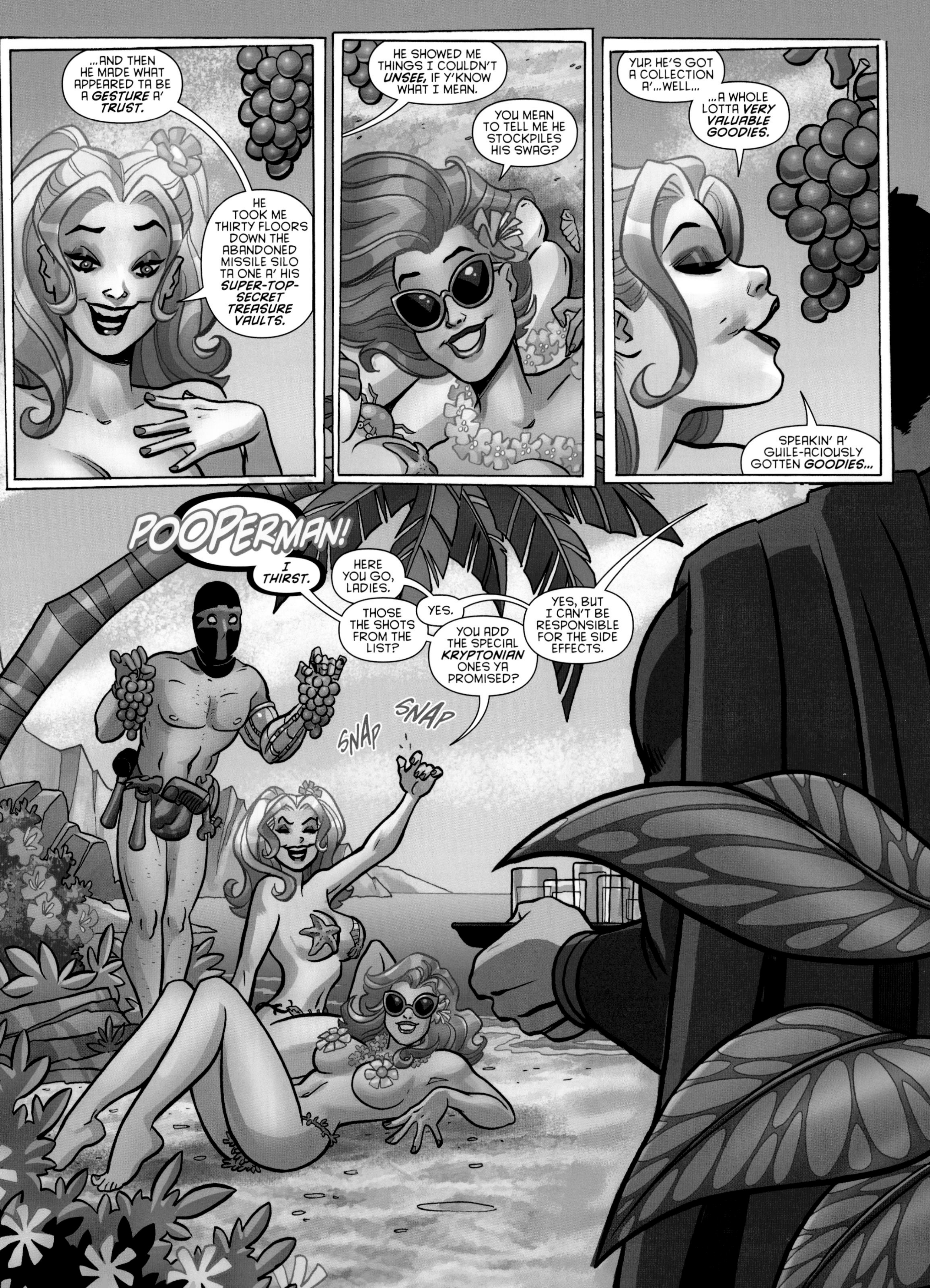
...AND THEN HE MADE WHAT APPEARED TA BE A GESTURE A' TRUST.
HE TOOK ME THIRTY FLOORS DOWN THE ABANDONED MISSILE SILO TA ONE A' HIS SUPER-TOP-SECRET TREASURE VAULTS.
HE SHOWED ME THINGS I COULDN'T UNSEE, IF Y'KNOW WHAT I MEAN.
YOU MEAN TO TELL ME HE STOCKPILES HIS SWAG?
YUP. HE'S GOT A COLLECTION A'...WELL...
...A WHOLE LOTTA VERY VALUABLE GOODIES.
SPEAKIN' A' GUILE-ACIOUSLY GOTTEN GOODIES...
POOPERMAN!
I THIRST.
HERE YOU GO, LADIES.
THOSE THE SHOTS FROM THE LIST?
YES.
YOU ADD THE SPECIAL KRYPTONIAN ONES YA PROMISED?
YES, BUT I CAN'T BE RESPONSIBLE FOR THE SIDE EFFECTS.
SNAP
SNAP

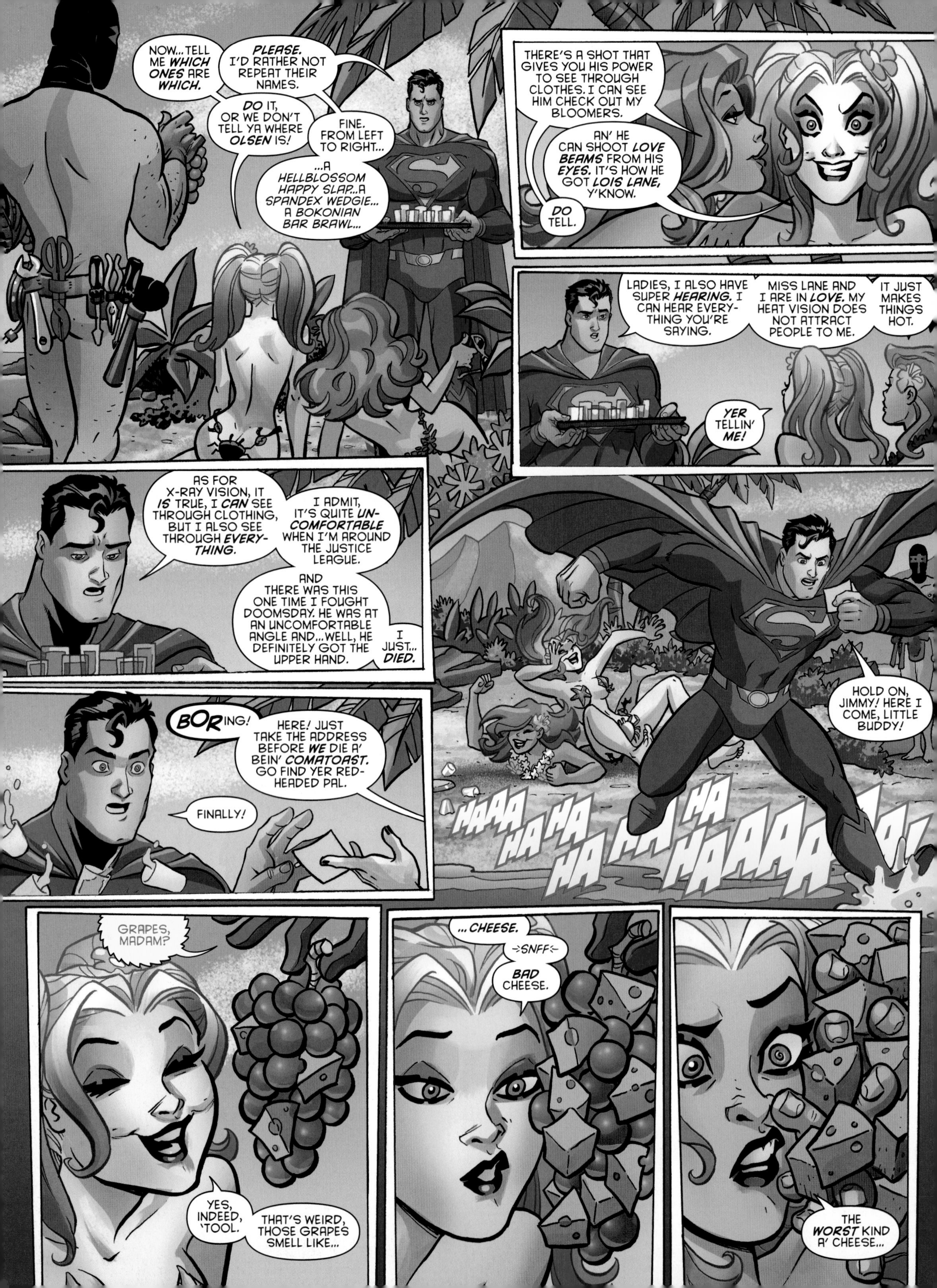
NOW... TELL ME WHICH ONES ARE WHICH.
PLEASE. I'D RATHER NOT REPEAT THEIR NAMES.
DO IT, OR WE DON'T TELL YA WHERE OLSEN IS!
FINE. FROM LEFT TO RIGHT...
...A HELLBLOSSOM HAPPY SLAP...A SPANDEX WEDGIE... A BOKONIAN BAR BRAWL...
THERE'S A SHOT THAT GIVES YOU HIS POWER TO SEE THROUGH CLOTHES. I CAN SEE HIM CHECK OUT MY BLOOMERS.
AN' HE CAN SHOOT LOVE BEAMS FROM HIS EYES. IT'S HOW HE GOT LOIS LANE, Y'KNOW.
DO TELL.
LADIES, I ALSO HAVE SUPER HEARING. I CAN HEAR EVERYTHING YOU'RE SAYING.
MISS LANE AND I ARE IN LOVE. MY HEAT VISION DOES NOT ATTRACT PEOPLE TO ME.
IT JUST MAKES THINGS HOT.
YER TELLIN' ME!
AS FOR X-RAY VISION, IT IS TRUE, I CAN SEE THROUGH CLOTHING, BUT I ALSO SEE THROUGH EVERYTHING.
I ADMIT, IT'S QUITE UNCOMFORTABLE WHEN I'M AROUND THE JUSTICE LEAGUE.
AND THERE WAS THIS ONE TIME I FOUGHT DOOMSDAY. HE WAS AT AN UNCOMFORTABLE ANGLE AND...WELL, HE DEFINITELY GOT THE UPPER HAND.
I JUST... DIED.
BORING!
HERE! JUST TAKE THE ADDRESS BEFORE WE DIE A' BEIN' COMATOAST. GO FIND YER RED-HEADED PAL.
FINALLY!
HOLD ON, JIMMY! HERE I COME, LITTLE BUDDY!
HAAA HA HA HA HA HA HAAAAA!
GRAPES, MADAM?
YES, INDEED, 'TOOL.
THAT'S WEIRD, THOSE GRAPES SMELL LIKE...
...CHEESE.
SNFF
BAD CHEESE.
THE WORST KIND A' CHEESE...

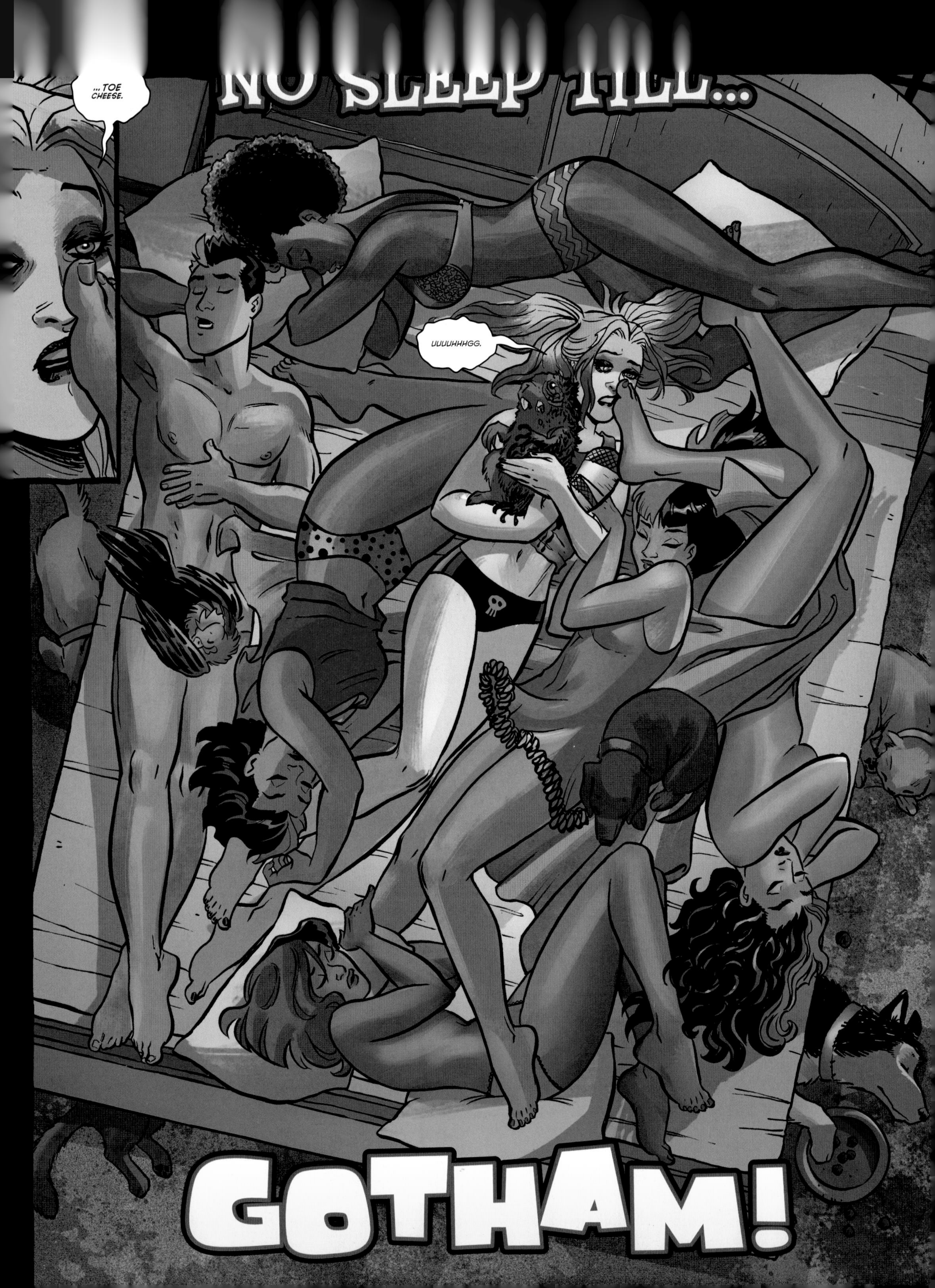
NO SLEEP TILL...
... TOE CHEESE.
UUUUHHHGG.
GOTHAM!

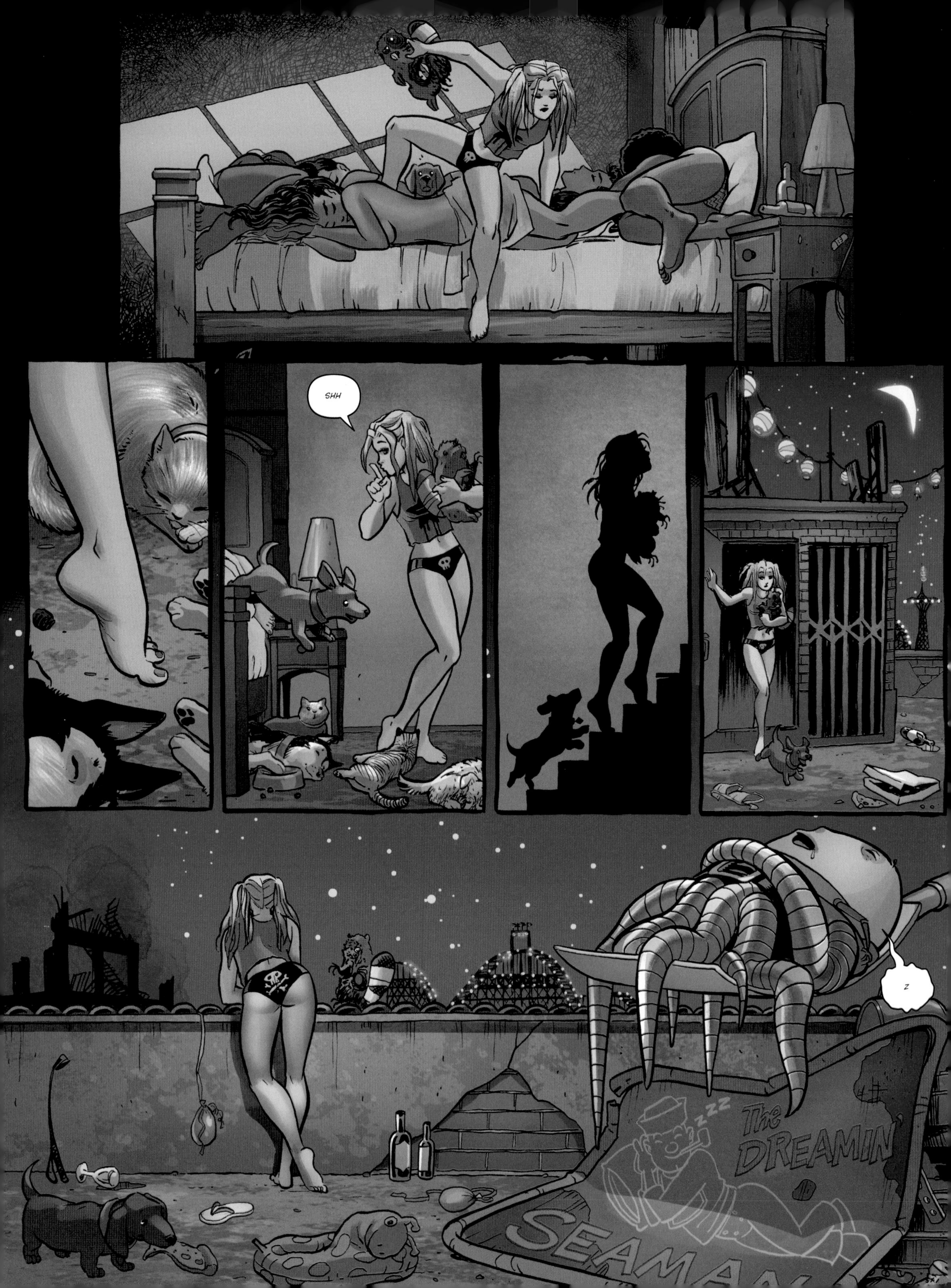
SHH
Z
The DREAMIN'
SEAMA
ZZZ

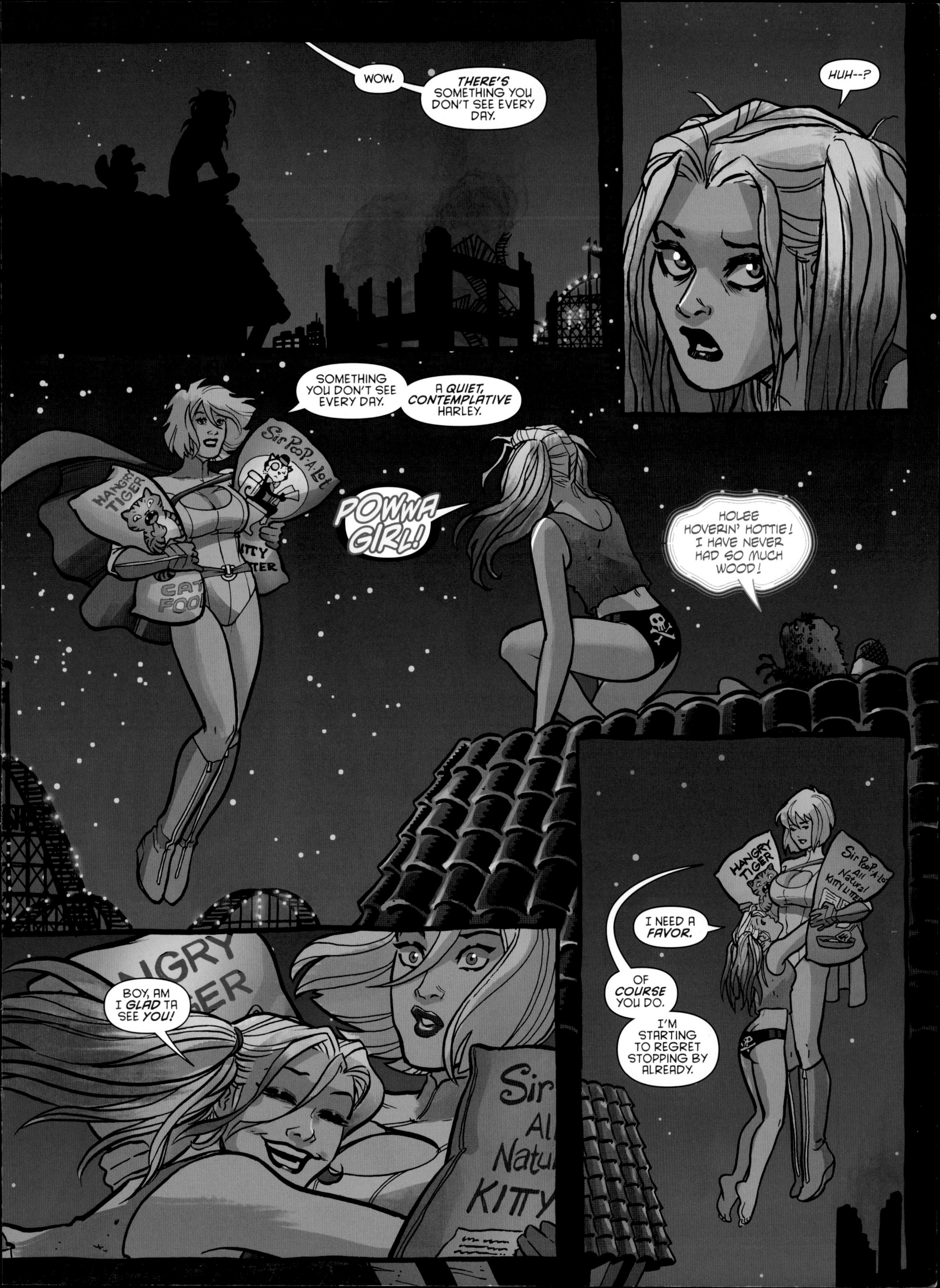
WOW.
THERE'S SOMETHING YOU DON'T SEE EVERY DAY.
HUH--?
SOMETHING YOU DON'T SEE EVERY DAY.
A QUIET, CONTEMPLATIVE HARLEY.
Sir PooP-A-Lot
HANGRY TIGER
KITTY LITTER
CAT FOOD
POWWA GIRL!
HOLEE HOVERIN' HOTTIE! I HAVE NEVER HAD SO MUCH WOOD!
BOY, AM I GLAD TA SEE YOU!
I NEED A FAVOR.
OF COURSE YOU DO.
I'M STARTING TO REGRET STOPPING BY ALREADY.

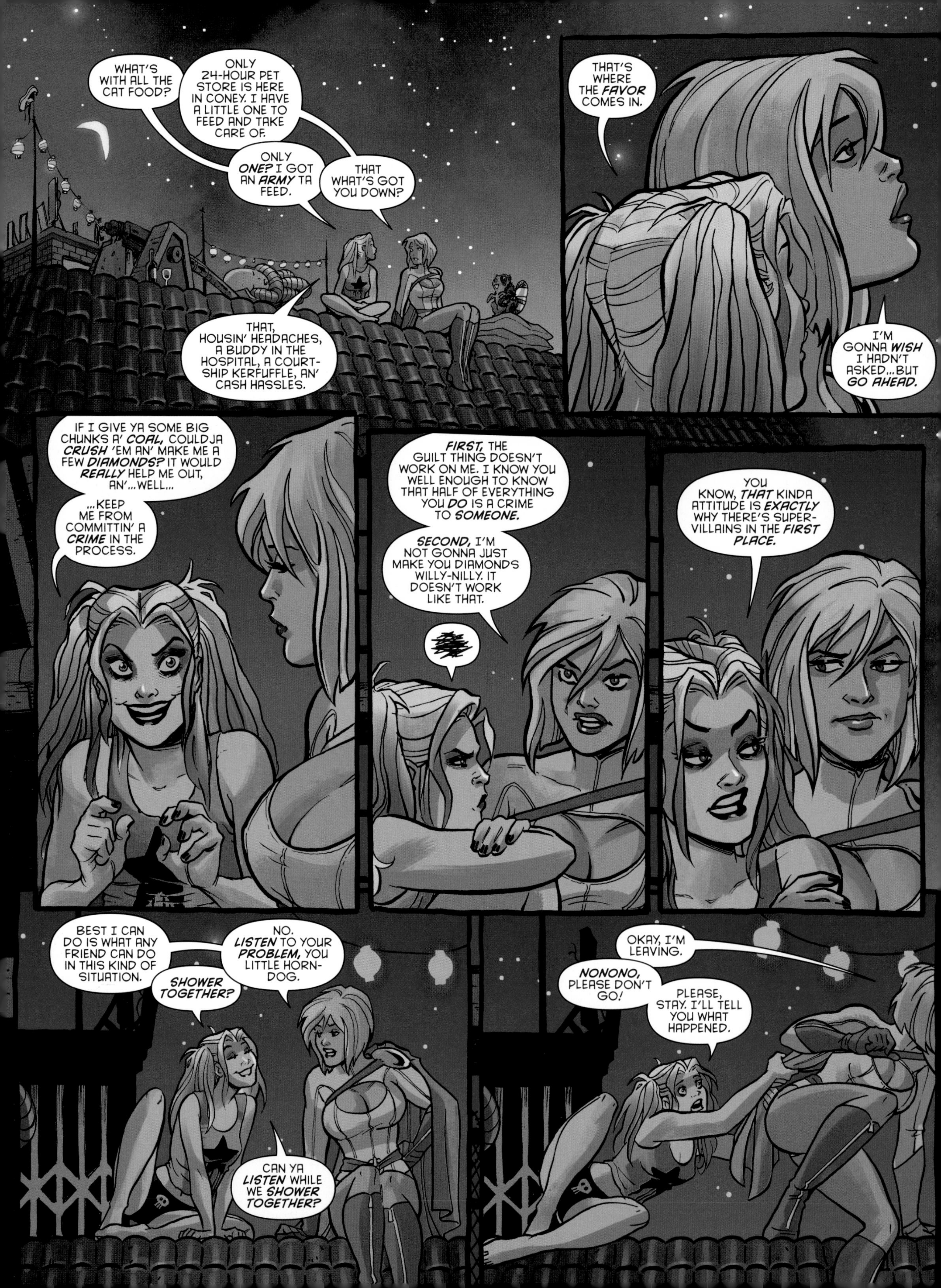
WHAT'S WITH ALL THE CAT FOOD?
ONLY 24-HOUR PET STORE IS HERE IN CONEY. I HAVE A LITTLE ONE TO FEED AND TAKE CARE OF.
ONLY ONE? I GOT AN ARMY TA FEED.
THAT WHAT'S GOT YOU DOWN?
THAT, HOUSIN' HEADACHES, A BUDDY IN THE HOSPITAL, A COURTSHIP KERFUFFLE, AN' CASH HASSLES.
THAT'S WHERE THE FAVOR COMES IN.
I'M GONNA WISH I HADN'T ASKED...BUT GO AHEAD.
IF I GIVE YA SOME BIG CHUNKS A' COAL, COULDJA CRUSH 'EM AN' MAKE ME A FEW DIAMONDS? IT WOULD REALLY HELP ME OUT, AN'...WELL...
...KEEP ME FROM COMMITTIN' A CRIME IN THE PROCESS.
FIRST, THE GUILT THING DOESN'T WORK ON ME. I KNOW YOU WELL ENOUGH TO KNOW THAT HALF OF EVERYTHING YOU DO IS A CRIME TO SOMEONE.
SECOND, I'M NOT GONNA JUST MAKE YOU DIAMONDS WILLY-NILLY. IT DOESN'T WORK LIKE THAT.
YOU KNOW, THAT KINDA ATTITUDE IS EXACTLY WHY THERE'S SUPER-VILLAINS IN THE FIRST PLACE.
BEST I CAN DO IS WHAT ANY FRIEND CAN DO IN THIS KIND OF SITUATION.
SHOWER TOGETHER?
NO. LISTEN TO YOUR PROBLEM, YOU LITTLE HORN-DOG.
CAN YA LISTEN WHILE WE SHOWER TOGETHER?
OKAY, I'M LEAVING.
NONONO, PLEASE DON'T GO!
PLEASE, STAY. I'LL TELL YOU WHAT HAPPENED.

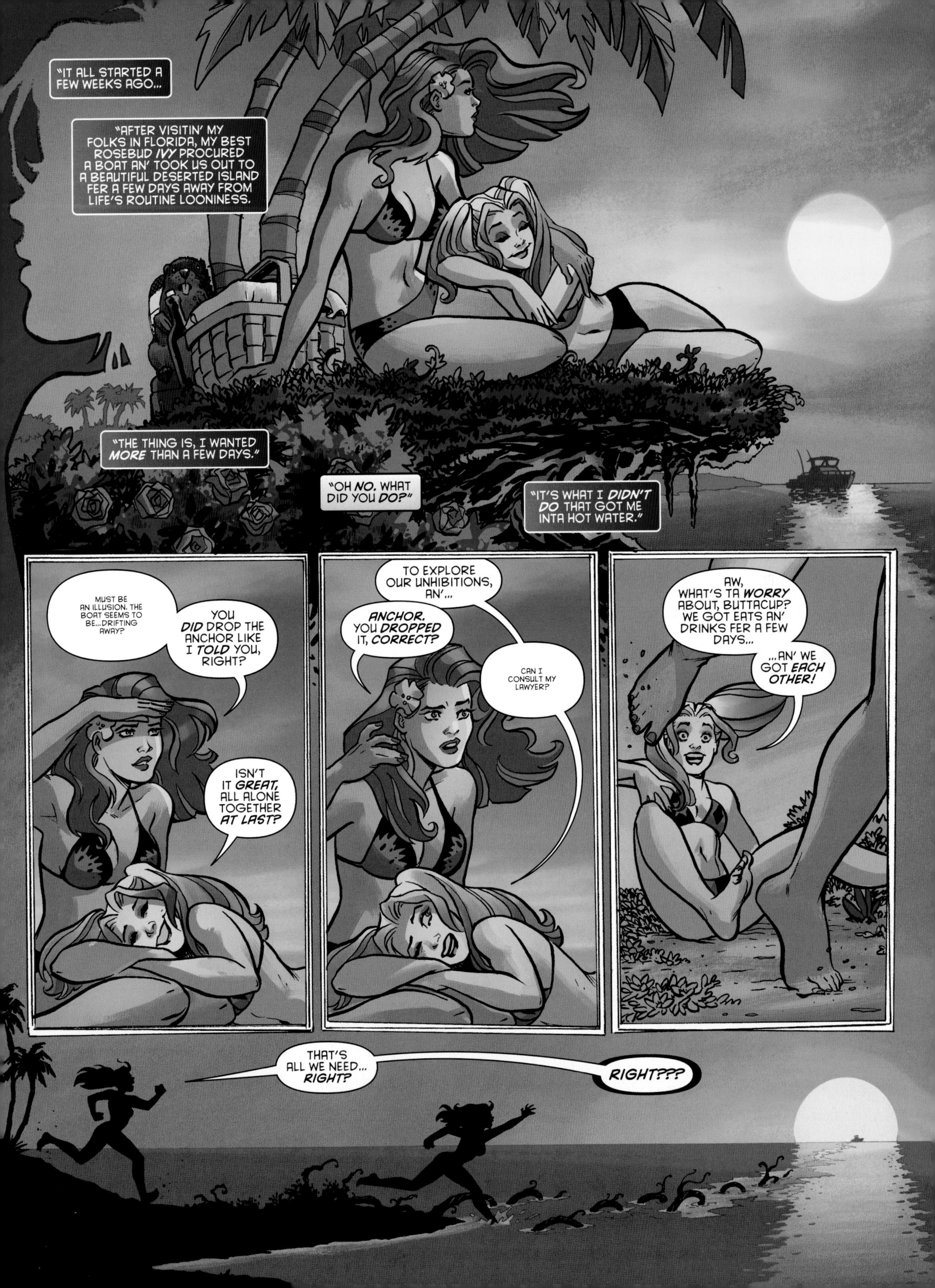
"IT ALL STARTED A FEW WEEKS AGO...
"AFTER VISITIN' MY FOLKS IN FLORIDA, MY BEST ROSEBUD IVY PROCURED A BOAT AN' TOOK US OUT TO A BEAUTIFUL DESERTED ISLAND FER A FEW DAYS AWAY FROM LIFE'S ROUTINE LOONINESS.
"THE THING IS, I WANTED MORE THAN A FEW DAYS."
"OH NO. WHAT DID YOU DO?"
"IT'S WHAT I DIDN'T DO THAT GOT ME INTA HOT WATER."
MUST BE AN ILLUSION. THE BOAT SEEMS TO BE...DRIFTING AWAY?
YOU DID DROP THE ANCHOR LIKE I TOLD YOU, RIGHT?
ISN'T IT GREAT, ALL ALONE TOGETHER AT LAST?
TO EXPLORE OUR UNHIBITIONS, AN'...
ANCHOR. YOU DROPPED IT, CORRECT?
CAN I CONSULT MY LAWYER?
AW, WHAT'S TA WORRY ABOUT, BUTTACUP? WE GOT EATS AN' DRINKS FER A FEW DAYS...
...AN' WE GOT EACH OTHER!
THAT'S ALL WE NEED... RIGHT?
RIGHT???

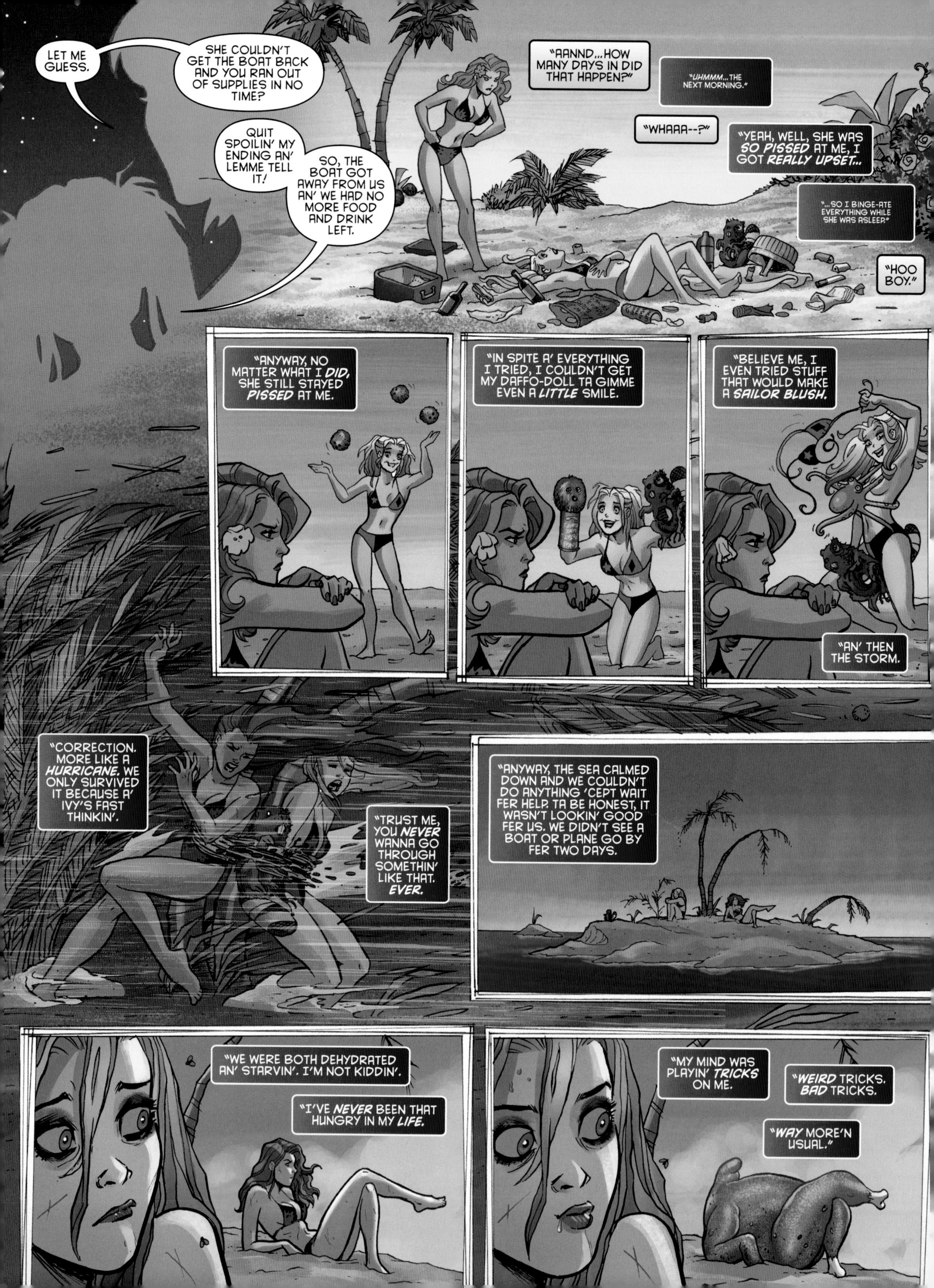
LET ME GUESS.
SHE COULDN'T GET THE BOAT BACK AND YOU RAN OUT OF SUPPLIES IN NO TIME?
QUIT SPOILIN' MY ENDING AN' LEMME TELL IT!
SO, THE BOAT GOT AWAY FROM US AN' WE HAD NO MORE FOOD AND DRINK LEFT.
"AANND...HOW MANY DAYS IN DID THAT HAPPEN?"
"UHMMM...THE NEXT MORNING."
"WHAAA--?"
"YEAH, WELL, SHE WAS SO PISSED AT ME, I GOT REALLY UPSET...
"...SO I BINGE-ATE EVERYTHING WHILE SHE WAS ASLEEP."
"HOO BOY."
"ANYWAY, NO MATTER WHAT I DID, SHE STILL STAYED PISSED AT ME.
"IN SPITE A' EVERYTHING I TRIED, I COULDN'T GET MY DAFFO-DOLL TA GIMME EVEN A LITTLE SMILE.
"BELIEVE ME, I EVEN TRIED STUFF THAT WOULD MAKE A SAILOR BLUSH.
"AN' THEN THE STORM.
"CORRECTION. MORE LIKE A HURRICANE. WE ONLY SURVIVED IT BECAUSE A' IVY'S FAST THINKIN'.
"TRUST ME, YOU NEVER WANNA GO THROUGH SOMETHIN' LIKE THAT. EVER.
"ANYWAY, THE SEA CALMED DOWN AND WE COULDN'T DO ANYTHING 'CEPT WAIT FER HELP. TA BE HONEST, IT WASN'T LOOKIN' GOOD FER US. WE DIDN'T SEE A BOAT OR PLANE GO BY FER TWO DAYS.
"WE WERE BOTH DEHYDRATED AN' STARVIN'. I'M NOT KIDDIN'.
"I'VE NEVER BEEN THAT HUNGRY IN MY LIFE.
"MY MIND WAS PLAYIN' TRICKS ON ME.
"WEIRD TRICKS. BAD TRICKS.
"WAY MORE'N USUAL."

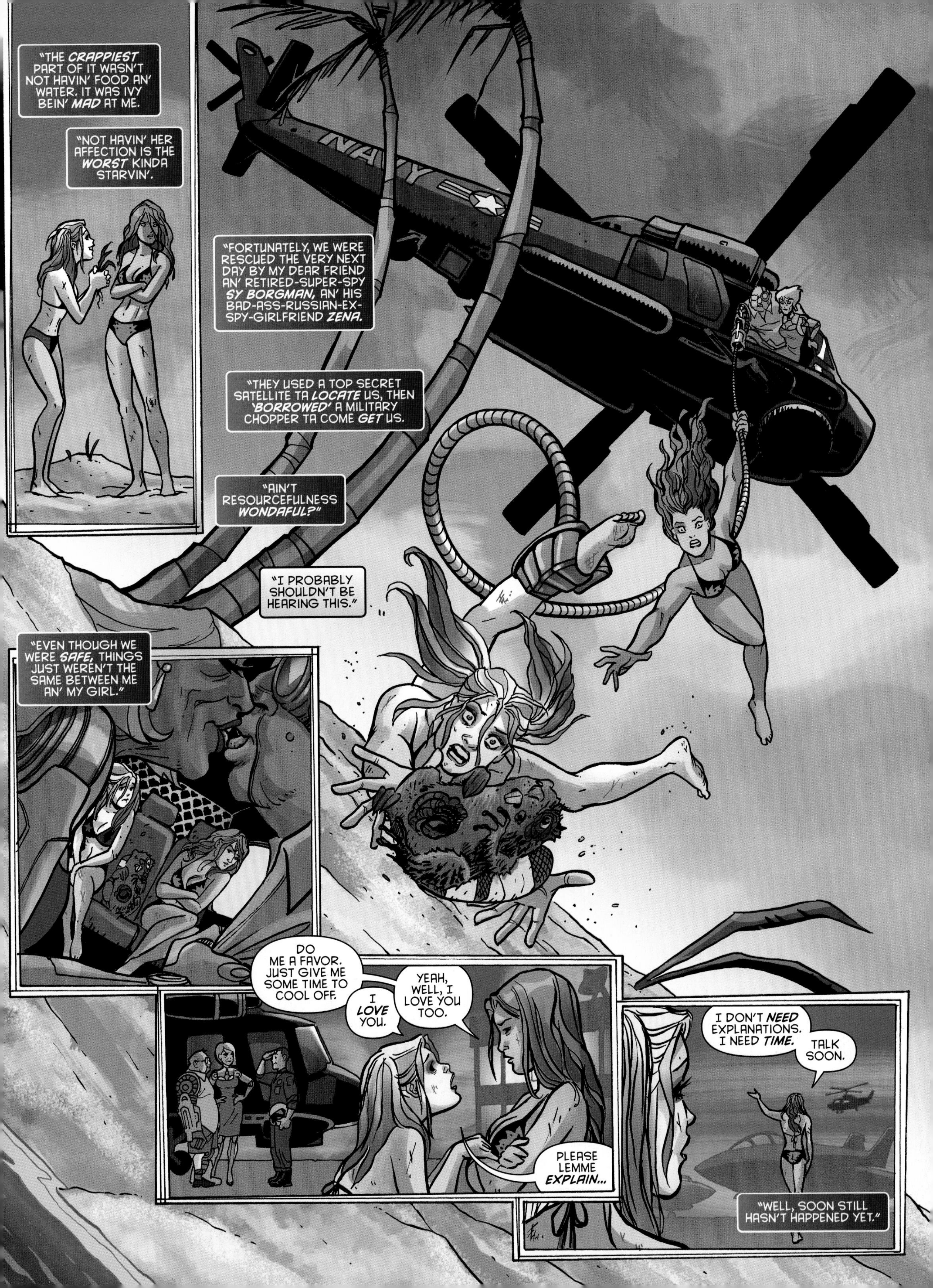
"THE CRAPPIEST PART OF IT WASN'T NOT HAVIN' FOOD AN' WATER. IT WAS IVY BEIN' MAD AT ME.
"NOT HAVIN' HER AFFECTION IS THE WORST KINDA STARVIN'.
NAVY
"FORTUNATELY, WE WERE RESCUED THE VERY NEXT DAY BY MY DEAR FRIEND AN' RETIRED-SUPER-SPY SY BORGMAN, AN' HIS BAD-ASS-RUSSIAN-EX-SPY-GIRLFRIEND ZENA.
"THEY USED A TOP SECRET SATELLITE TA LOCATE US, THEN 'BORROWED' A MILITARY CHOPPER TA COME GET US.
"AIN'T RESOURCEFULNESS WONDAFUL?"
"I PROBABLY SHOULDN'T BE HEARING THIS."
"EVEN THOUGH WE WERE SAFE, THINGS JUST WEREN'T THE SAME BETWEEN ME AN' MY GIRL."
DO ME A FAVOR. JUST GIVE ME SOME TIME TO COOL OFF.
I LOVE YOU.
YEAH, WELL, I LOVE YOU TOO.
PLEASE LEMME EXPLAIN...
I DON'T NEED EXPLANATIONS. I NEED TIME.
TALK SOON.
"WELL, SOON STILL HASN'T HAPPENED YET."

IVY MAD AT ME IS MISERABLE ENOUGH, BUT *HERE*...

...HERE I *REALLY* SCREWED UP, AN' MY FRIENDS GOT HURT. I DIDN'T KEEP UP WITH THE MORTGAGE ON THE DREAMIN' SEAMAN HOTEL. MY RIGHT-HAND MAN *TONY* TOOK THE *BRUNT* A' THAT MISTAKE.

WHAT *HAPPENED?* DID YOU HAVE TO PAY *PENALTIES* ON THE LOAN?

I THINK THAT ONLY HAPPENS WHEN YA GET A MORTGAGE FROM A *LEGITIMATE* COMPANY, BUT I COULDN'T GET ONE FER THE HOTEL, SO I WENT TA...

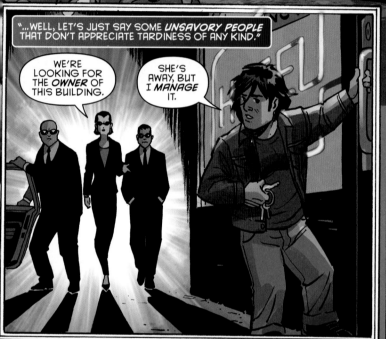

"...WELL, LET'S JUST SAY SOME *UNSAVORY PEOPLE* THAT DON'T APPRECIATE TARDINESS OF ANY KIND."

WE'RE LOOKING FOR THE *OWNER* OF THIS BUILDING.

SHE'S AWAY, BUT I *MANAGE* IT.

CAN I HELP YOU?

WE'RE WITH THE *DEFEO MORTGAGE COMPANY.*

SEEMS YOU AND YOUR BOSS HAVEN'T PAID YOUR MORTGAGE IN A WHILE.

THAT'S *UNACCEPTABLE.*

"NEEDLESS TA SAY, THEY MADE AN *EXAMPLE* OUTTA MY POOR TONY."

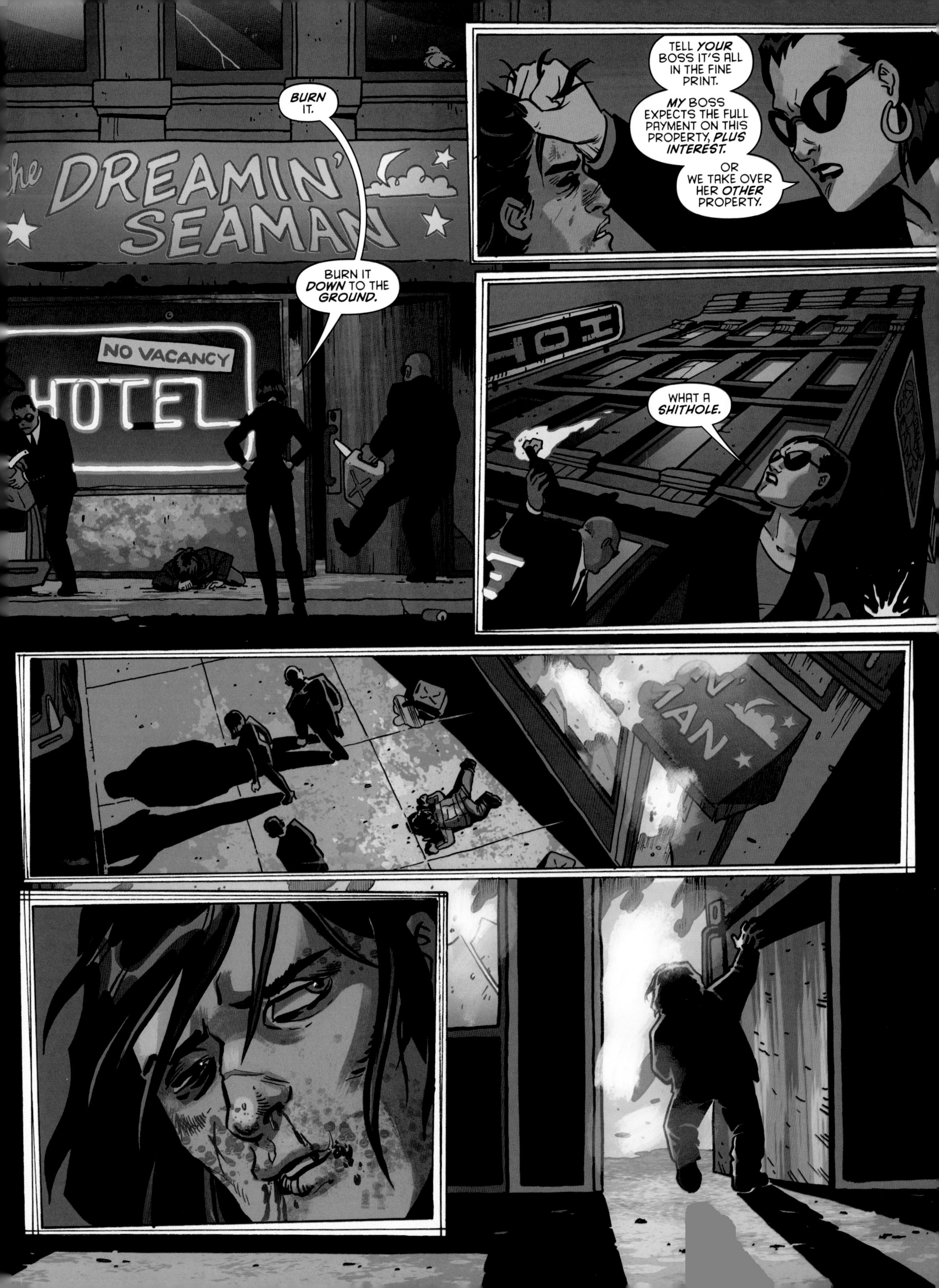
the DREAMIN' SEAMAN
NO VACANCY
HOTEL
BURN IT.
BURN IT DOWN TO THE GROUND.
TELL YOUR BOSS IT'S ALL IN THE FINE PRINT.
MY BOSS EXPECTS THE FULL PAYMENT ON THIS PROPERTY, PLUS INTEREST.
OR WE TAKE OVER HER OTHER PROPERTY.
WHAT A SHITHOLE.

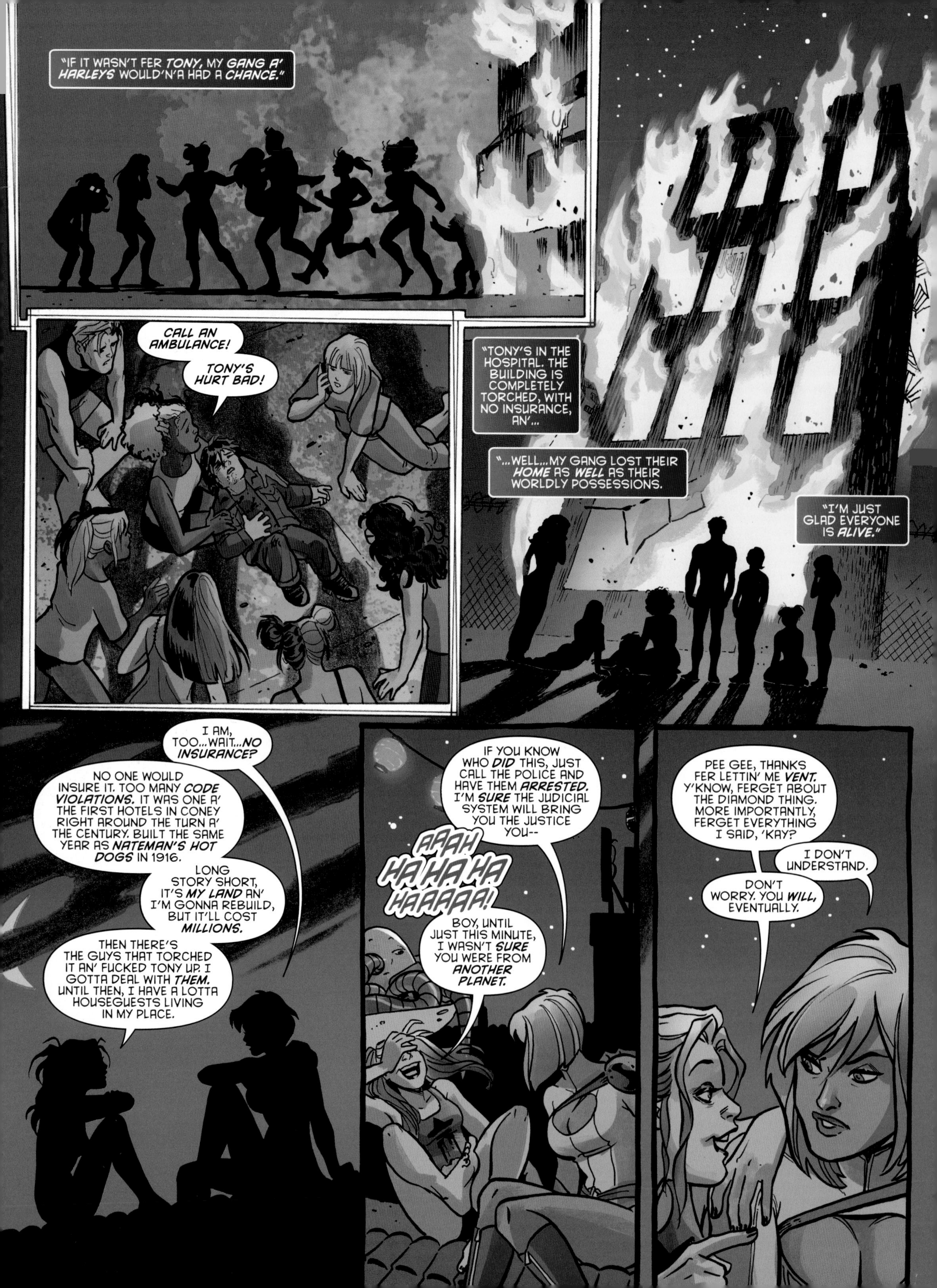
"IF IT WASN'T FER TONY, MY GANG A' HARLEYS WOULD'N'A HAD A CHANCE."
CALL AN AMBULANCE!
TONY'S HURT BAD!
"TONY'S IN THE HOSPITAL. THE BUILDING IS COMPLETELY TORCHED, WITH NO INSURANCE, AN'...
"...WELL...MY GANG LOST THEIR HOME AS WELL AS THEIR WORLDLY POSSESSIONS.
"I'M JUST GLAD EVERYONE IS ALIVE."
I AM, TOO...WAIT...NO INSURANCE?
NO ONE WOULD INSURE IT. TOO MANY CODE VIOLATIONS. IT WAS ONE A' THE FIRST HOTELS IN CONEY RIGHT AROUND THE TURN A' THE CENTURY. BUILT THE SAME YEAR AS NATEMAN'S HOT DOGS IN 1916.
LONG STORY SHORT, IT'S MY LAND AN' I'M GONNA REBUILD, BUT IT'LL COST MILLIONS.
THEN THERE'S THE GUYS THAT TORCHED IT AN' FUCKED TONY UP. I GOTTA DEAL WITH THEM. UNTIL THEN, I HAVE A LOTTA HOUSEGUESTS LIVING IN MY PLACE.
IF YOU KNOW WHO DID THIS, JUST CALL THE POLICE AND HAVE THEM ARRESTED. I'M SURE THE JUDICIAL SYSTEM WILL BRING YOU THE JUSTICE YOU--
AAAH HA HA HA HAAAAA!
BOY, UNTIL JUST THIS MINUTE, I WASN'T SURE YOU WERE FROM ANOTHER PLANET.
PEE GEE, THANKS FER LETTIN' ME VENT. Y'KNOW, FERGET ABOUT THE DIAMOND THING. MORE IMPORTANTLY, FERGET EVERYTHING I SAID, 'KAY?
I DON'T UNDERSTAND.
DON'T WORRY. YOU WILL, EVENTUALLY.

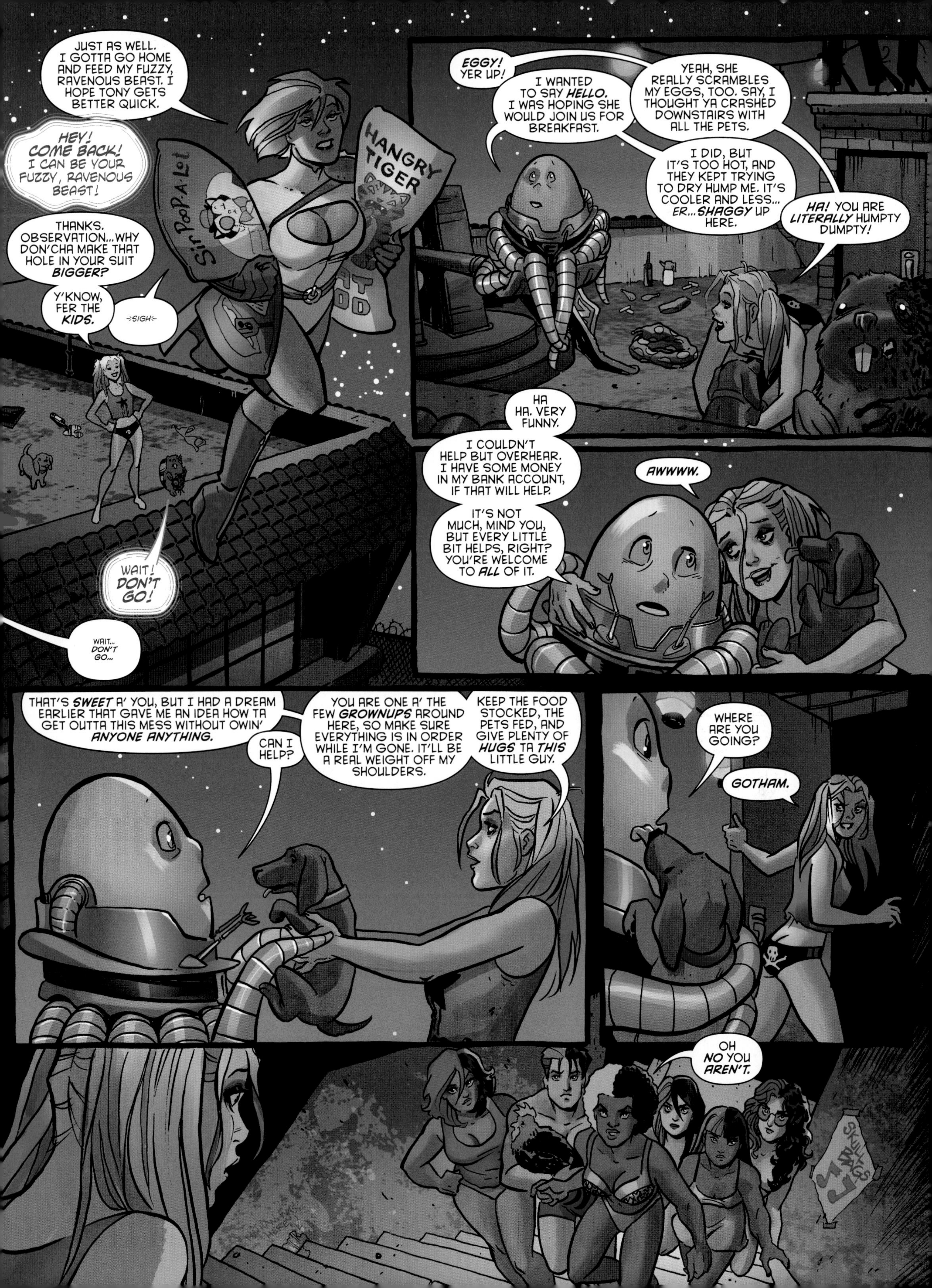
JUST AS WELL. I GOTTA GO HOME AND FEED MY FUZZY, RAVENOUS BEAST. I HOPE TONY GETS BETTER QUICK.
HEY! COME BACK! I CAN BE YOUR FUZZY, RAVENOUS BEAST!
THANKS. OBSERVATION...WHY DON'CHA MAKE THAT HOLE IN YOUR SUIT BIGGER?
Y'KNOW, FER THE KIDS.
SIGH
HANGRY TIGER
Sir Poop-A-Lot
WAIT! DON'T GO!
WAIT... DON'T GO...
EGGY! YER UP!
I WANTED TO SAY HELLO. I WAS HOPING SHE WOULD JOIN US FOR BREAKFAST.
YEAH, SHE REALLY SCRAMBLES MY EGGS, TOO. SAY, I THOUGHT YA CRASHED DOWNSTAIRS WITH ALL THE PETS.
I DID, BUT IT'S TOO HOT, AND THEY KEPT TRYING TO DRY HUMP ME. IT'S COOLER AND LESS... ER...SHAGGY UP HERE.
HA! YOU ARE LITERALLY HUMPTY DUMPTY!
HA HA. VERY FUNNY.
I COULDN'T HELP BUT OVERHEAR. I HAVE SOME MONEY IN MY BANK ACCOUNT, IF THAT WILL HELP.
IT'S NOT MUCH, MIND YOU, BUT EVERY LITTLE BIT HELPS, RIGHT? YOU'RE WELCOME TO ALL OF IT.
AWWWW.
THAT'S SWEET A' YOU, BUT I HAD A DREAM EARLIER THAT GAVE ME AN IDEA HOW TA GET OUTTA THIS MESS WITHOUT OWIN' ANYONE ANYTHING.
CAN I HELP?
YOU ARE ONE A' THE FEW GROWNUPS AROUND HERE, SO MAKE SURE EVERYTHING IS IN ORDER WHILE I'M GONE. IT'LL BE A REAL WEIGHT OFF MY SHOULDERS.
KEEP THE FOOD STOCKED, THE PETS FED, AND GIVE PLENTY OF HUGS TA THIS LITTLE GUY.
WHERE ARE YOU GOING?
GOTHAM.
OH NO YOU AREN'T.

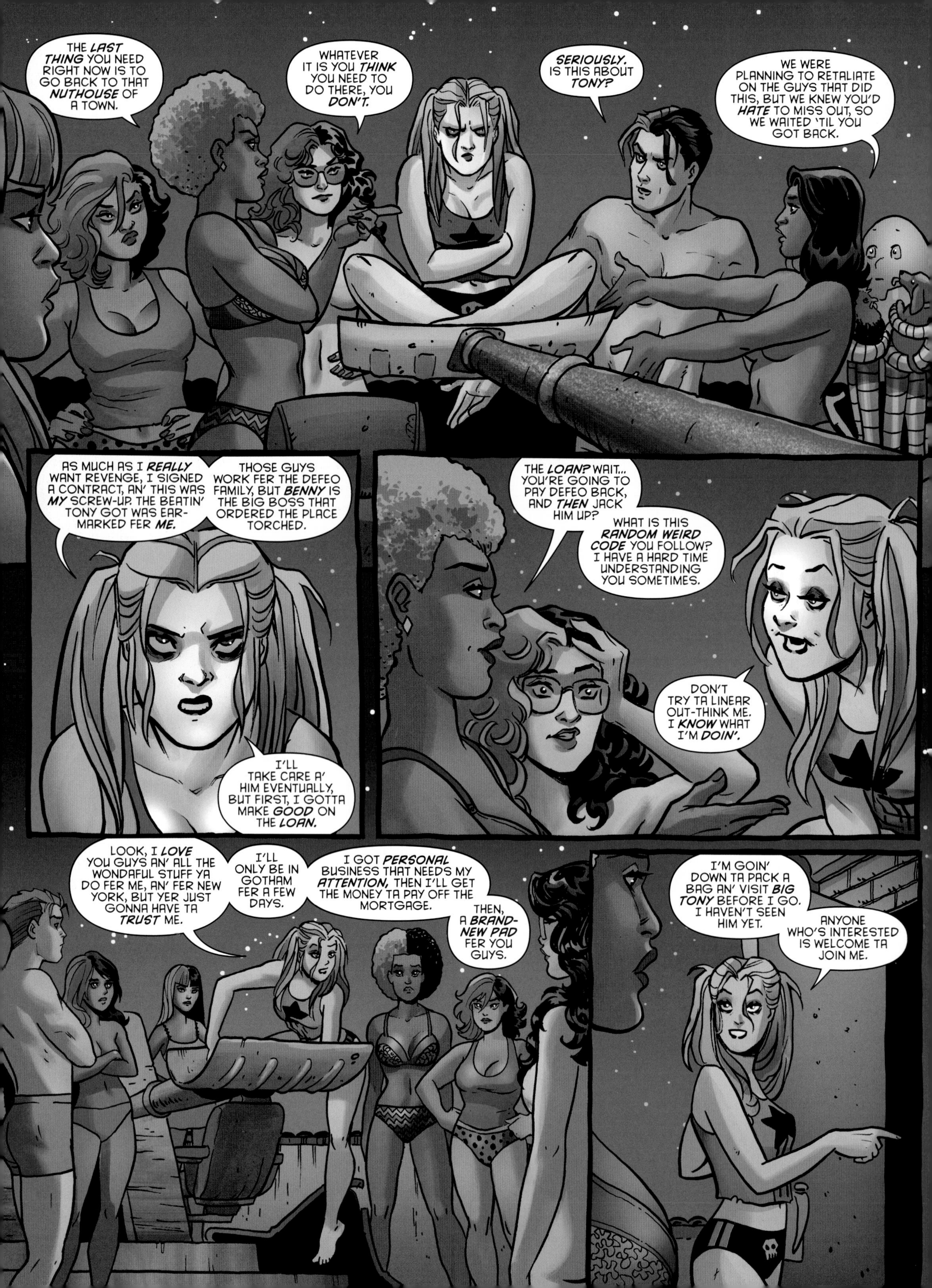
THE LAST THING YOU NEED RIGHT NOW IS TO GO BACK TO THAT NUTHOUSE OF A TOWN.
WHATEVER IT IS YOU THINK YOU NEED TO DO THERE, YOU DON'T.
SERIOUSLY. IS THIS ABOUT TONY?
WE WERE PLANNING TO RETALIATE ON THE GUYS THAT DID THIS, BUT WE KNEW YOU'D HATE TO MISS OUT, SO WE WAITED 'TIL YOU GOT BACK.
AS MUCH AS I REALLY WANT REVENGE, I SIGNED A CONTRACT, AN' THIS WAS MY SCREW-UP. THE BEATIN' TONY GOT WAS EAR-MARKED FER ME.
THOSE GUYS WORK FER THE DEFEO FAMILY, BUT BENNY IS THE BIG BOSS THAT ORDERED THE PLACE TORCHED.
I'LL TAKE CARE A' HIM EVENTUALLY, BUT FIRST, I GOTTA MAKE GOOD ON THE LOAN.
THE LOAN? WAIT... YOU'RE GOING TO PAY DEFEO BACK, AND THEN JACK HIM UP?
WHAT IS THIS RANDOM WEIRD CODE YOU FOLLOW? I HAVE A HARD TIME UNDERSTANDING YOU SOMETIMES.
DON'T TRY TA LINEAR OUT-THINK ME. I KNOW WHAT I'M DOIN'.
LOOK, I LOVE YOU GUYS AN' ALL THE WONDAFUL STUFF YA DO FER ME, AN' FER NEW YORK, BUT YER JUST GONNA HAVE TA TRUST ME.
I'LL ONLY BE IN GOTHAM FER A FEW DAYS.
I GOT PERSONAL BUSINESS THAT NEEDS MY ATTENTION, THEN I'LL GET THE MONEY TA PAY OFF THE MORTGAGE.
THEN, A BRAND-NEW PAD FER YOU GUYS.
I'M GOIN' DOWN TA PACK A BAG AN' VISIT BIG TONY BEFORE I GO. I HAVEN'T SEEN HIM YET.
ANYONE WHO'S INTERESTED IS WELCOME TA JOIN ME.

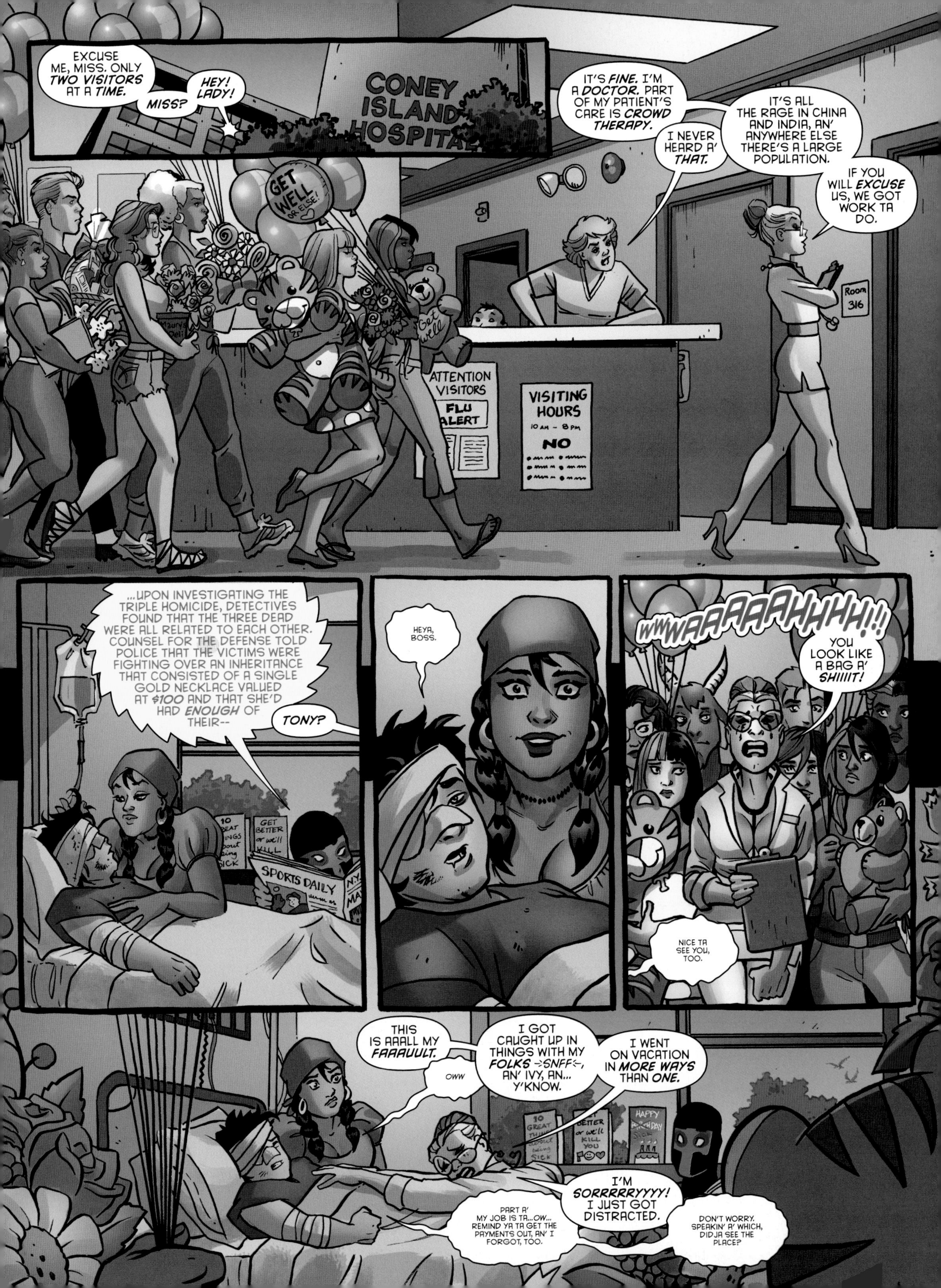
EXCUSE ME, MISS. ONLY TWO VISITORS AT A TIME.
MISS?
HEY! LADY!
CONEY ISLAND HOSPITAL
IT'S FINE. I'M A DOCTOR. PART OF MY PATIENT'S CARE IS CROWD THERAPY.
I NEVER HEARD A' THAT.
IT'S ALL THE RAGE IN CHINA AND INDIA, AN' ANYWHERE ELSE THERE'S A LARGE POPULATION.
IF YOU WILL EXCUSE US, WE GOT WORK TA DO.
GET WELL OR ELSE!
Room 316
ATTENTION VISITORS
FLU ALERT
VISITING HOURS
10 AM – 8 PM
NO
...UPON INVESTIGATING THE TRIPLE HOMICIDE, DETECTIVES FOUND THAT THE THREE DEAD WERE ALL RELATED TO EACH OTHER. COUNSEL FOR THE DEFENSE TOLD POLICE THAT THE VICTIMS WERE FIGHTING OVER AN INHERITANCE THAT CONSISTED OF A SINGLE GOLD NECKLACE VALUED AT $100 AND THAT SHE'D HAD ENOUGH OF THEIR--
TONY?
SPORTS DAILY
HEYA, BOSS.
WWWAAAAAAHHHH!!!
YOU LOOK LIKE A BAG A' SHIIIIT!
NICE TA SEE YOU, TOO.
THIS IS AAALL MY FAAAAUULT.
OWW
I GOT CAUGHT UP IN THINGS WITH MY FOLKS -SNFF-, AN' IVY, AN... Y'KNOW.
I WENT ON VACATION IN MORE WAYS THAN ONE.
I'M SORRRRRYYYY! I JUST GOT DISTRACTED.
PART A' MY JOB IS TA...OW... REMIND YA TA GET THE PAYMENTS OUT, AN' I FORGOT, TOO.
DON'T WORRY. SPEAKIN' A' WHICH, DIDJA SEE THE PLACE?

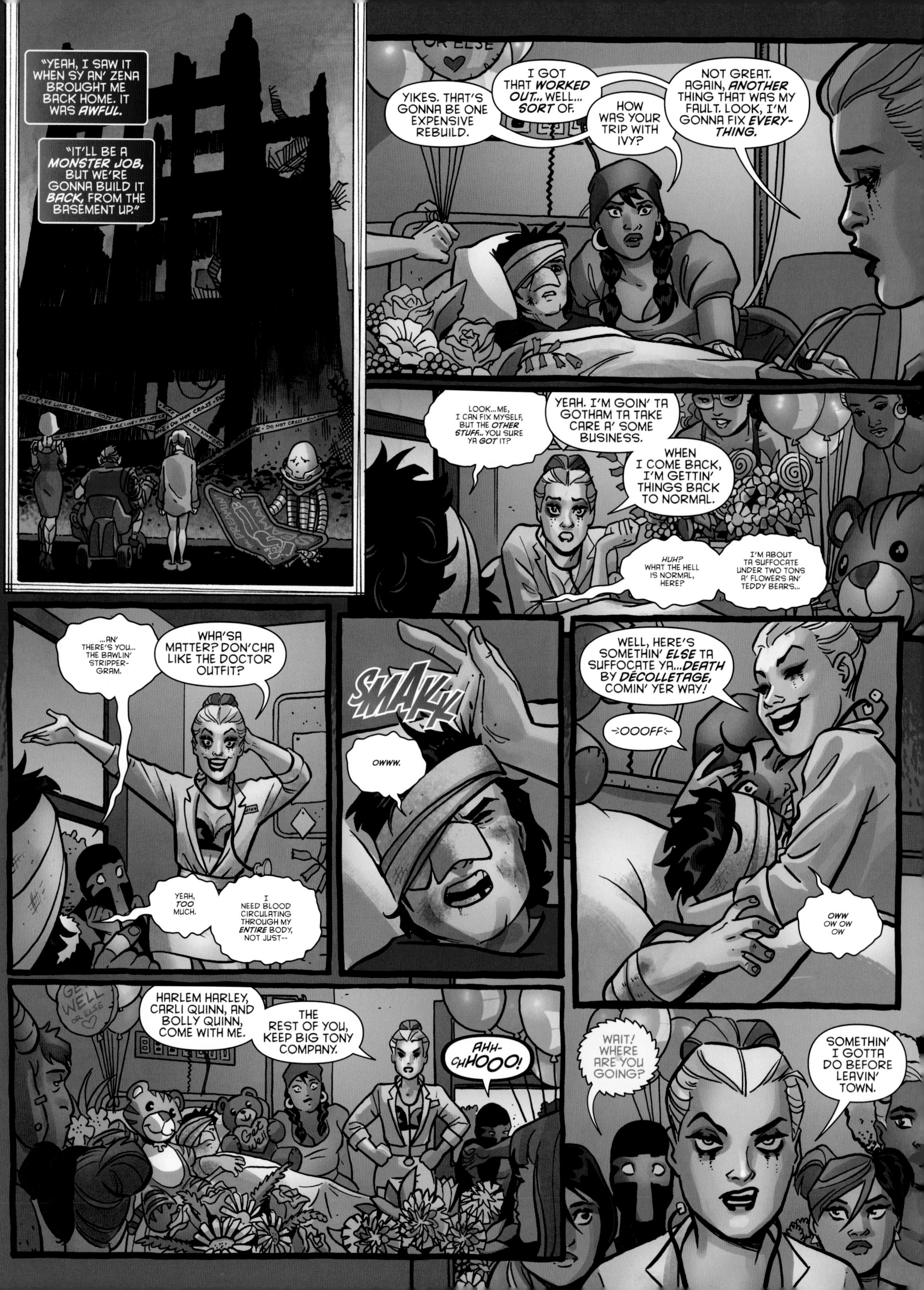

"YEAH, I SAW IT WHEN SY AN' ZENA BROUGHT ME BACK HOME. IT WAS *AWFUL.*
"IT'LL BE A *MONSTER JOB,* BUT WE'RE GONNA BUILD IT *BACK,* FROM THE BASEMENT UP."
FIRE LINE - DO NOT CROSS
DREAMIN'
SEAMAN
OR ELSE
YIKES. THAT'S GONNA BE ONE EXPENSIVE REBUILD.
I GOT THAT *WORKED OUT*... WELL... *SORT* OF.
HOW WAS YOUR TRIP WITH IVY?
NOT GREAT. AGAIN, *ANOTHER* THING THAT WAS MY FAULT. LOOK, I'M GONNA FIX *EVERY-THING.*
LOOK...ME, I CAN FIX MYSELF, BUT THE *OTHER STUFF*... YOU SURE YA *GOT* IT?
YEAH. I'M GOIN' TA GOTHAM TA TAKE CARE A' SOME BUSINESS.
WHEN I COME BACK, I'M GETTIN' THINGS BACK TO NORMAL.
HUH? WHAT THE HELL IS NORMAL, HERE?
I'M ABOUT TA SUFFOCATE UNDER TWO TONS A' FLOWERS AN' TEDDY BEARS...
...AN' THERE'S YOU... THE BAWLIN' STRIPPER-GRAM.
WHA'SA MATTER? DON'CHA LIKE THE DOCTOR OUTFIT?
YEAH, *TOO* MUCH.
I NEED BLOOD CIRCULATING THROUGH MY *ENTIRE* BODY, NOT JUST--
SMAKK
OWWW.
WELL, HERE'S SOMETHIN' *ELSE* TA SUFFOCATE YA... *DEATH* BY *DÉCOLLETAGE,* COMIN' YER WAY!
OOOFF
OWW OW OW OW
GET WELL OR ELSE
HARLEM HARLEY, CARLI QUINN, AND BOLLY QUINN, COME WITH ME.
THE REST OF YOU, KEEP BIG TONY COMPANY.
Get Well
AHH-CHHOOO!
WAIT! WHERE ARE YOU GOING?
SOMETHIN' I GOTTA DO BEFORE LEAVIN' TOWN.

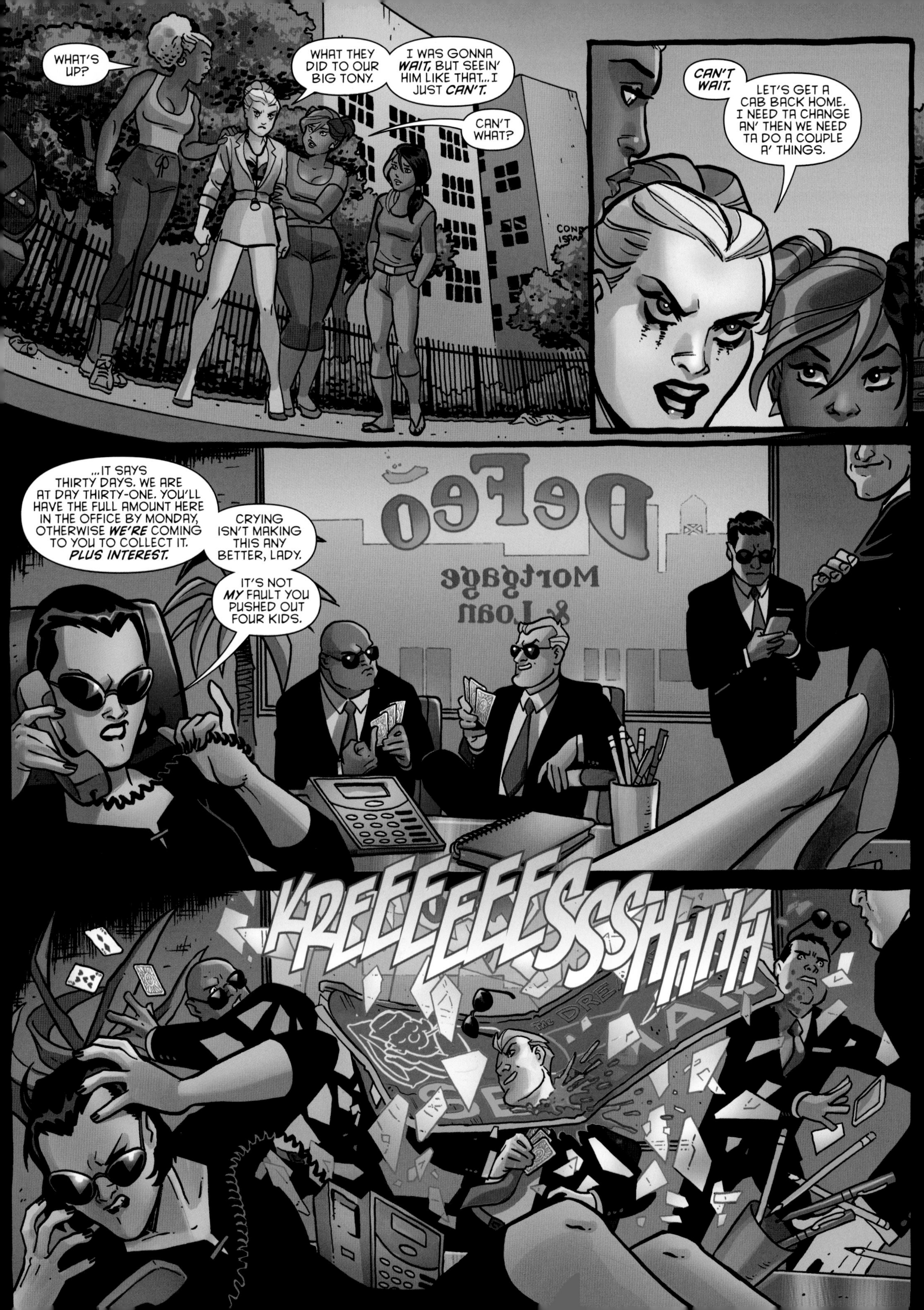
WHAT'S UP?
WHAT THEY DID TO OUR BIG TONY.
I WAS GONNA WAIT, BUT SEEIN' HIM LIKE THAT... I JUST CAN'T.
CAN'T WHAT?
CAN'T WAIT.
LET'S GET A CAB BACK HOME. I NEED TA CHANGE AN' THEN WE NEED TA DO A COUPLE A' THINGS.
DeFeo Mortgage & Loan
...IT SAYS THIRTY DAYS. WE ARE AT DAY THIRTY-ONE. YOU'LL HAVE THE FULL AMOUNT HERE IN THE OFFICE BY MONDAY, OTHERWISE WE'RE COMING TO YOU TO COLLECT IT. PLUS INTEREST.
CRYING ISN'T MAKING THIS ANY BETTER, LADY.
IT'S NOT MY FAULT YOU PUSHED OUT FOUR KIDS.
KREEEEEESSSHHHH

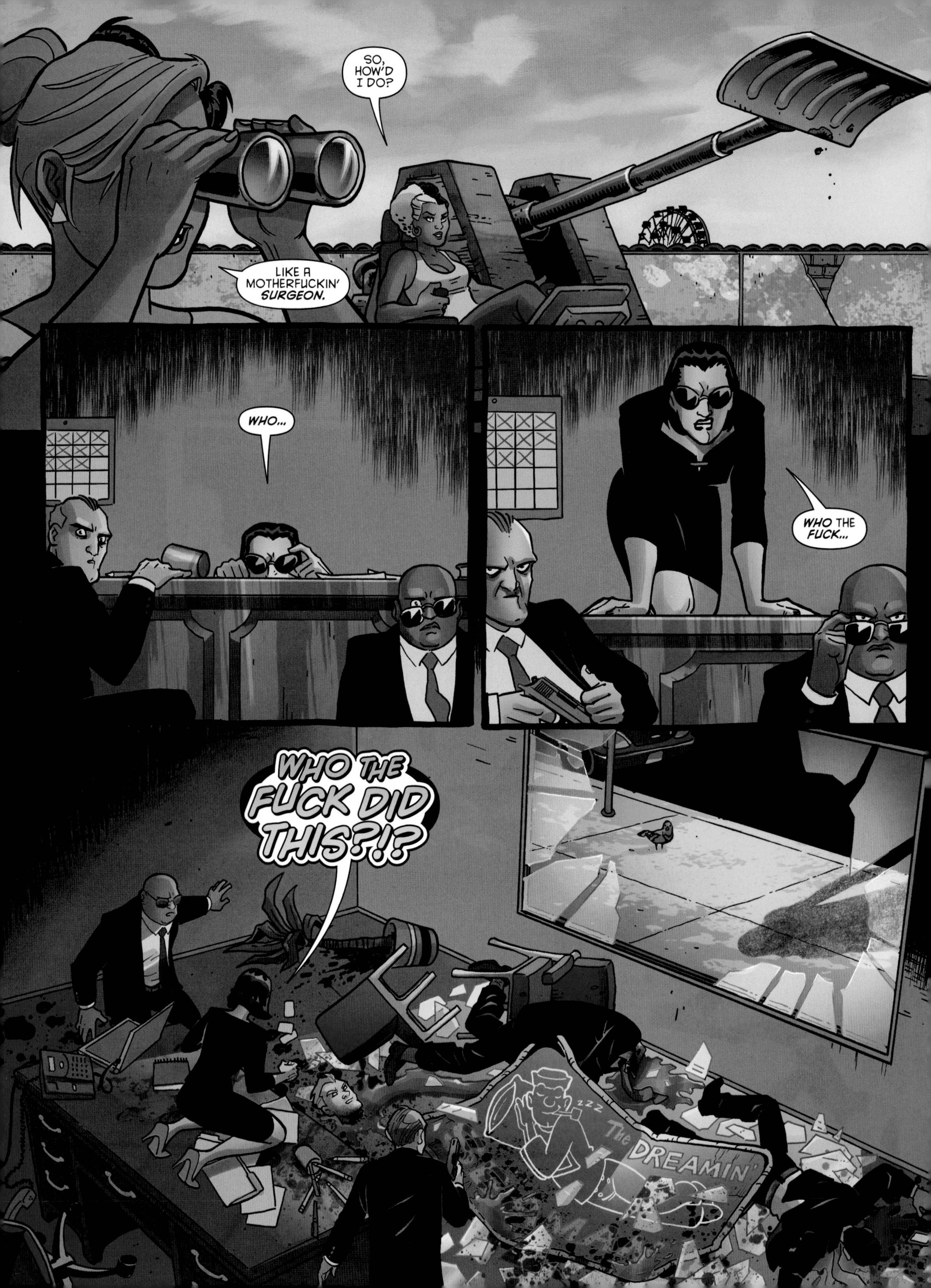
SO, HOW'D I DO?
LIKE A MOTHERFUCKIN' SURGEON.
WHO...
WHO THE FUCK...
WHO THE FUCK DID THIS?!?
THE DREAMIN'

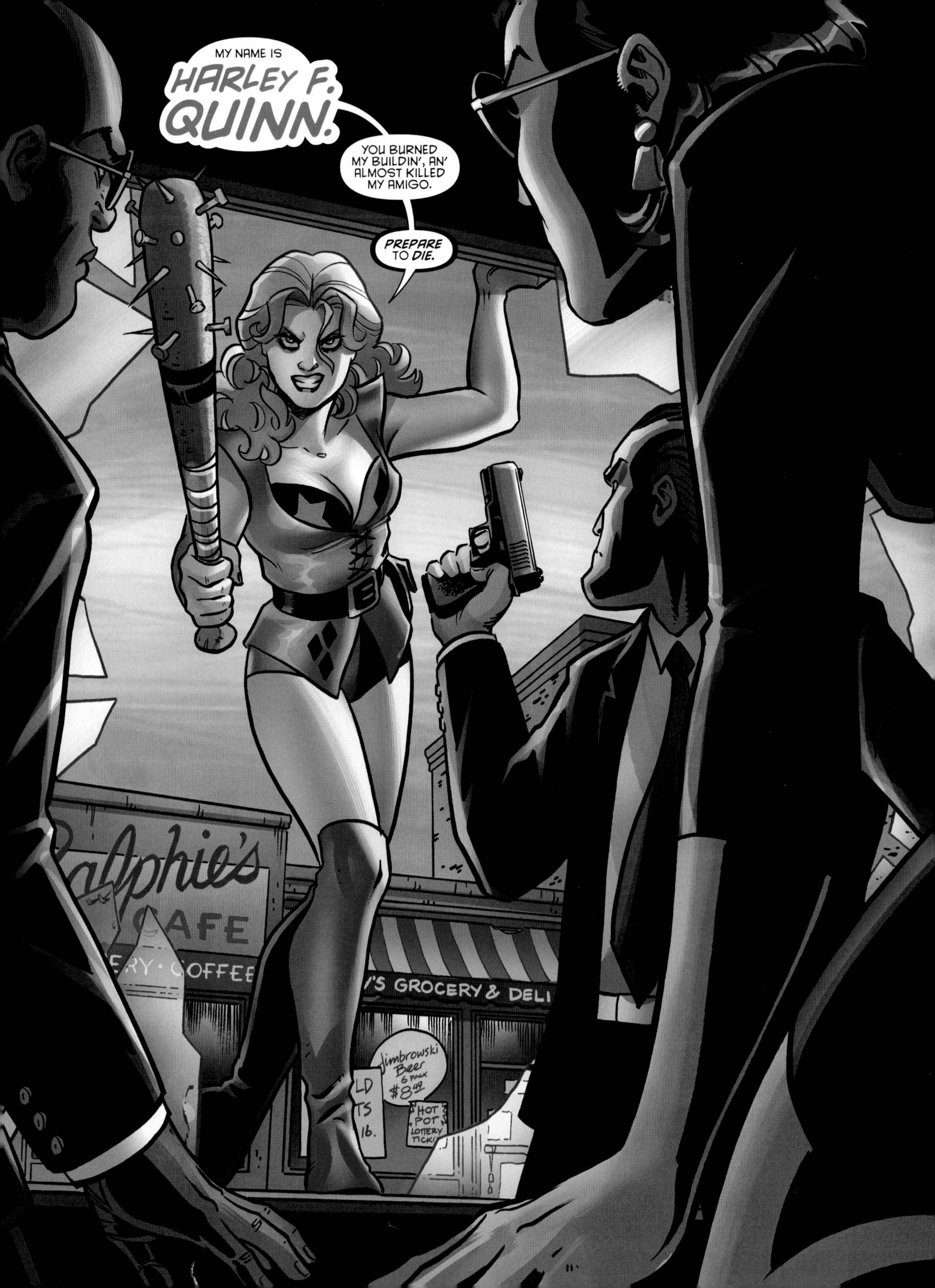
MY NAME IS HARLEY F. QUINN.
YOU BURNED MY BUILDIN', AN' ALMOST KILLED MY AMIGO.
PREPARE TO DIE.
CAFE
COFFEE
GROCERY & DELI
Jimbrowski Beer 6 PACK $8.49
HOT POT LOTTERY

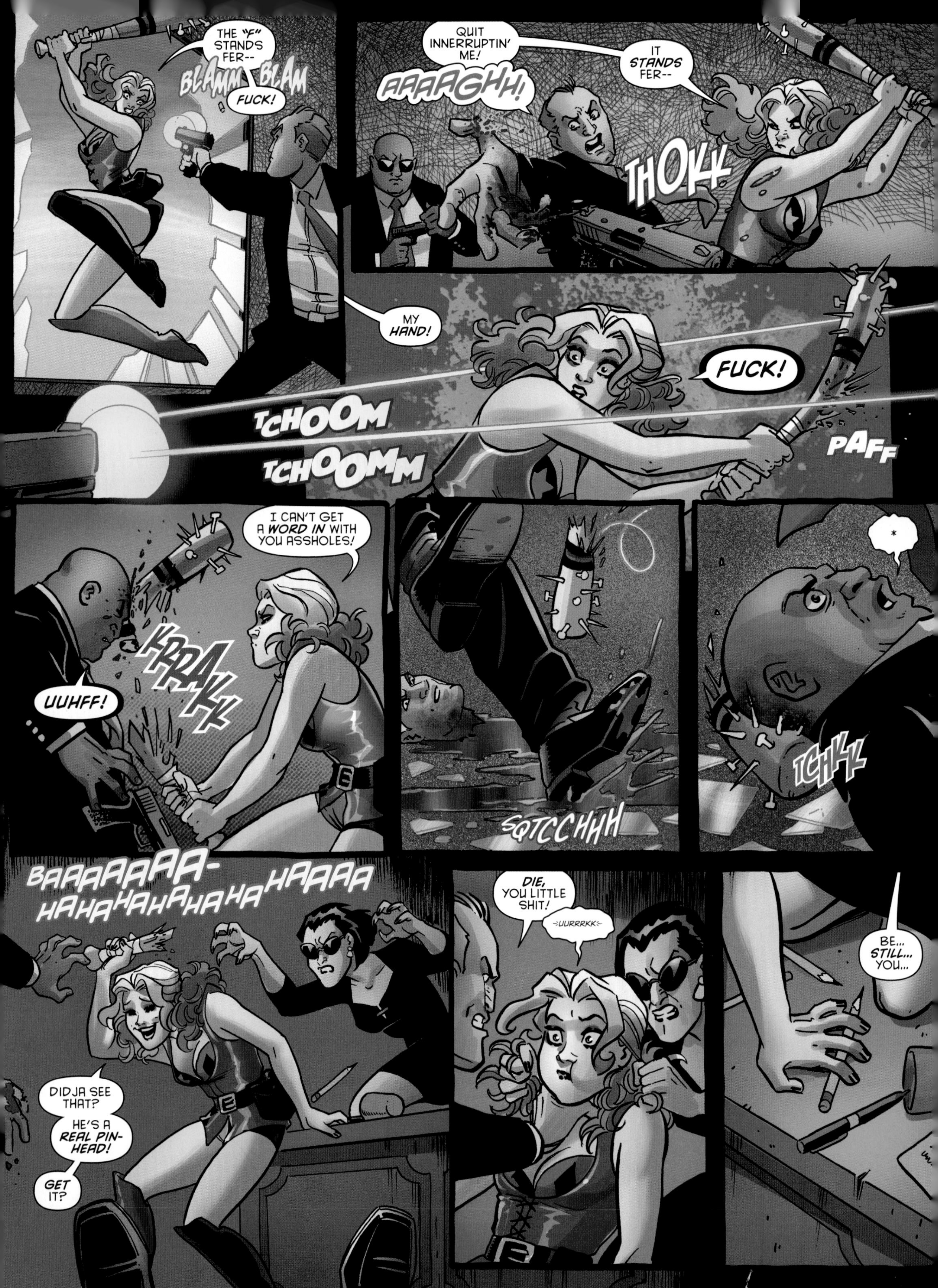
THE "F" STANDS FER--
BLAMM BLAM
FUCK!
QUIT INNERRUPTIN' ME!
AAAAGHH!
IT STANDS FER--
THOKK
MY HAND!
FUCK!
TCHOOM
TCHOOMM
PAFF
I CAN'T GET A WORD IN WITH YOU ASSHOLES!
KRRAKK
UUHFF!
SQTCCHHH
*
TCHKK
BAAAAAAA-HAHAHAHAHAHAHAHAAAAA
DIDJA SEE THAT?
HE'S A REAL PIN-HEAD!
GET IT?
DIE, YOU LITTLE SHIT!
UURRRKK
BE... STILL... YOU...

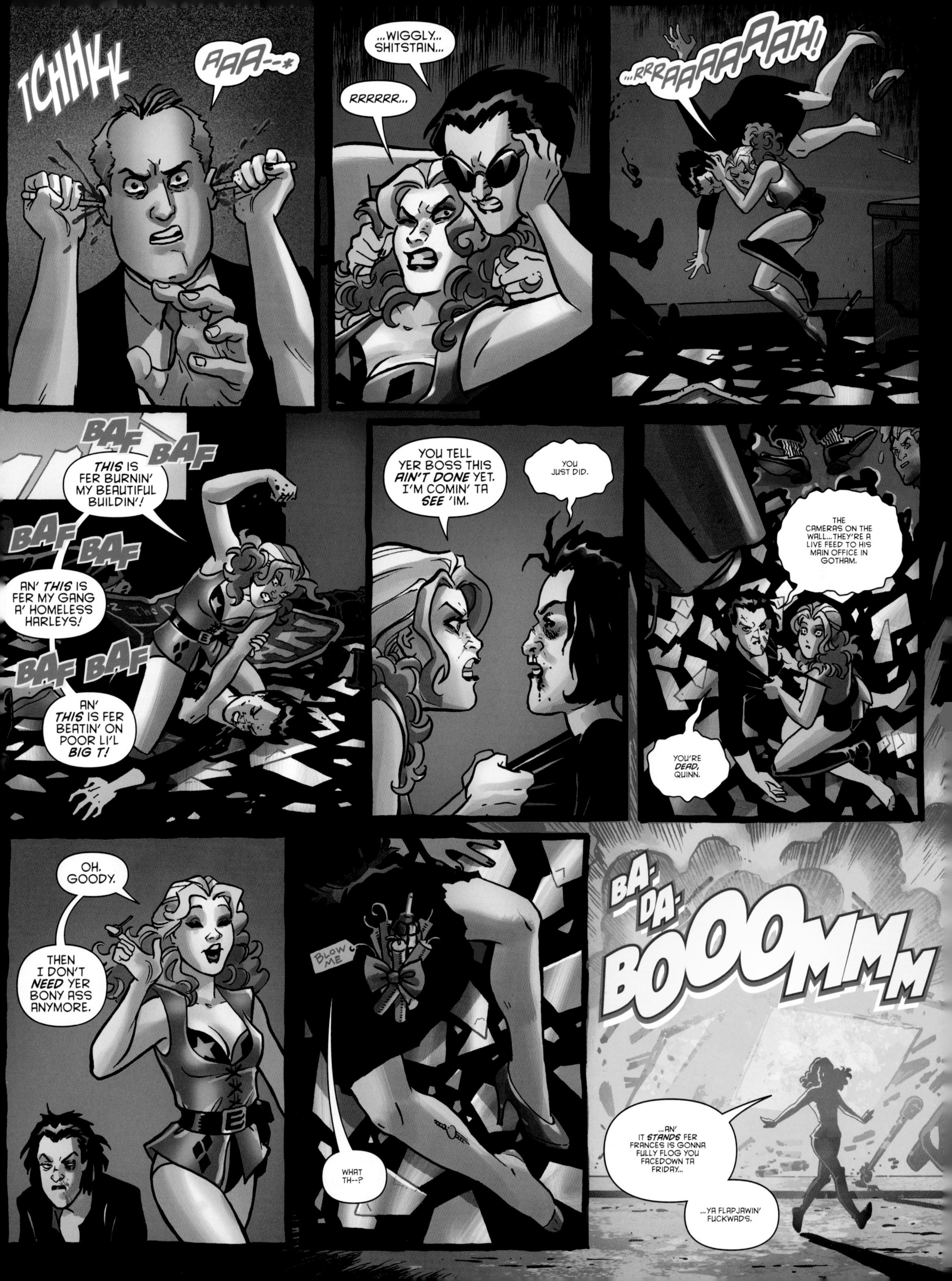
TCHHKK
AAA--*
...WIGGLY... SHITSTAIN...
RRRRRR...
...RRRAAAAAAAH!
BAF BAF
THIS IS FER BURNIN' MY BEAUTIFUL BUILDIN'!
BAF BAF
AN' THIS IS FER MY GANG A' HOMELESS HARLEYS!
BAF BAF
AN' THIS IS FER BEATIN' ON POOR LI'L BIG T!
YOU TELL YER BOSS THIS AIN'T DONE YET. I'M COMIN' TA SEE 'IM.
YOU JUST DID.
THE CAMERAS ON THE WALL...THEY'RE A LIVE FEED TO HIS MAIN OFFICE IN GOTHAM.
YOU'RE DEAD, QUINN.
OH. GOODY.
THEN I DON'T NEED YER BONY ASS ANYMORE.
BLOW ME
WHAT TH--?
BA-DA-BOOOMMMM
...AN' IT STANDS FER FRANCES IS GONNA FULLY FLOG YOU FACEDOWN TA FRIDAY...
...YA FLAPJAWIN' FUCKWADS.

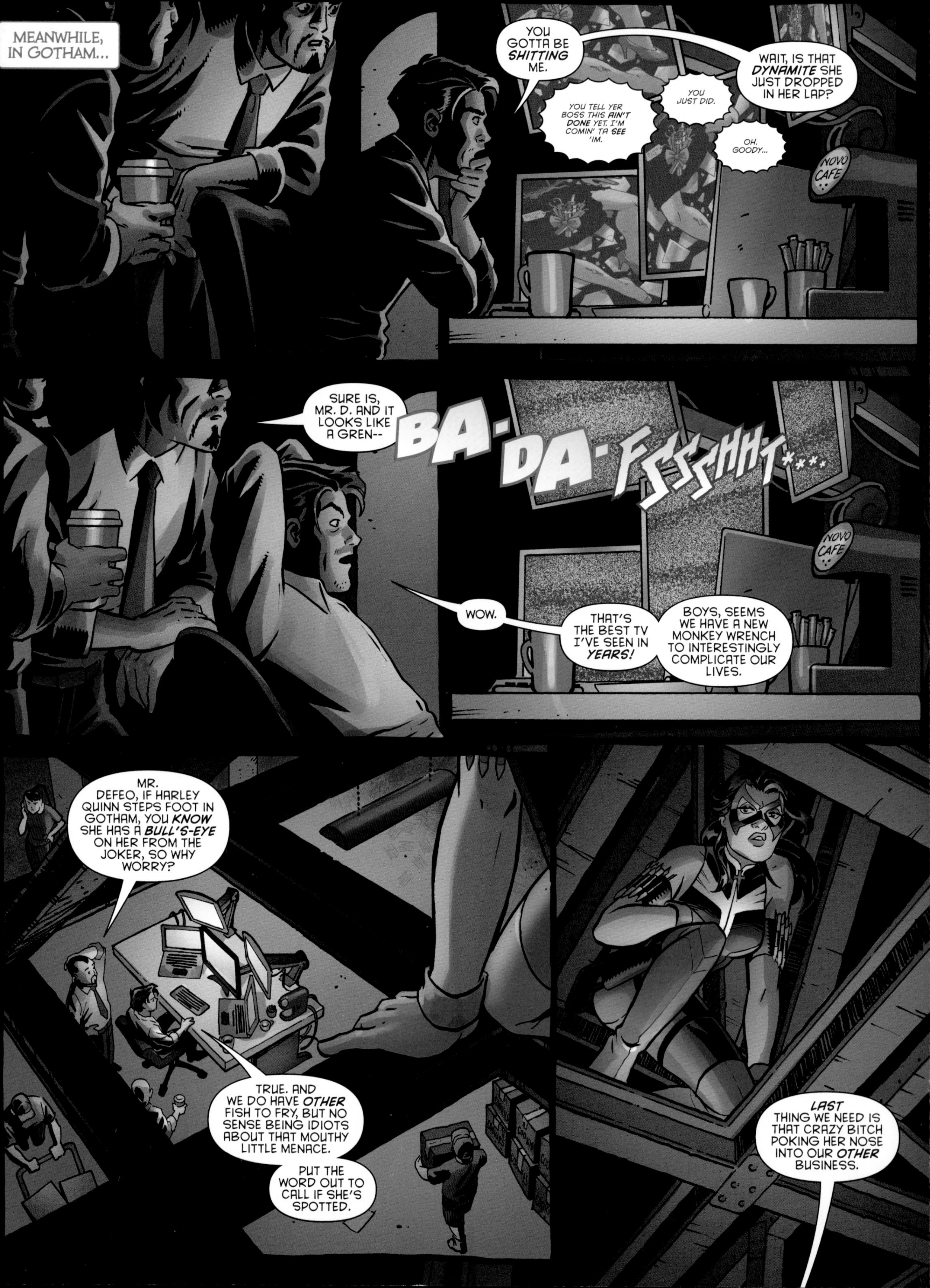
MEANWHILE, IN GOTHAM...
YOU GOTTA BE SHITTING ME.
WAIT, IS THAT DYNAMITE SHE JUST DROPPED IN HER LAP?
YOU TELL YER BOSS THIS AIN'T DONE YET. I'M COMIN' TA SEE 'IM.
YOU JUST DID.
OH. GOODY...
NOVO CAFE
SURE IS, MR. D. AND IT LOOKS LIKE A GREN--
BA-DA-FSSSHHT*...
WOW.
THAT'S THE BEST TV I'VE SEEN IN YEARS!
BOYS, SEEMS WE HAVE A NEW MONKEY WRENCH TO INTERESTINGLY COMPLICATE OUR LIVES.
NOVO CAFE
MR. DEFEO, IF HARLEY QUINN STEPS FOOT IN GOTHAM, YOU KNOW SHE HAS A BULL'S-EYE ON HER FROM THE JOKER, SO WHY WORRY?
TRUE. AND WE DO HAVE OTHER FISH TO FRY, BUT NO SENSE BEING IDIOTS ABOUT THAT MOUTHY LITTLE MENACE.
PUT THE WORD OUT TO CALL IF SHE'S SPOTTED.
LAST THING WE NEED IS THAT CRAZY BITCH POKING HER NOSE INTO OUR OTHER BUSINESS.

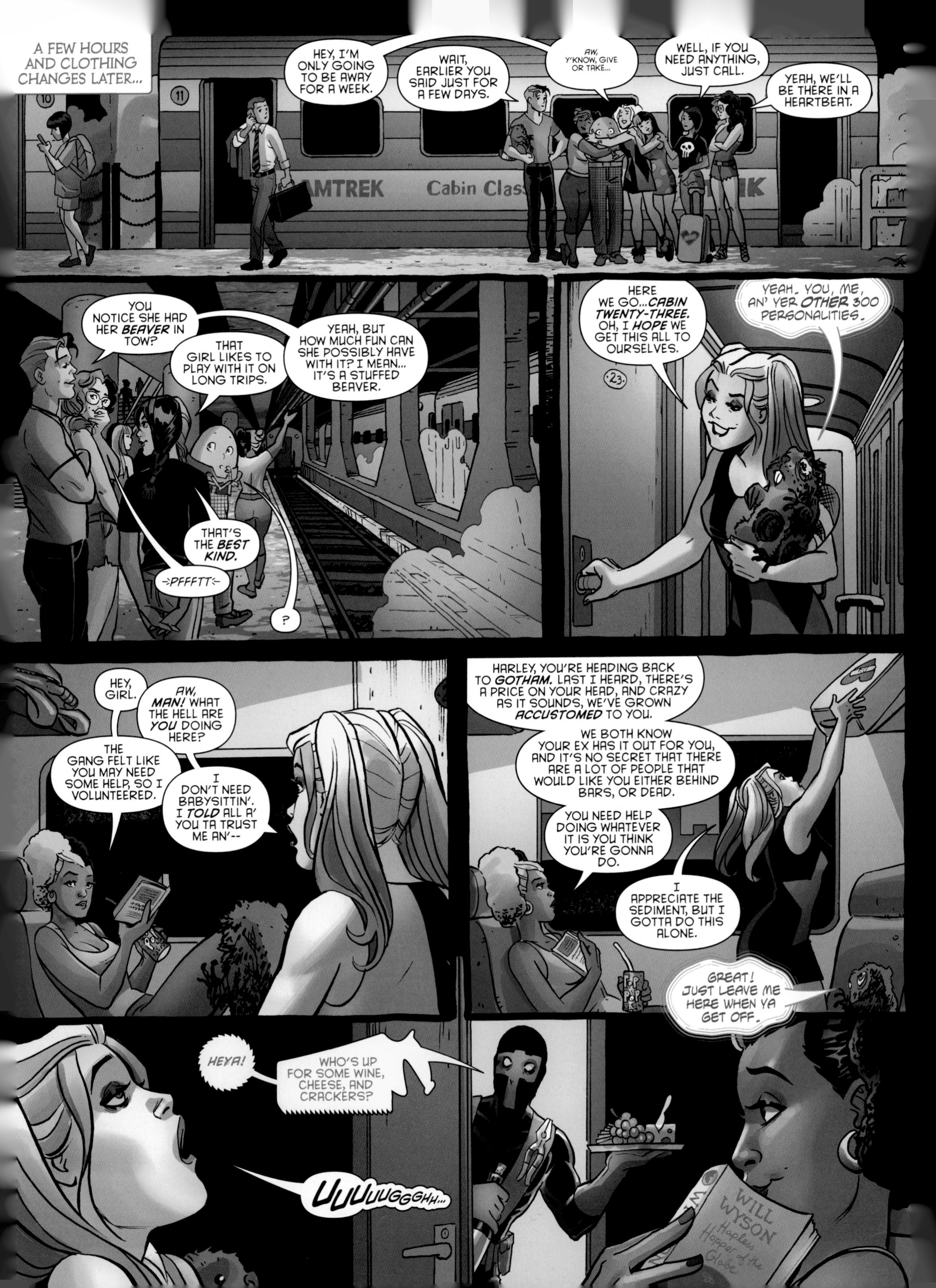

A FEW HOURS AND CLOTHING CHANGES LATER...
HEY, I'M ONLY GOING TO BE AWAY FOR A WEEK.
WAIT, EARLIER YOU SAID JUST FOR A FEW DAYS.
AW, Y'KNOW, GIVE OR TAKE...
WELL, IF YOU NEED ANYTHING, JUST CALL.
YEAH, WE'LL BE THERE IN A HEARTBEAT.
AMTREK Cabin Class
YOU NOTICE SHE HAD HER BEAVER IN TOW?
THAT GIRL LIKES TO PLAY WITH IT ON LONG TRIPS.
YEAH, BUT HOW MUCH FUN CAN SHE POSSIBLY HAVE WITH IT? I MEAN... IT'S A STUFFED BEAVER.
THAT'S THE BEST KIND.
PFFFTT
?
HERE WE GO...CABIN TWENTY-THREE. OH, I HOPE WE GET THIS ALL TO OURSELVES.
YEAH. YOU, ME, AN' YER OTHER 300 PERSONALITIES.
23
HEY, GIRL.
AW, MAN! WHAT THE HELL ARE YOU DOING HERE?
THE GANG FELT LIKE YOU MAY NEED SOME HELP, SO I VOLUNTEERED.
I DON'T NEED BABYSITTIN'. I TOLD ALL A' YOU TA TRUST ME AN'--
HARLEY, YOU'RE HEADING BACK TO GOTHAM. LAST I HEARD, THERE'S A PRICE ON YOUR HEAD, AND CRAZY AS IT SOUNDS, WE'VE GROWN ACCUSTOMED TO YOU.
WE BOTH KNOW YOUR EX HAS IT OUT FOR YOU, AND IT'S NO SECRET THAT THERE ARE A LOT OF PEOPLE THAT WOULD LIKE YOU EITHER BEHIND BARS, OR DEAD.
YOU NEED HELP DOING WHATEVER IT IS YOU THINK YOU'RE GONNA DO.
I APPRECIATE THE SEDIMENT, BUT I GOTTA DO THIS ALONE.
GREAT! JUST LEAVE ME HERE WHEN YA GET OFF.
HEYA!
WHO'S UP FOR SOME WINE, CHEESE, AND CRACKERS?
UUUUUGGGHH...
WILL WYSON
Hapless Hopper of the Globe

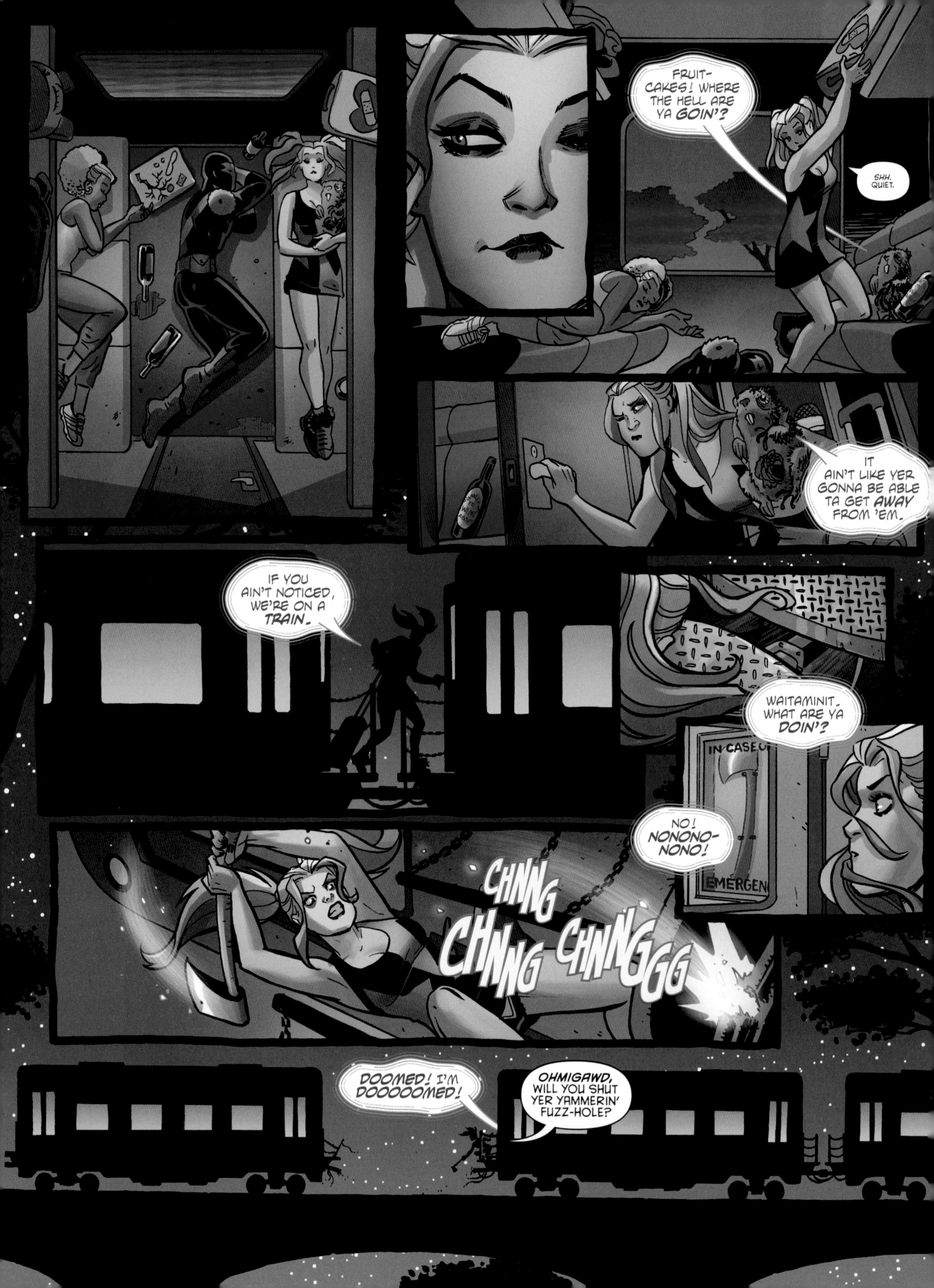
FRUIT-CAKES! WHERE THE HELL ARE YA GOIN'?
SHH. QUIET.
IT AIN'T LIKE YER GONNA BE ABLE TA GET AWAY FROM 'EM.
IF YOU AIN'T NOTICED, WE'RE ON A TRAIN.
WAITAMINIT. WHAT ARE YA DOIN'?
IN CASE O
EMERGEN
NO! NONONO-NONO!
CHNNG
CHNNG CHNNGGG
DOOMED! I'M DOOOOOMED!
OHMIGAWD, WILL YOU SHUT YER YAMMERIN' FUZZ-HOLE?

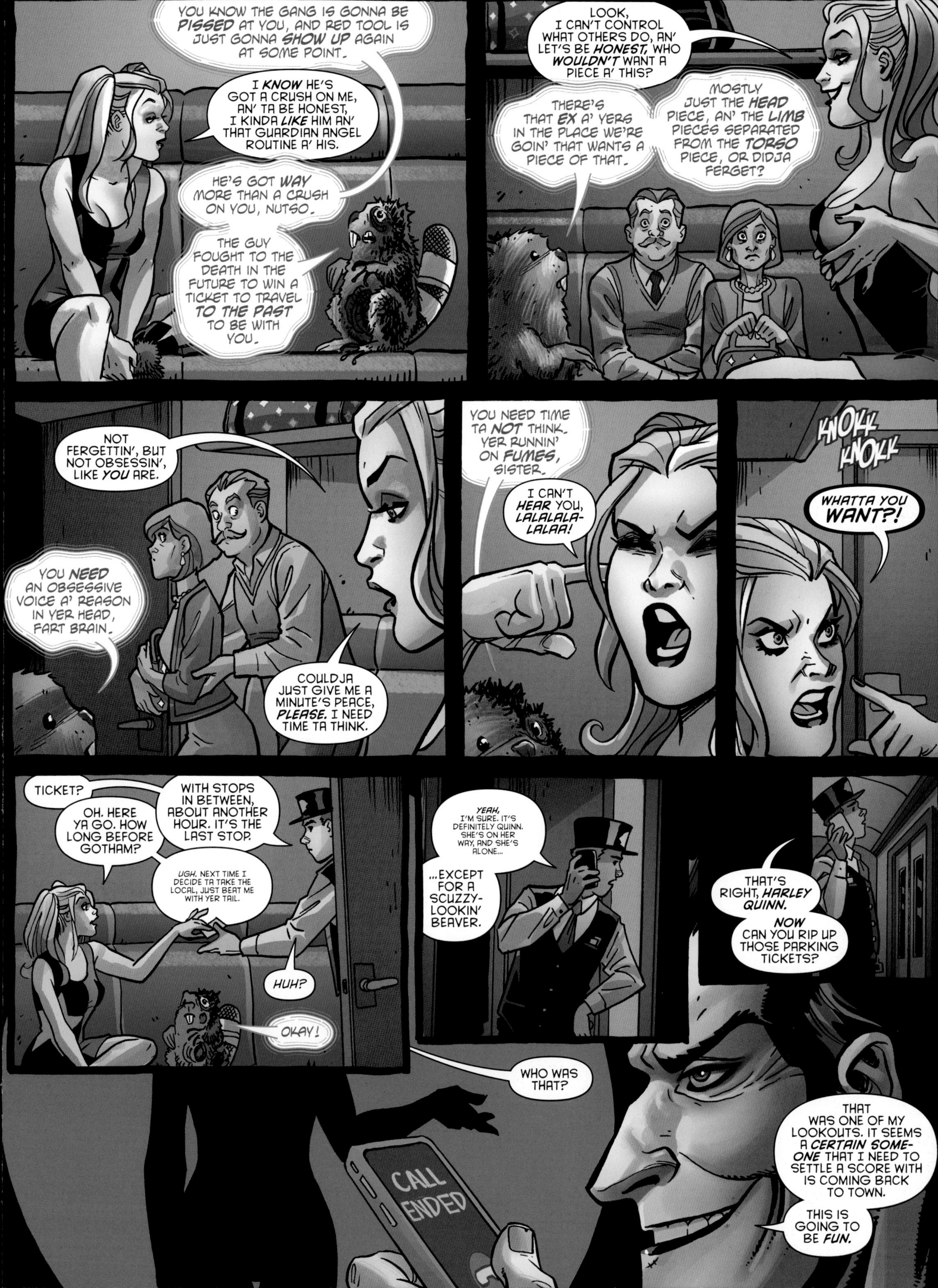
YOU KNOW THE GANG IS GONNA BE PISSED AT YOU, AND RED TOOL IS JUST GONNA SHOW UP AGAIN AT SOME POINT.
I KNOW HE'S GOT A CRUSH ON ME, AN' TA BE HONEST, I KINDA LIKE HIM AN' THAT GUARDIAN ANGEL ROUTINE A' HIS.
HE'S GOT WAY MORE THAN A CRUSH ON YOU, NUTSO.
THE GUY FOUGHT TO THE DEATH IN THE FUTURE TO WIN A TICKET TO TRAVEL TO THE PAST TO BE WITH YOU.
LOOK, I CAN'T CONTROL WHAT OTHERS DO, AN' LET'S BE HONEST, WHO WOULDN'T WANT A PIECE A' THIS?
THERE'S THAT EX A' YERS IN THE PLACE WE'RE GOIN' THAT WANTS A PIECE OF THAT.
MOSTLY JUST THE HEAD PIECE, AN' THE LIMB PIECES SEPARATED FROM THE TORSO PIECE, OR DIDJA FERGET?
NOT FERGETTIN', BUT NOT OBSESSIN', LIKE YOU ARE.
YOU NEED AN OBSESSIVE VOICE A' REASON IN YER HEAD, FART BRAIN.
COULDJA JUST GIVE ME A MINUTE'S PEACE, PLEASE. I NEED TIME TA THINK.
YOU NEED TIME TA NOT THINK. YER RUNNIN' ON FUMES, SISTER.
I CAN'T HEAR YOU, LALALALA-LALAA!
KNOKK KNOKK
WHATTA YOU WANT?!
TICKET?
OH. HERE YA GO. HOW LONG BEFORE GOTHAM?
WITH STOPS IN BETWEEN, ABOUT ANOTHER HOUR. IT'S THE LAST STOP.
UGH. NEXT TIME I DECIDE TA TAKE THE LOCAL, JUST BEAT ME WITH YER TAIL.
HUH?
OKAY!
YEAH, I'M SURE. IT'S DEFINITELY QUINN. SHE'S ON HER WAY, AND SHE'S ALONE...
...EXCEPT FOR A SCUZZY-LOOKIN' BEAVER.
THAT'S RIGHT, HARLEY QUINN.
NOW CAN YOU RIP UP THOSE PARKING TICKETS?
WHO WAS THAT?
CALL ENDED
THAT WAS ONE OF MY LOOKOUTS. IT SEEMS A CERTAIN SOME-ONE THAT I NEED TO SETTLE A SCORE WITH IS COMING BACK TO TOWN.
THIS IS GOING TO BE FUN.

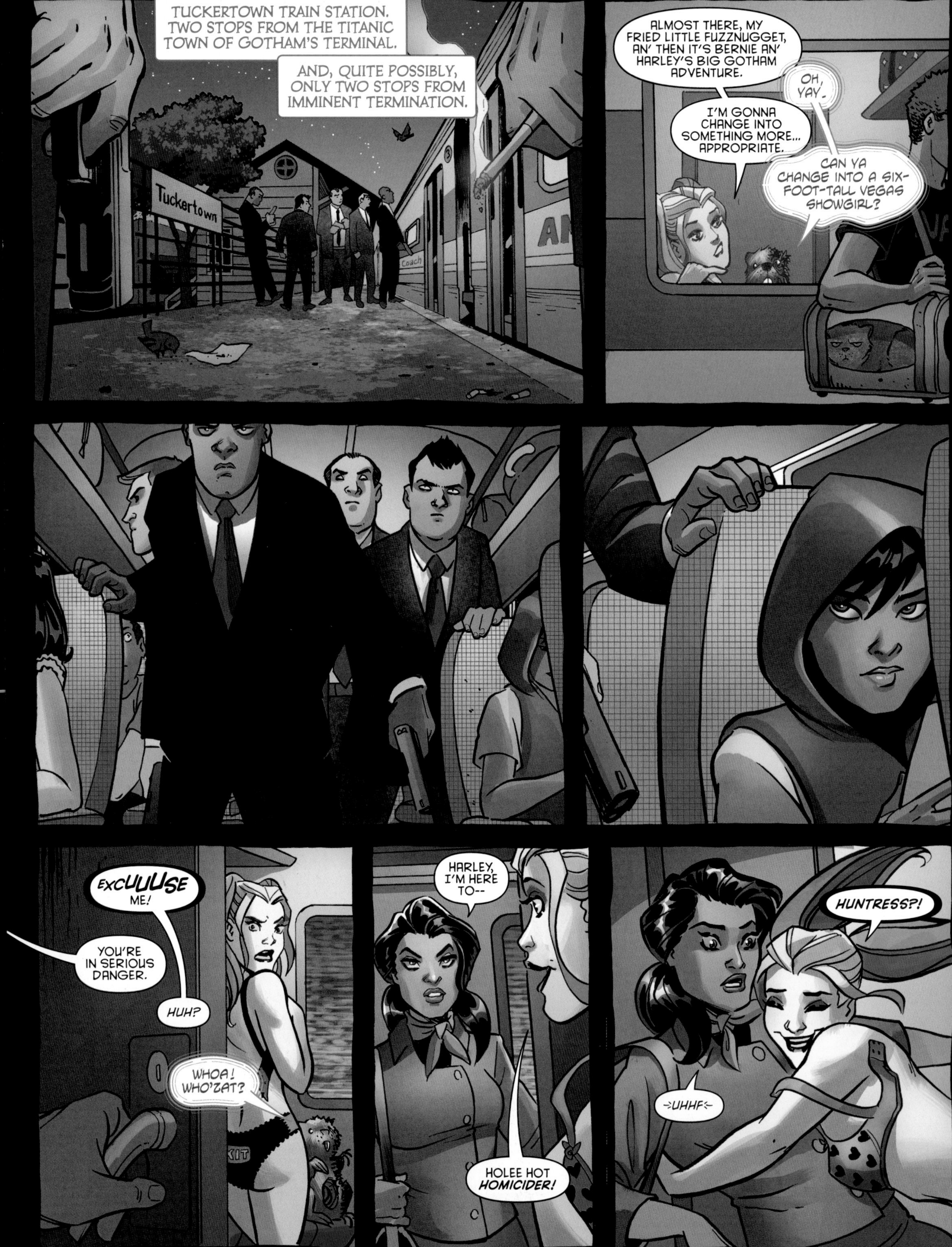
TUCKERTOWN TRAIN STATION. TWO STOPS FROM THE TITANIC TOWN OF GOTHAM'S TERMINAL.
AND, QUITE POSSIBLY, ONLY TWO STOPS FROM IMMINENT TERMINATION.
Tuckertown
ALMOST THERE, MY FRIED LITTLE FUZZNUGGET, AN' THEN IT'S BERNIE AN' HARLEY'S BIG GOTHAM ADVENTURE.
OH, YAY.
I'M GONNA CHANGE INTO SOMETHING MORE... APPROPRIATE.
CAN YA CHANGE INTO A SIX-FOOT-TALL VEGAS SHOWGIRL?
EXCUUUSE ME!
YOU'RE IN SERIOUS DANGER.
HUH?
WHOA! WHO'ZAT?
HARLEY, I'M HERE TO--
HOLEE HOT HOMICIDER!
HUNTRESS?!
UHHF

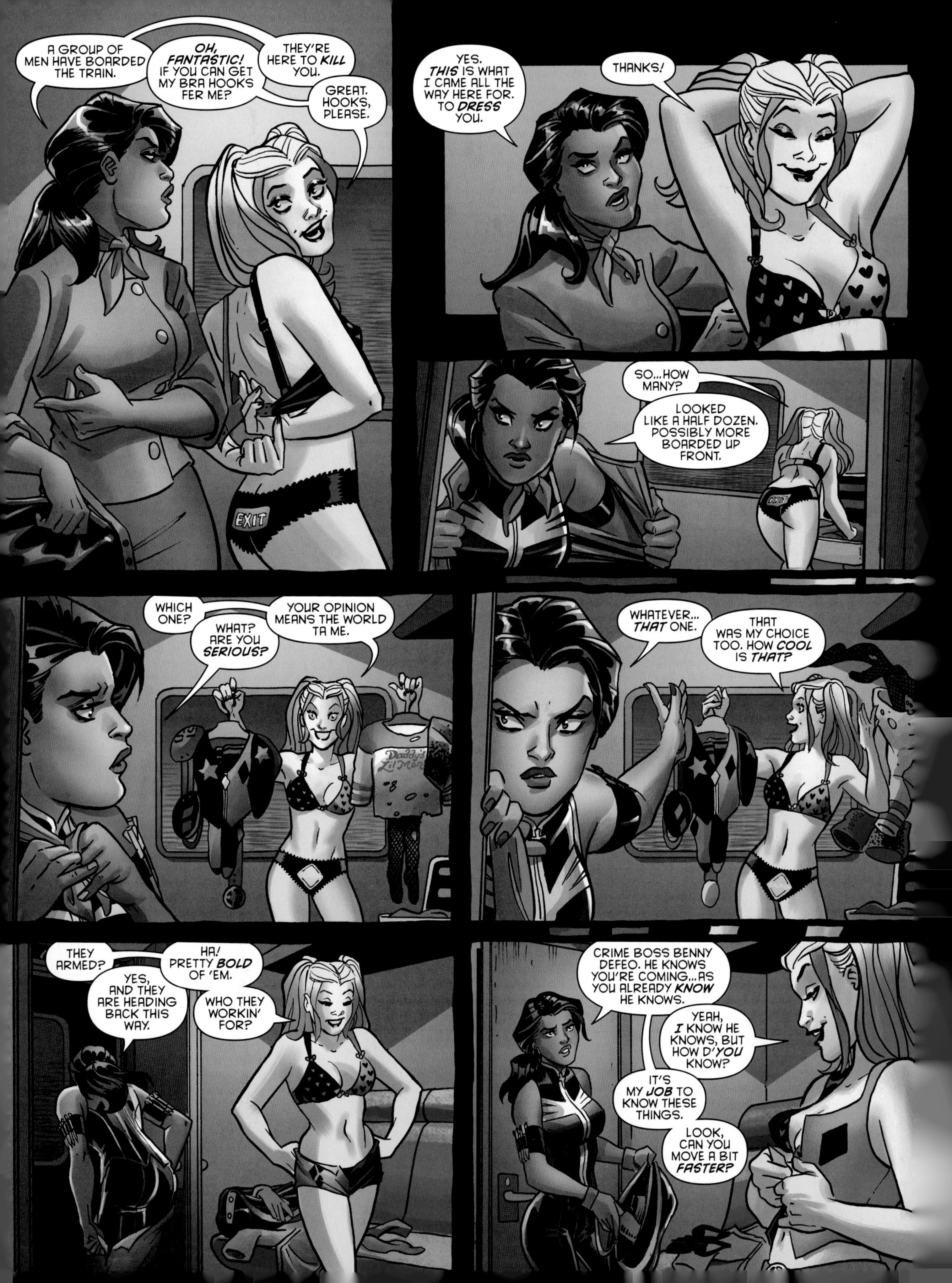

A GROUP OF MEN HAVE BOARDED THE TRAIN.
OH, FANTASTIC! IF YOU CAN GET MY BRA HOOKS FER ME?
THEY'RE HERE TO KILL YOU.
GREAT. HOOKS, PLEASE.
YES. THIS IS WHAT I CAME ALL THE WAY HERE FOR. TO DRESS YOU.
THANKS!
SO...HOW MANY?
LOOKED LIKE A HALF DOZEN. POSSIBLY MORE BOARDED UP FRONT.
EXIT
WHICH ONE?
WHAT? ARE YOU SERIOUS?
YOUR OPINION MEANS THE WORLD TA ME.
WHATEVER... THAT ONE.
THAT WAS MY CHOICE TOO. HOW COOL IS THAT?
THEY ARMED?
YES, AND THEY ARE HEADING BACK THIS WAY.
HA! PRETTY BOLD OF 'EM.
WHO THEY WORKIN' FOR?
CRIME BOSS BENNY DEFEO. HE KNOWS YOU'RE COMING...AS YOU ALREADY KNOW HE KNOWS.
YEAH, I KNOW HE KNOWS, BUT HOW D'YOU KNOW?
IT'S MY JOB TO KNOW THESE THINGS.
LOOK, CAN YOU MOVE A BIT FASTER?

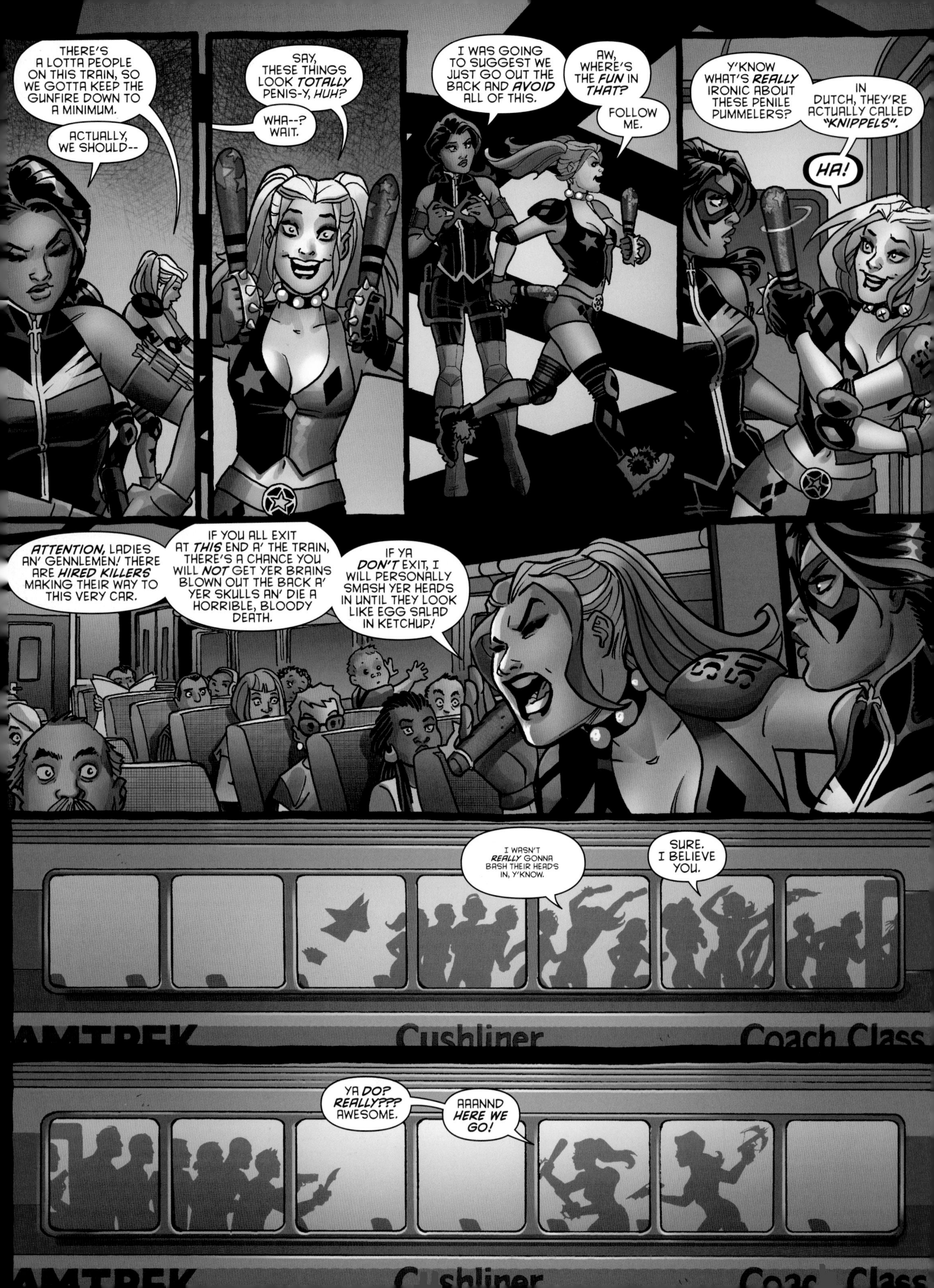

THERE'S A LOTTA PEOPLE ON THIS TRAIN, SO WE GOTTA KEEP THE GUNFIRE DOWN TO A MINIMUM.
ACTUALLY, WE SHOULD--
SAY, THESE THINGS LOOK TOTALLY PENIS-Y, HUH?
WHA--? WAIT.
I WAS GOING TO SUGGEST WE JUST GO OUT THE BACK AND AVOID ALL OF THIS.
AW, WHERE'S THE FUN IN THAT?
FOLLOW ME.
Y'KNOW WHAT'S REALLY IRONIC ABOUT THESE PENILE PUMMELERS?
IN DUTCH, THEY'RE ACTUALLY CALLED "KNIPPELS".
HA!
ATTENTION, LADIES AN' GENNLEMEN! THERE ARE HIRED KILLERS MAKING THEIR WAY TO THIS VERY CAR.
IF YOU ALL EXIT AT THIS END A' THE TRAIN, THERE'S A CHANCE YOU WILL NOT GET YER BRAINS BLOWN OUT THE BACK A' YER SKULLS AN' DIE A HORRIBLE, BLOODY DEATH.
IF YA DON'T EXIT, I WILL PERSONALLY SMASH YER HEADS IN UNTIL THEY LOOK LIKE EGG SALAD IN KETCHUP!
I WASN'T REALLY GONNA BASH THEIR HEADS IN, Y'KNOW.
SURE. I BELIEVE YOU.
AMTREK
Cushliner
Coach Class
YA DO? REALLY??? AWESOME.
AAANND HERE WE GO!
AMTREK
Cushliner
Coach Class

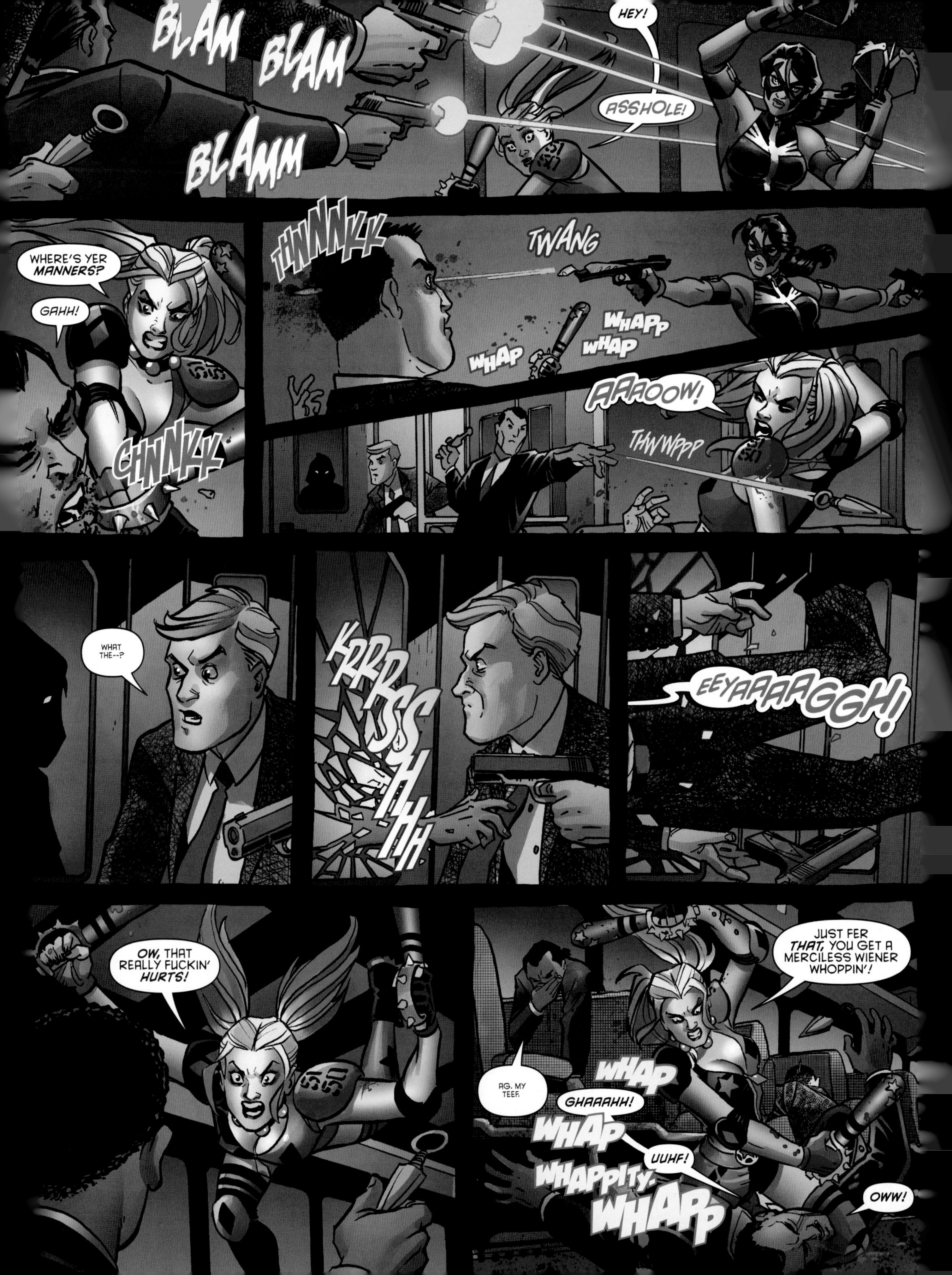

BLAM
BLAM
BLAMM
HEY!
ASSHOLE!
WHERE'S YER MANNERS?
GAHH!
CHNNKK
THNNNKK
TWANG
WHAP
WHAPP
WHAP
AAAOOW!
THWWPPP
WHAT THE--?
KRRRSSHHH.
EEYAAAAAGGH!
OW, THAT REALLY FUCKIN' HURTS!
JUST FER THAT, YOU GET A MERCILESS WIENER WHOPPIN'!
AG. MY TEEF.
WHAP
GHAAAHH!
WHAP
UUHF!
WHAPPITY.
WHAPP
OWW!

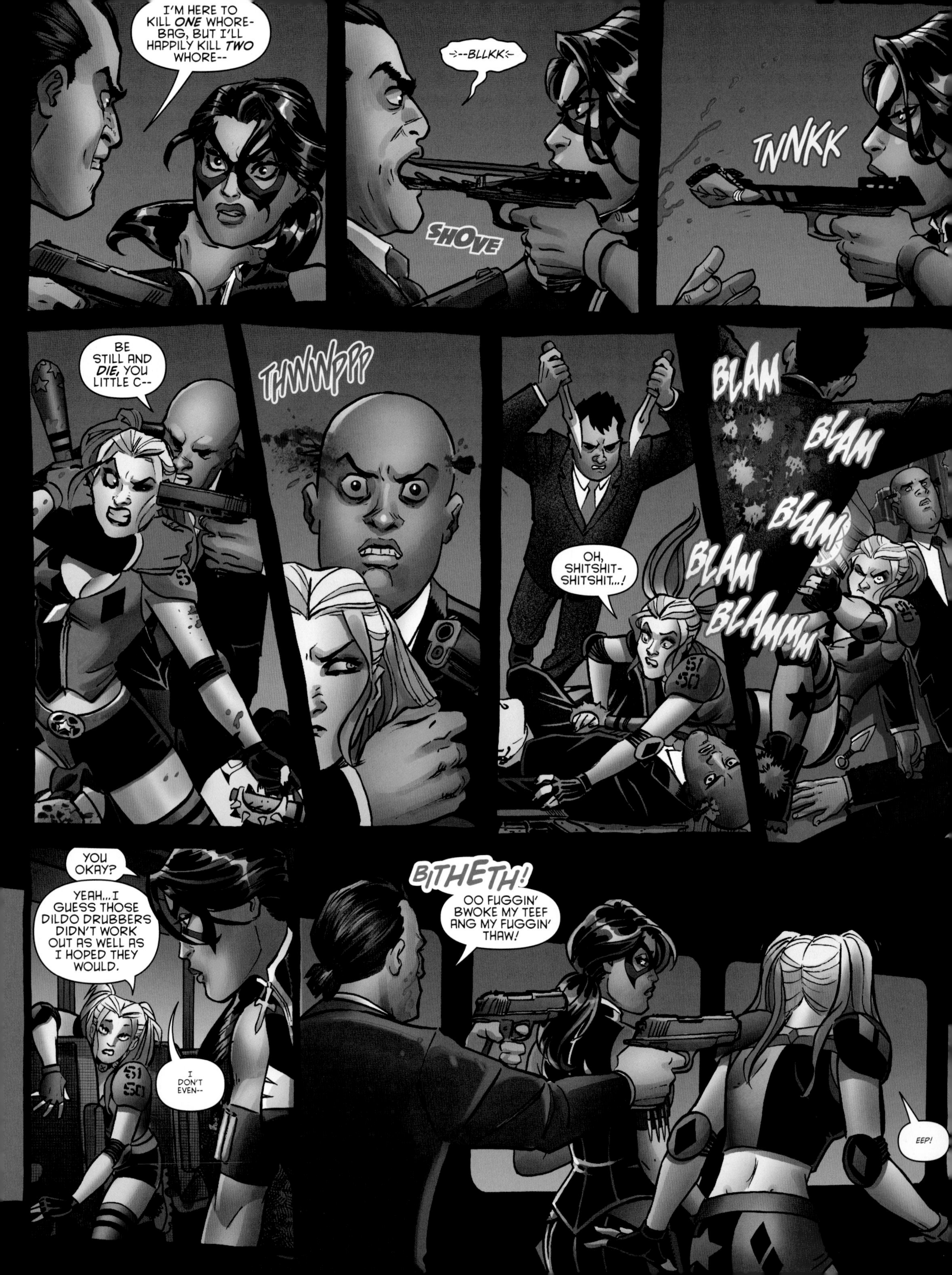
I'M HERE TO KILL ONE WHORE-BAG, BUT I'LL HAPPILY KILL TWO WHORE--
--BLLKK--
SHOVE
TNNKK
BE STILL AND DIE, YOU LITTLE C--
THWWPPP
OH, SHITSHIT-SHITSHIT...!
BLAM
BLAM
BLAM
BLAM
BLAMMM
YOU OKAY?
YEAH... I GUESS THOSE DILDO DRUBBERS DIDN'T WORK OUT AS WELL AS I HOPED THEY WOULD.
I DON'T EVEN--
BITHETH!
OO FUGGIN' BWOKE MY TEEF ANG MY FUGGIN' THAW!
EEP!

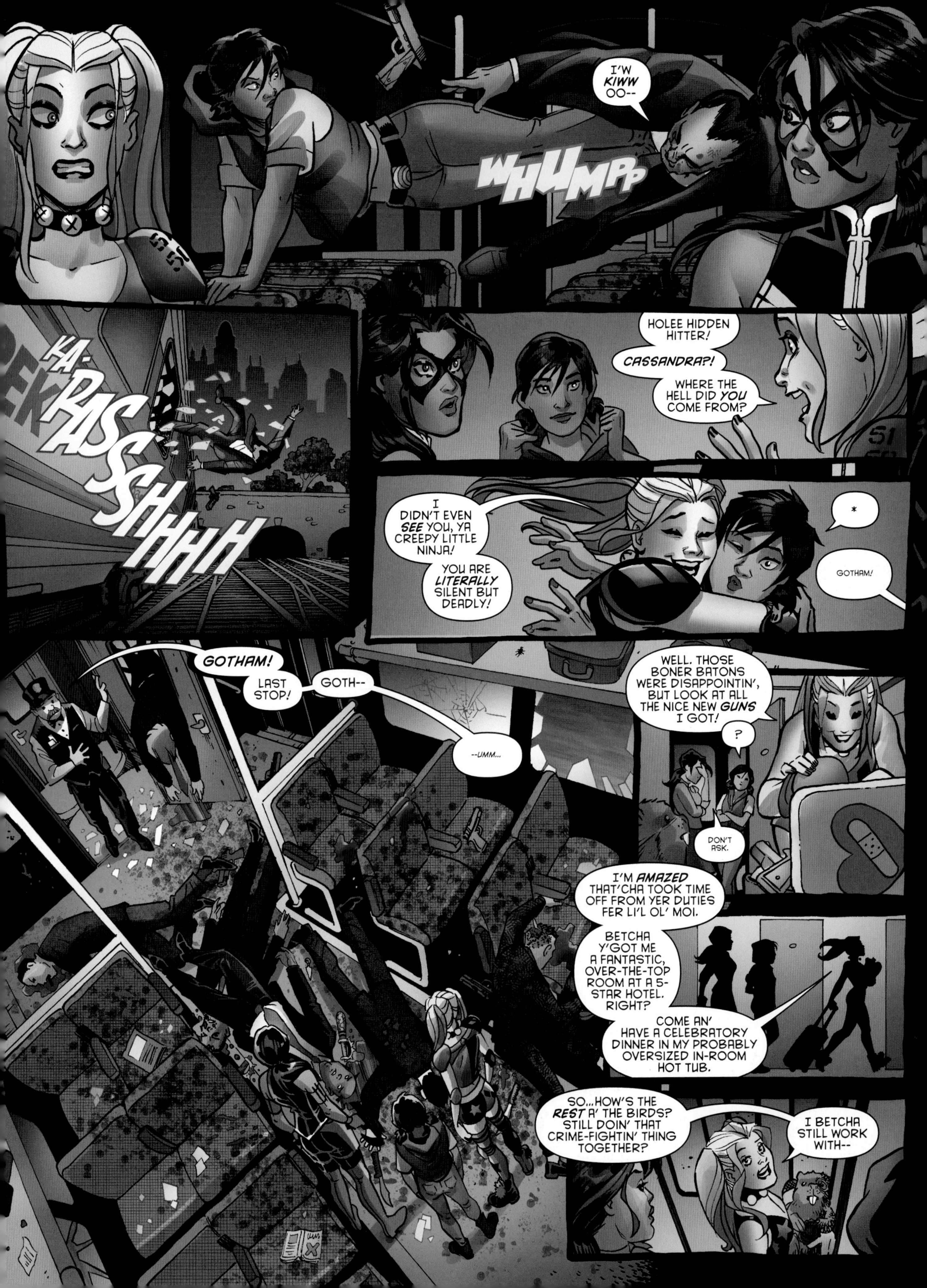
I'W KIWW OO--
WHUMPP
KA-RASSHHHH
HOLEE HIDDEN HITTER!
CASSANDRA?!
WHERE THE HELL DID YOU COME FROM?
I DIDN'T EVEN SEE YOU, YA CREEPY LITTLE NINJA!
YOU ARE LITERALLY SILENT BUT DEADLY!
*
GOTHAM!
GOTHAM!
LAST STOP!
GOTH--
--UMM...
WELL. THOSE BONER BATONS WERE DISAPPOINTIN', BUT LOOK AT ALL THE NICE NEW GUNS I GOT!
?
DON'T ASK.
I'M AMAZED THAT'CHA TOOK TIME OFF FROM YER DUTIES FER LI'L OL' MOI.
BETCHA Y'GOT ME A FANTASTIC, OVER-THE-TOP ROOM AT A 5-STAR HOTEL. RIGHT?
COME AN' HAVE A CELEBRATORY DINNER IN MY PROBABLY OVERSIZED IN-ROOM HOT TUB.
SO...HOW'S THE REST A' THE BIRDS? STILL DOIN' THAT CRIME-FIGHTIN' THING TOGETHER?
I BETCHA STILL WORK WITH--

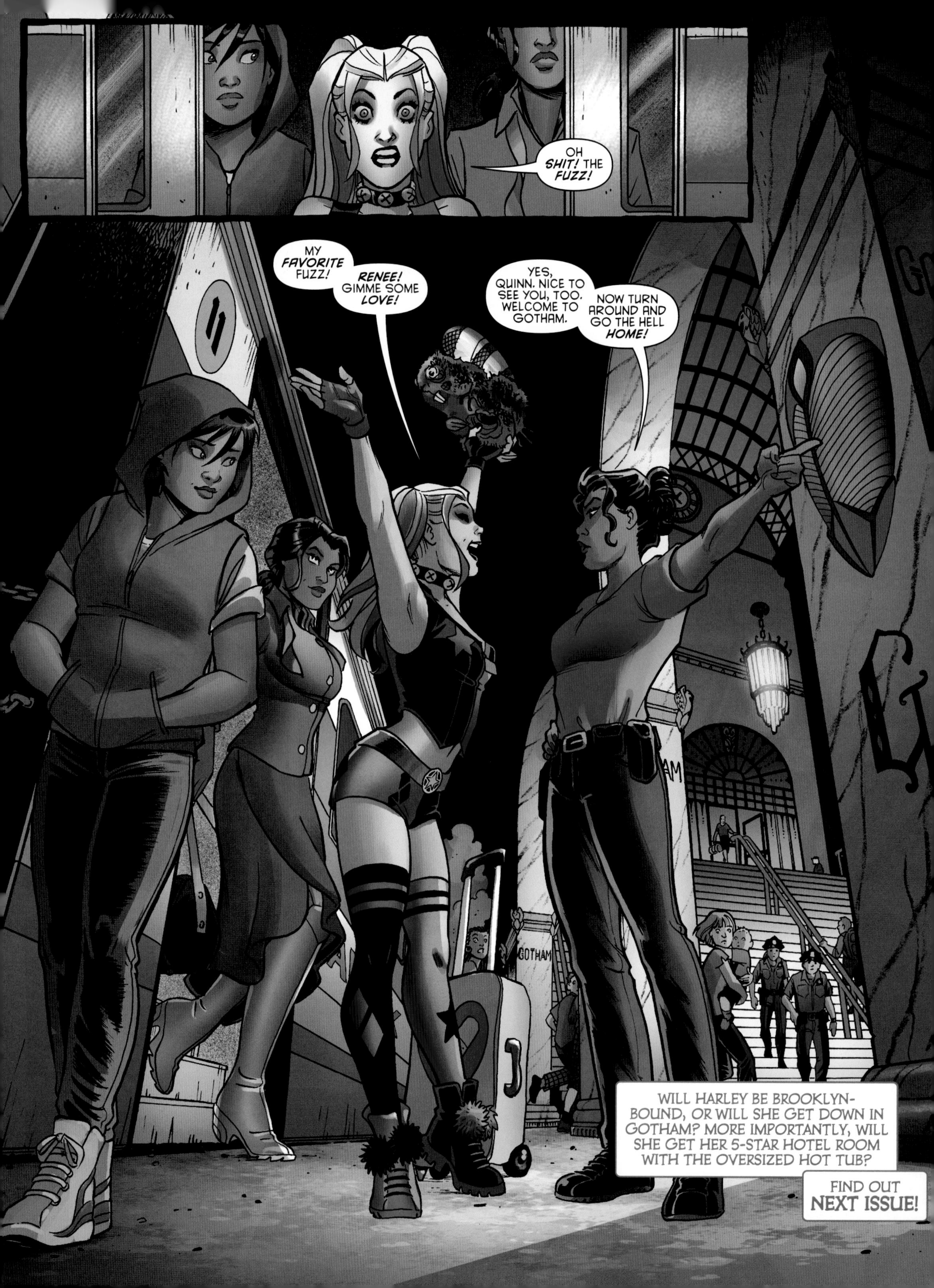
OH SHIT! THE FUZZ!
MY FAVORITE FUZZ!
RENEE! GIMME SOME LOVE!
YES, QUINN. NICE TO SEE YOU, TOO. WELCOME TO GOTHAM.
NOW TURN AROUND AND GO THE HELL HOME!
GOTHAM
WILL HARLEY BE BROOKLYN-BOUND, OR WILL SHE GET DOWN IN GOTHAM? MORE IMPORTANTLY, WILL SHE GET HER 5-STAR HOTEL ROOM WITH THE OVERSIZED HOT TUB?
FIND OUT NEXT ISSUE!

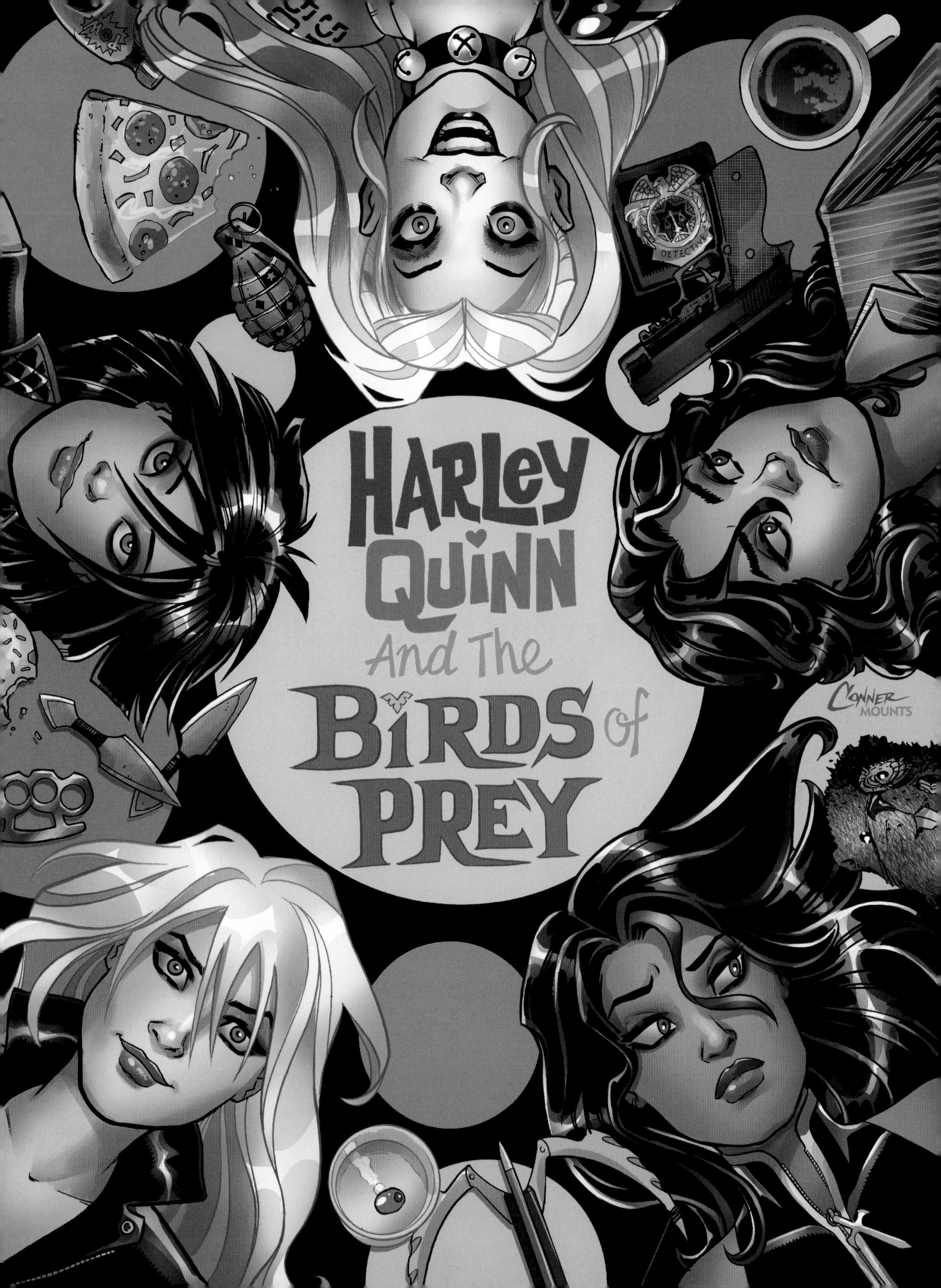
HARLEY QUINN
And The
BIRDS of
PREY
CONNER
MOUNTS
DETECTIVE

BOOK TWO
BELOW & BEYOND THE CALL OF DOODY

"Let me handle this MY way, in MY town."

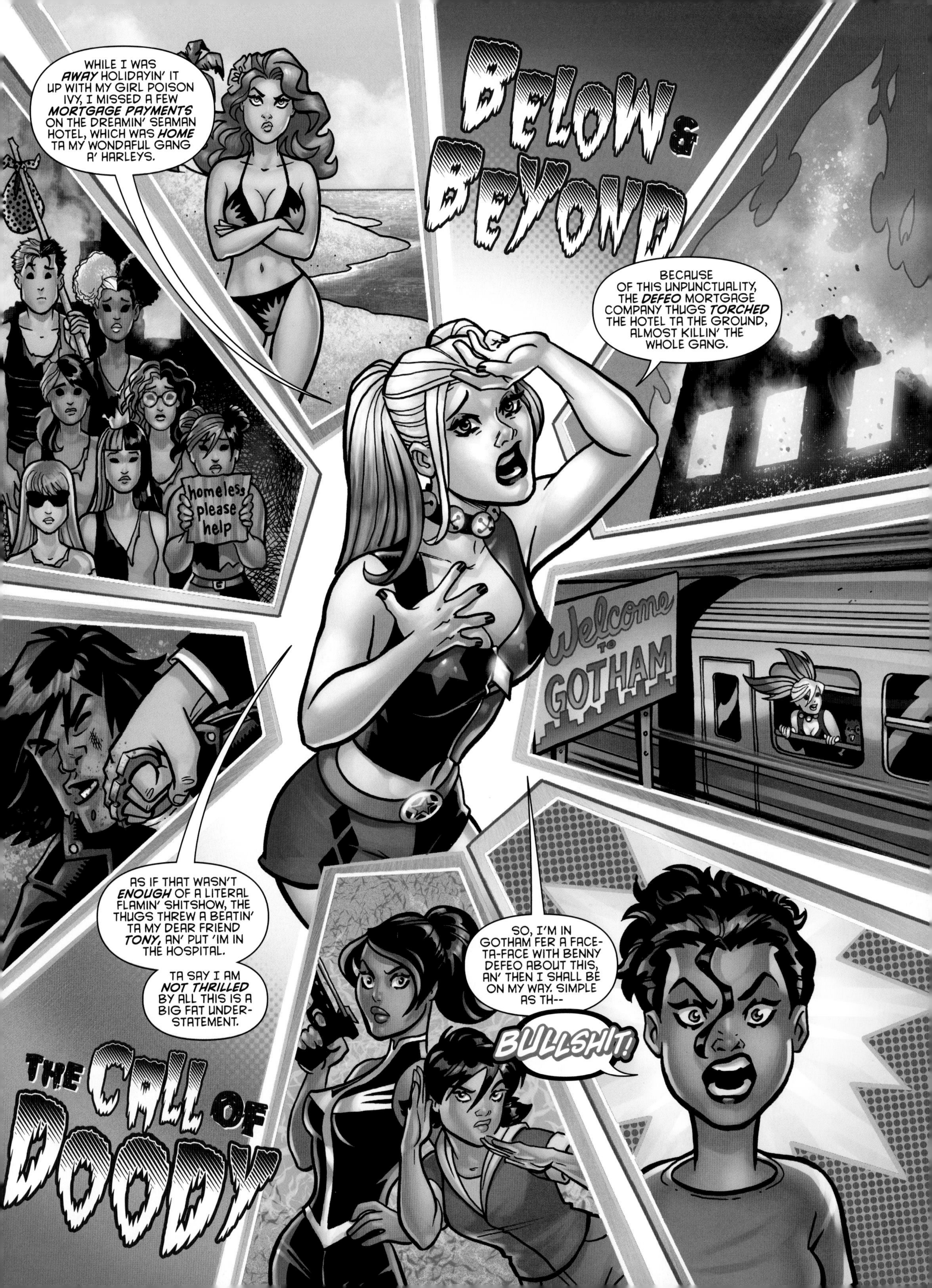
WHILE I WAS AWAY HOLIDAYIN' IT UP WITH MY GIRL POISON IVY, I MISSED A FEW MORTGAGE PAYMENTS ON THE DREAMIN' SEAMAN HOTEL, WHICH WAS HOME TA MY WONDAFUL GANG A' HARLEYS.
homeless please help
BELOW & BEYOND
BECAUSE OF THIS UNPUNCTUALITY, THE DEFEO MORTGAGE COMPANY THUGS TORCHED THE HOTEL TA THE GROUND, ALMOST KILLIN' THE WHOLE GANG.
Welcome TO GOTHAM
AS IF THAT WASN'T ENOUGH OF A LITERAL FLAMIN' SHITSHOW, THE THUGS THREW A BEATIN' TA MY DEAR FRIEND TONY, AN' PUT 'IM IN THE HOSPITAL.
TA SAY I AM NOT THRILLED BY ALL THIS IS A BIG FAT UNDER-STATEMENT.
SO, I'M IN GOTHAM FER A FACE-TA-FACE WITH BENNY DEFEO ABOUT THIS, AN' THEN I SHALL BE ON MY WAY. SIMPLE AS TH--
BULLSHIT!
THE CALL OF DOODY

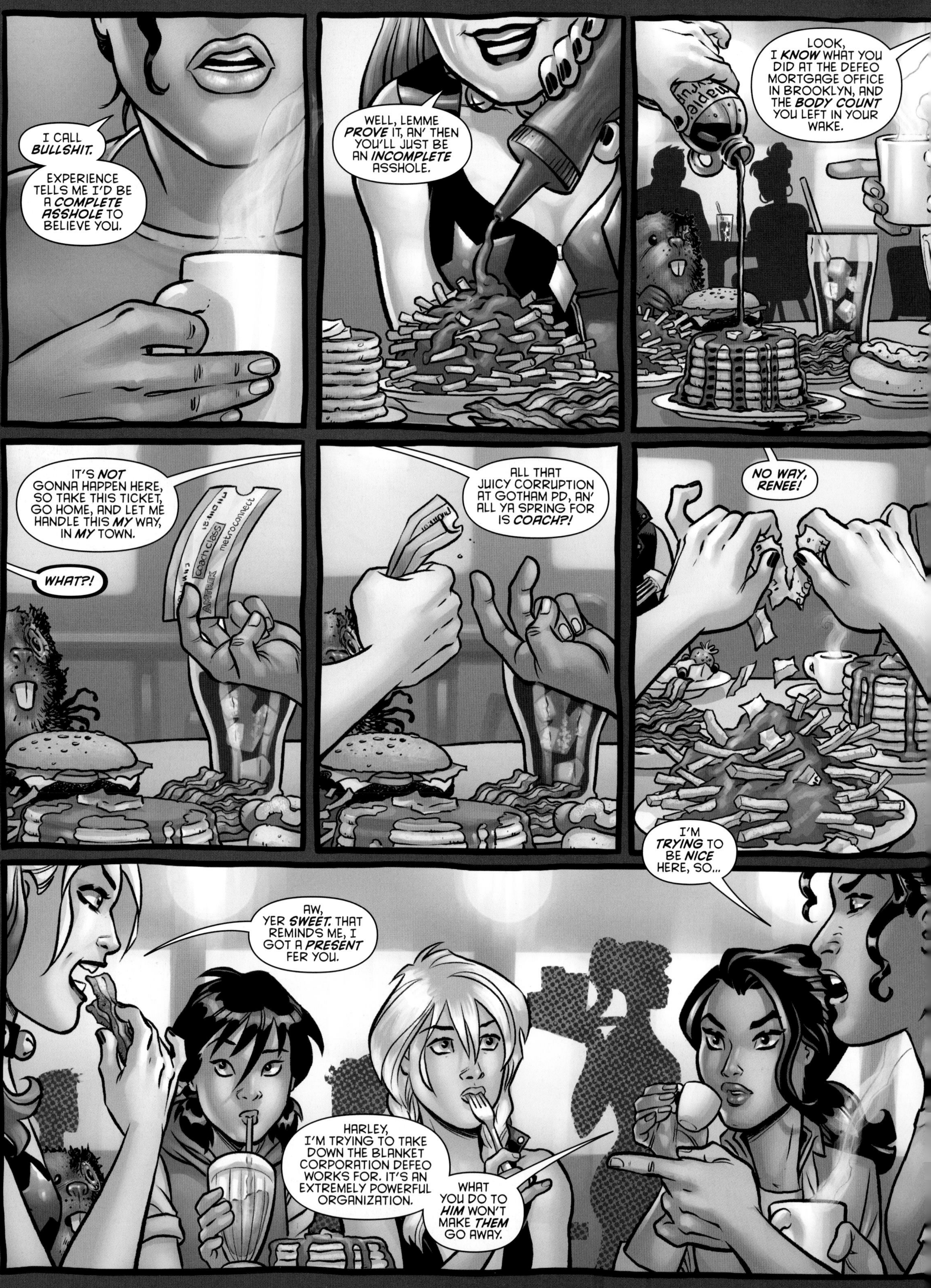
I CALL BULLSHIT.
EXPERIENCE TELLS ME I'D BE A COMPLETE ASSHOLE TO BELIEVE YOU.
WELL, LEMME PROVE IT, AN' THEN YOU'LL JUST BE AN INCOMPLETE ASSHOLE.
LOOK, I KNOW WHAT YOU DID AT THE DEFEO MORTGAGE OFFICE IN BROOKLYN, AND THE BODY COUNT YOU LEFT IN YOUR WAKE.
IT'S NOT GONNA HAPPEN HERE, SO TAKE THIS TICKET, GO HOME, AND LET ME HANDLE THIS MY WAY, IN MY TOWN.
WHAT?!
ALL THAT JUICY CORRUPTION AT GOTHAM PD, AN' ALL YA SPRING FOR IS COACH?!
NO WAY, RENEE!
I'M TRYING TO BE NICE HERE, SO...
AW, YER SWEET. THAT REMINDS ME, I GOT A PRESENT FER YOU.
HARLEY, I'M TRYING TO TAKE DOWN THE BLANKET CORPORATION DEFEO WORKS FOR. IT'S AN EXTREMELY POWERFUL ORGANIZATION.
WHAT YOU DO TO HIM WON'T MAKE THEM GO AWAY.

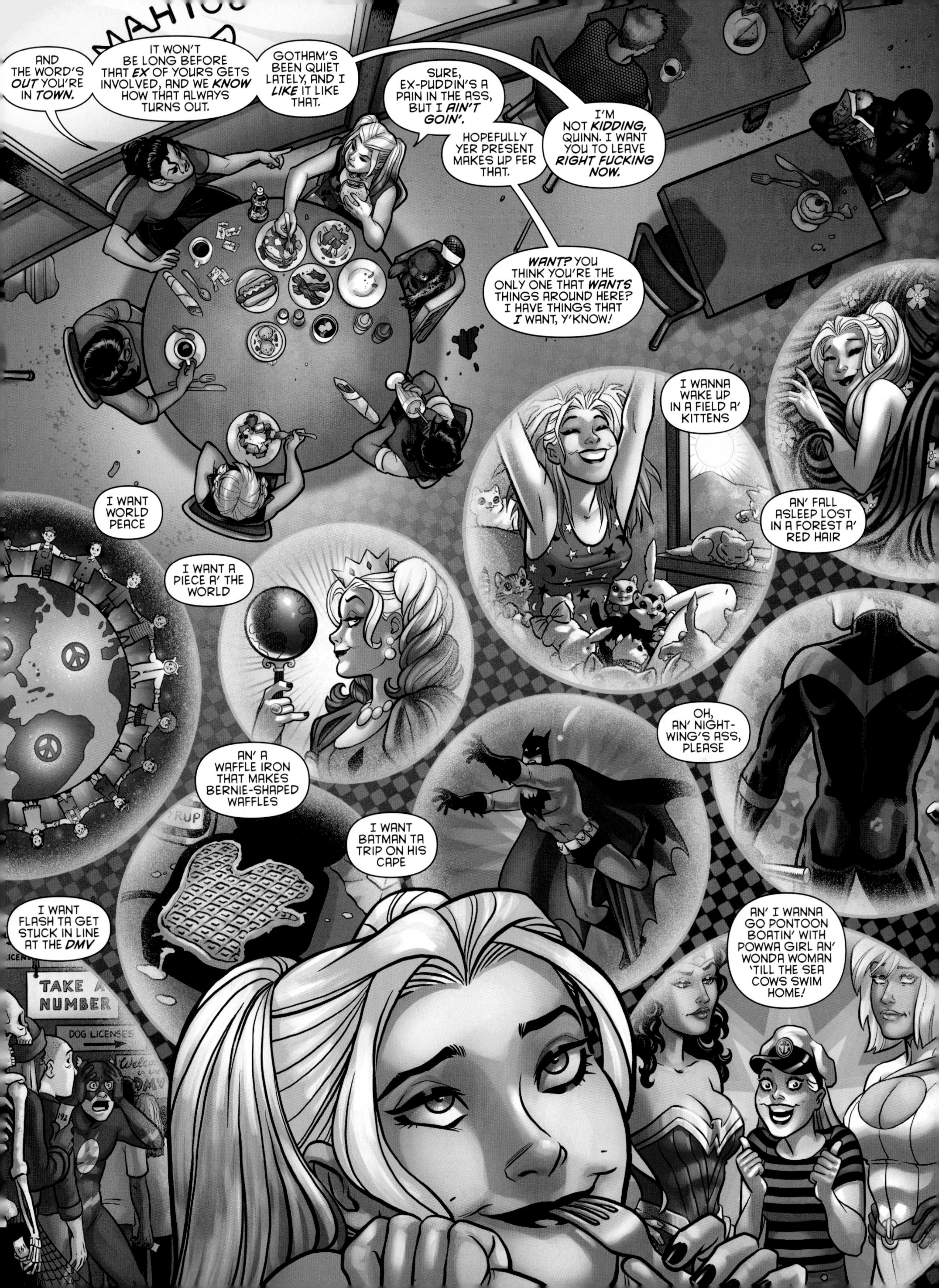
AND THE WORD'S OUT YOU'RE IN TOWN.
IT WON'T BE LONG BEFORE THAT EX OF YOURS GETS INVOLVED, AND WE KNOW HOW THAT ALWAYS TURNS OUT.
GOTHAM'S BEEN QUIET LATELY, AND I LIKE IT LIKE THAT.
SURE, EX-PUDDIN'S A PAIN IN THE ASS, BUT I AIN'T GOIN'.
HOPEFULLY YER PRESENT MAKES UP FER THAT.
I'M NOT KIDDING, QUINN. I WANT YOU TO LEAVE RIGHT FUCKING NOW.
WANT? YOU THINK YOU'RE THE ONLY ONE THAT WANTS THINGS AROUND HERE? I HAVE THINGS THAT I WANT, Y'KNOW!
I WANNA WAKE UP IN A FIELD A' KITTENS
AN' FALL ASLEEP LOST IN A FOREST A' RED HAIR
I WANT WORLD PEACE
I WANT A PIECE A' THE WORLD
OH, AN' NIGHT-WING'S ASS, PLEASE
AN' A WAFFLE IRON THAT MAKES BERNIE-SHAPED WAFFLES
I WANT BATMAN TA TRIP ON HIS CAPE
I WANT FLASH TA GET STUCK IN LINE AT THE DMV
AN' I WANNA GO PONTOON BOATIN' WITH POWWA GIRL AN' WONDA WOMAN 'TILL THE SEA COWS SWIM HOME!
TAKE A NUMBER
DOG LICENSES

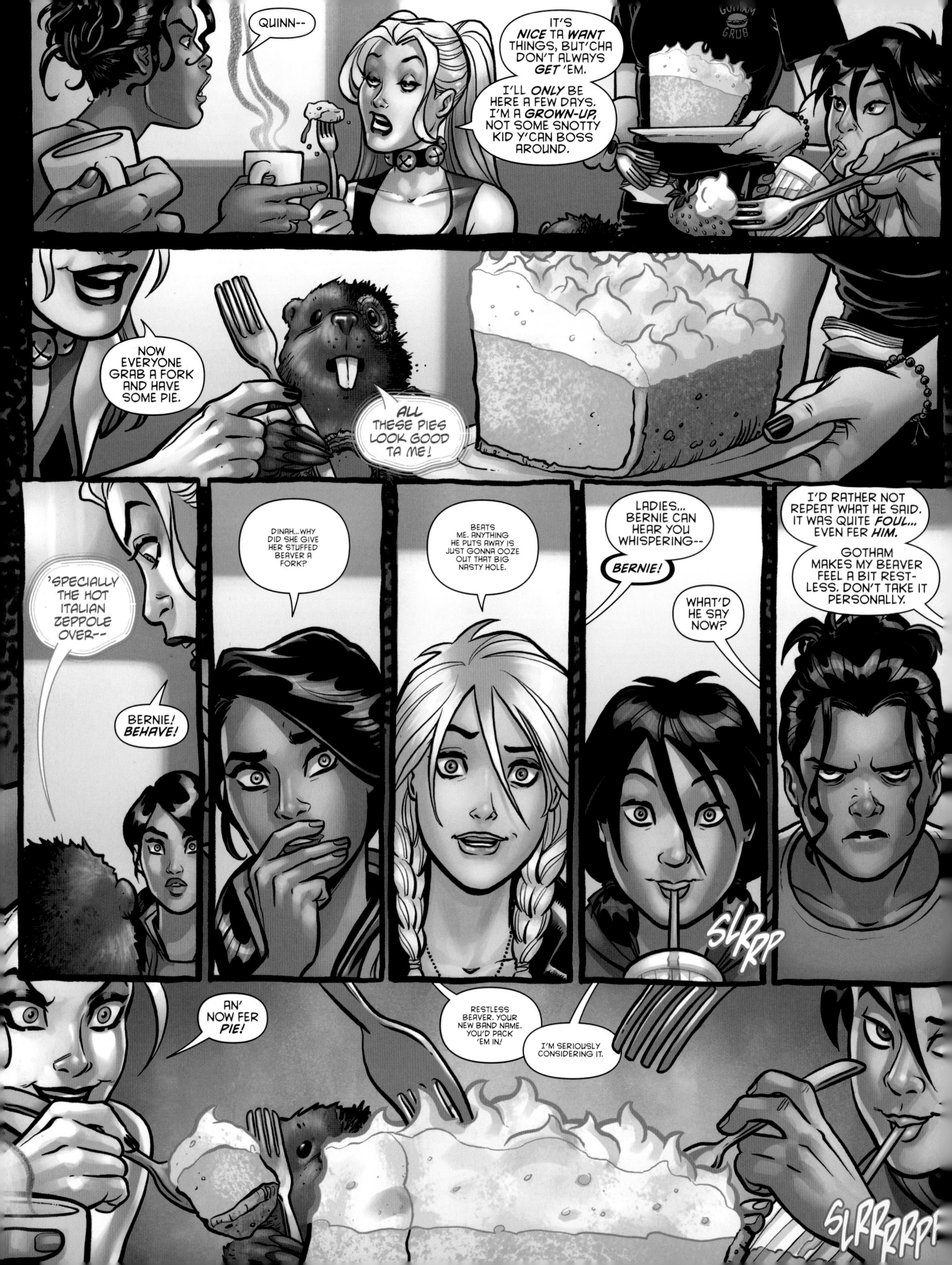
QUINN--
IT'S NICE TA WANT THINGS, BUT'CHA DON'T ALWAYS GET 'EM.
I'LL ONLY BE HERE A FEW DAYS. I'M A GROWN-UP, NOT SOME SNOTTY KID Y'CAN BOSS AROUND.
GOTHAM GRUB
NOW EVERYONE GRAB A FORK AND HAVE SOME PIE.
ALL THESE PIES LOOK GOOD TA ME!
'SPECIALLY THE HOT ITALIAN ZEPPOLE OVER--
BERNIE! BEHAVE!
DINAH...WHY DID SHE GIVE HER STUFFED BEAVER A FORK?
BEATS ME. ANYTHING HE PUTS AWAY IS JUST GONNA OOZE OUT THAT BIG NASTY HOLE.
LADIES... BERNIE CAN HEAR YOU WHISPERING--
BERNIE!
WHAT'D HE SAY NOW?
I'D RATHER NOT REPEAT WHAT HE SAID. IT WAS QUITE FOUL... EVEN FER HIM.
GOTHAM MAKES MY BEAVER FEEL A BIT RESTLESS. DON'T TAKE IT PERSONALLY.
SLRRP
AN' NOW FER PIE!
RESTLESS BEAVER. YOUR NEW BAND NAME. YOU'D PACK 'EM IN!
I'M SERIOUSLY CONSIDERING IT.
SLRRRRRPF

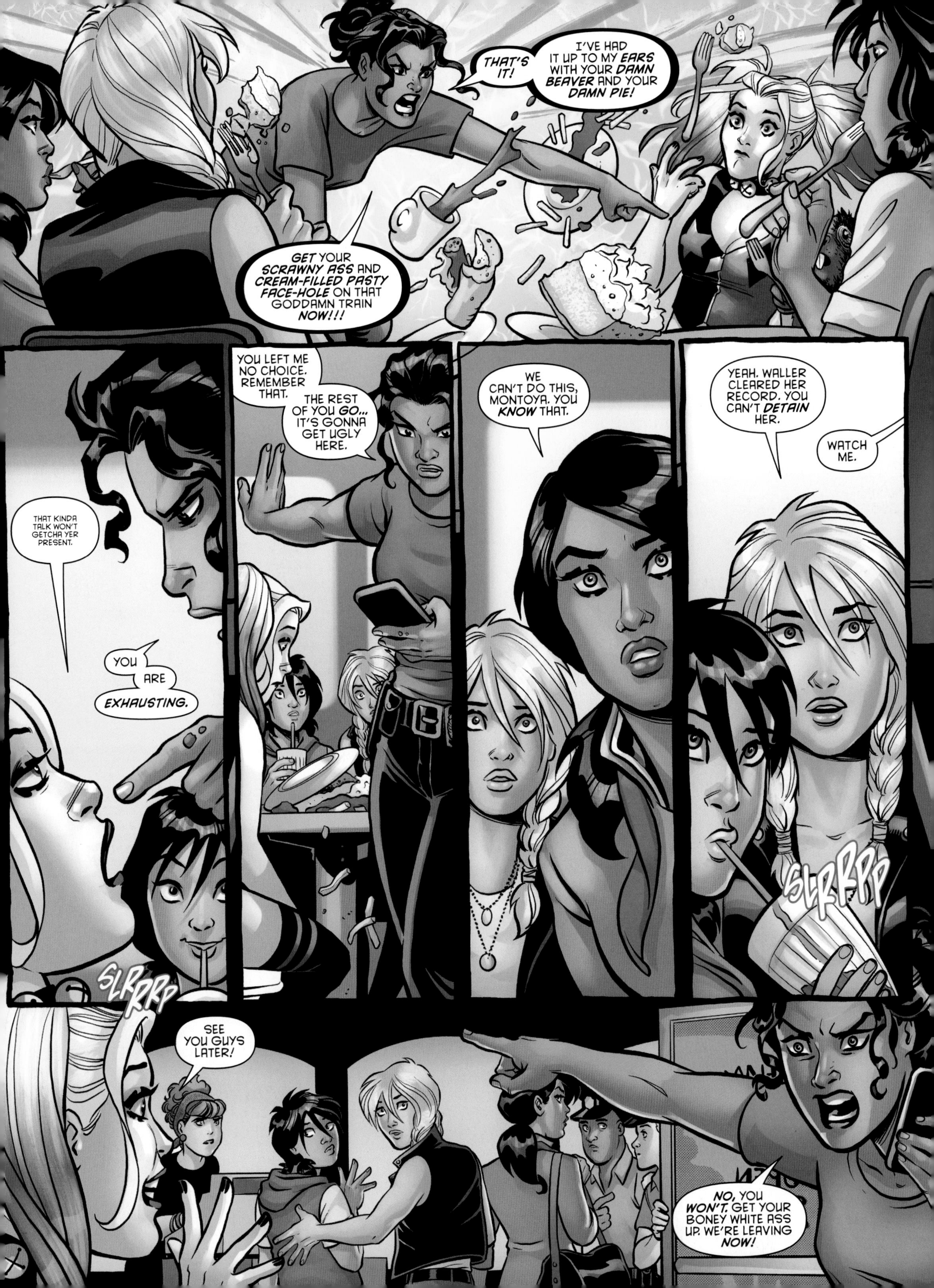
THAT'S IT!
I'VE HAD IT UP TO MY EARS WITH YOUR DAMN BEAVER AND YOUR DAMN PIE!
GET YOUR SCRAWNY ASS AND CREAM-FILLED PASTY FACE-HOLE ON THAT GODDAMN TRAIN NOW!!!
THAT KINDA TALK WON'T GETCHA YER PRESENT.
YOU
ARE
EXHAUSTING.
SLRRRP
YOU LEFT ME NO CHOICE. REMEMBER THAT.
THE REST OF YOU GO... IT'S GONNA GET UGLY HERE.
WE CAN'T DO THIS, MONTOYA. YOU KNOW THAT.
YEAH. WALLER CLEARED HER RECORD. YOU CAN'T DETAIN HER.
WATCH ME.
SLRRPP
SEE YOU GUYS LATER!
NO, YOU WON'T. GET YOUR BONEY WHITE ASS UP. WE'RE LEAVING NOW!

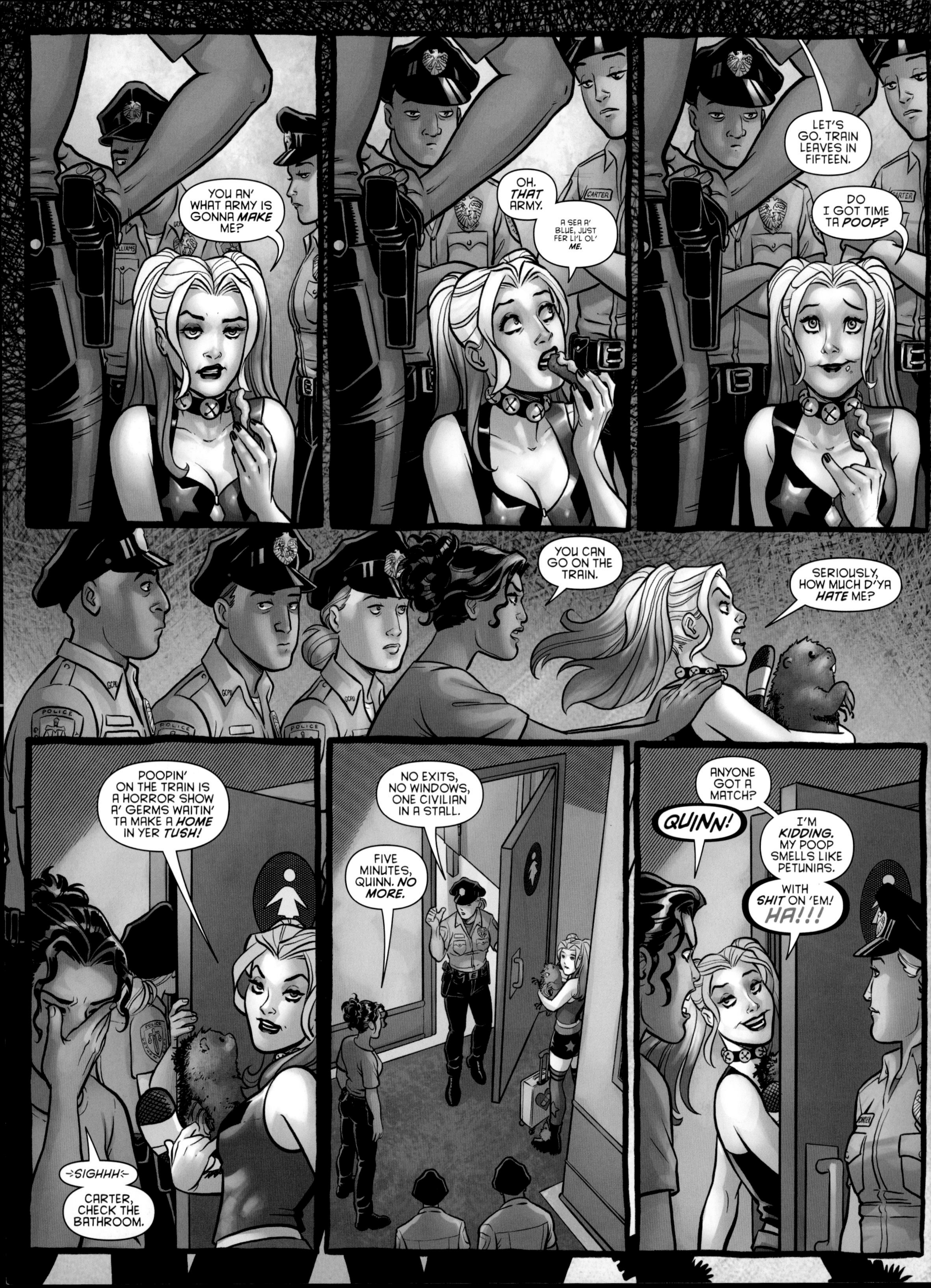

YOU AN' WHAT ARMY IS GONNA *MAKE* ME?
OH. *THAT* ARMY.
A SEA A' BLUE, JUST FER LI'L OL' *ME.*
LET'S GO. TRAIN LEAVES IN FIFTEEN.
DO I GOT TIME TA *POOP?*
YOU CAN GO ON THE TRAIN.
SERIOUSLY, HOW MUCH D'YA *HATE* ME?
POOPIN' ON THE TRAIN IS A HORROR SHOW A' GERMS WAITIN' TA MAKE A *HOME* IN YER *TUSH!*
-SIGHHH-
CARTER, CHECK THE BATHROOM.
NO EXITS, NO WINDOWS, ONE CIVILIAN IN A STALL.
FIVE MINUTES, QUINN. *NO MORE.*
ANYONE GOT A MATCH?
QUINN!
I'M *KIDDING.* MY POOP SMELLS LIKE PETUNIAS.
WITH *SHIT* ON 'EM! HA!!!

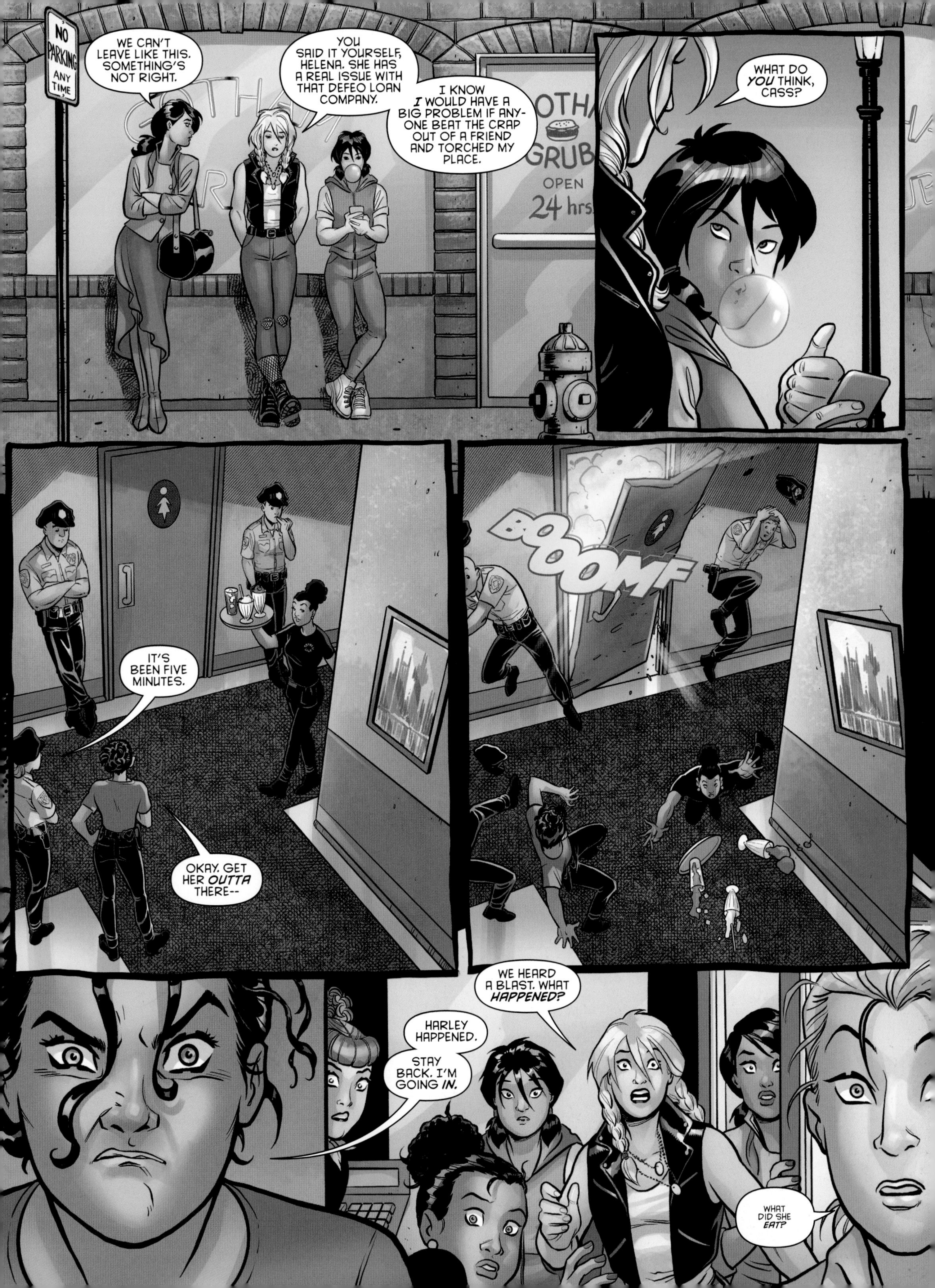
NO PARKING ANY TIME
WE CAN'T LEAVE LIKE THIS. SOMETHING'S NOT RIGHT.
YOU SAID IT YOURSELF, HELENA. SHE HAS A REAL ISSUE WITH THAT DEFEO LOAN COMPANY.
I KNOW *I* WOULD HAVE A BIG PROBLEM IF ANY-ONE BEAT THE CRAP OUT OF A FRIEND AND TORCHED MY PLACE.
OPEN 24 hrs.
WHAT DO *YOU* THINK, CASS?
IT'S BEEN FIVE MINUTES.
OKAY. GET HER *OUTTA* THERE--
BOOOMF
WE HEARD A BLAST. WHAT *HAPPENED?*
HARLEY HAPPENED.
STAY BACK. I'M GOING *IN.*
WHAT DID SHE *EAT?*

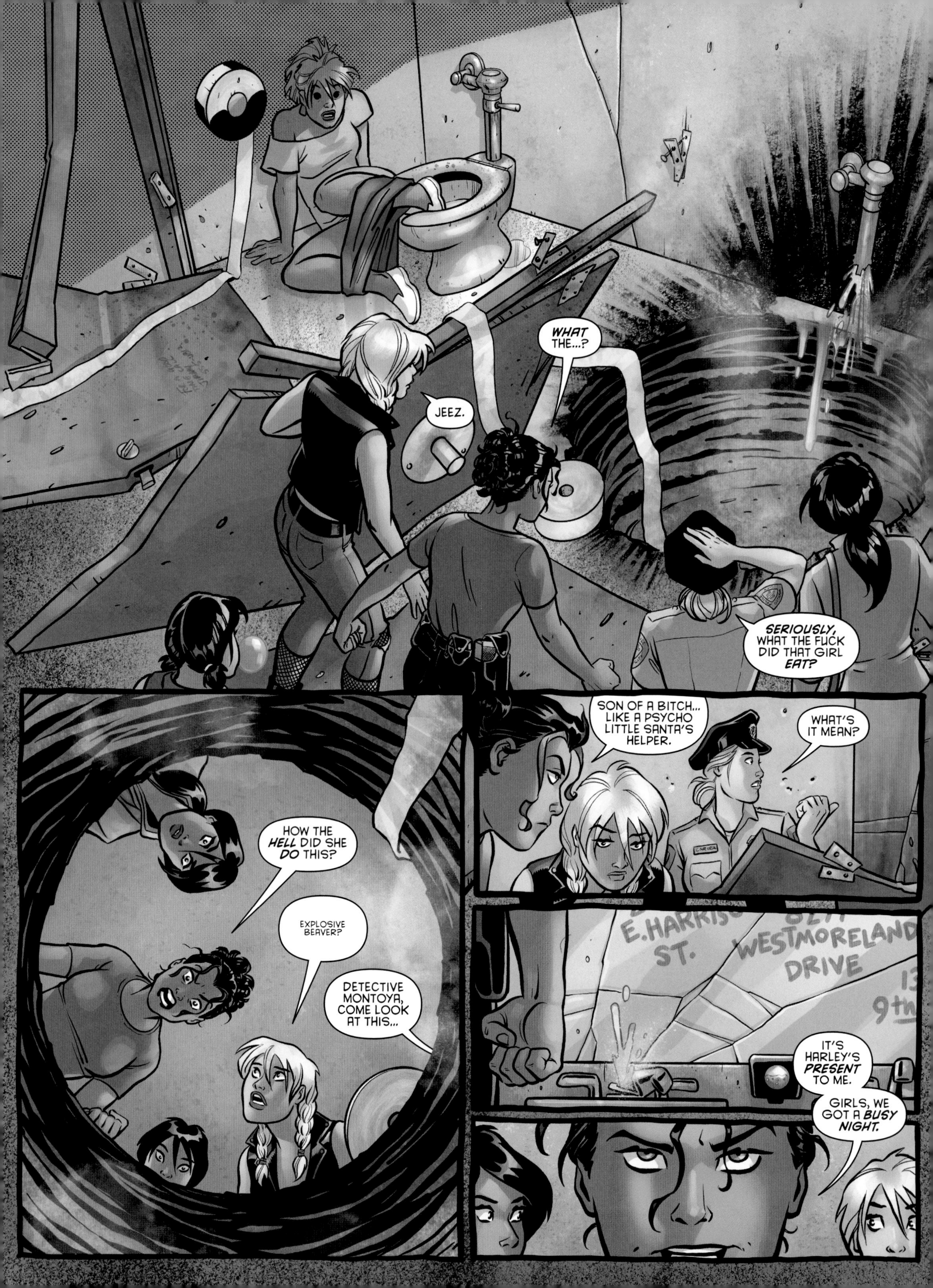
JEEZ.
WHAT THE...?
SERIOUSLY, WHAT THE FUCK DID THAT GIRL EAT?
HOW THE HELL DID SHE DO THIS?
EXPLOSIVE BEAVER?
DETECTIVE MONTOYA, COME LOOK AT THIS...
SON OF A BITCH... LIKE A PSYCHO LITTLE SANTA'S HELPER.
WHAT'S IT MEAN?
ST.
WESTMORELAND
DRIVE
IT'S HARLEY'S PRESENT TO ME.
GIRLS, WE GOT A BUSY NIGHT.

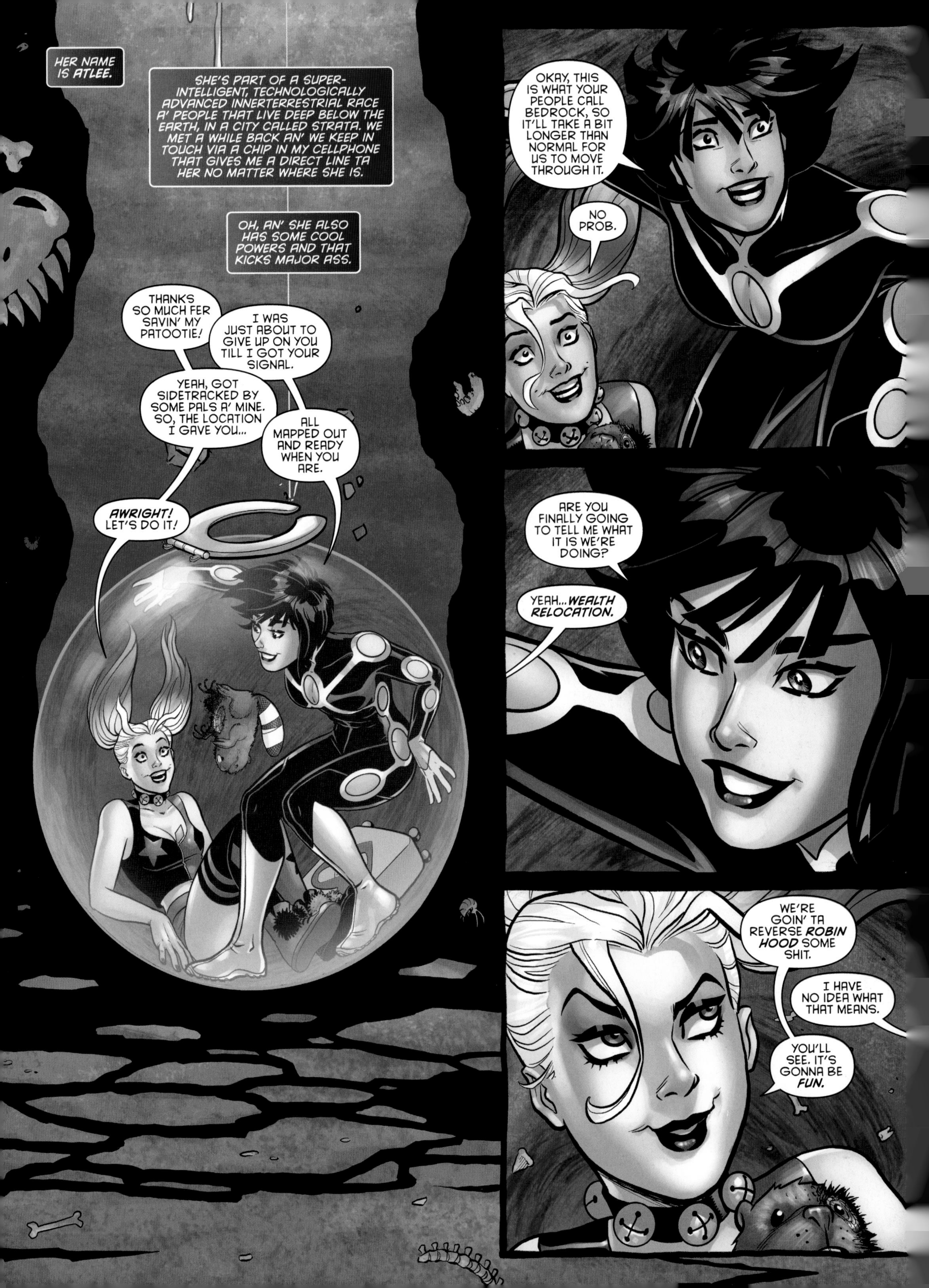
HER NAME IS ATLEE.
SHE'S PART OF A SUPER-INTELLIGENT, TECHNOLOGICALLY ADVANCED INNERTERRESTRIAL RACE A' PEOPLE THAT LIVE DEEP BELOW THE EARTH, IN A CITY CALLED STRATA. WE MET A WHILE BACK AN' WE KEEP IN TOUCH VIA A CHIP IN MY CELLPHONE THAT GIVES ME A DIRECT LINE TA HER NO MATTER WHERE SHE IS.
OH, AN' SHE ALSO HAS SOME COOL POWERS AND THAT KICKS MAJOR ASS.
THANKS SO MUCH FER SAVIN' MY PATOOTIE!
I WAS JUST ABOUT TO GIVE UP ON YOU TILL I GOT YOUR SIGNAL.
YEAH, GOT SIDETRACKED BY SOME PALS A' MINE. SO, THE LOCATION I GAVE YOU...
ALL MAPPED OUT AND READY WHEN YOU ARE.
AWRIGHT! LET'S DO IT!
OKAY, THIS IS WHAT YOUR PEOPLE CALL BEDROCK, SO IT'LL TAKE A BIT LONGER THAN NORMAL FOR US TO MOVE THROUGH IT.
NO PROB.
ARE YOU FINALLY GOING TO TELL ME WHAT IT IS WE'RE DOING?
YEAH...WEALTH RELOCATION.
WE'RE GOIN' TA REVERSE ROBIN HOOD SOME SHIT.
I HAVE NO IDEA WHAT THAT MEANS.
YOU'LL SEE. IT'S GONNA BE FUN.

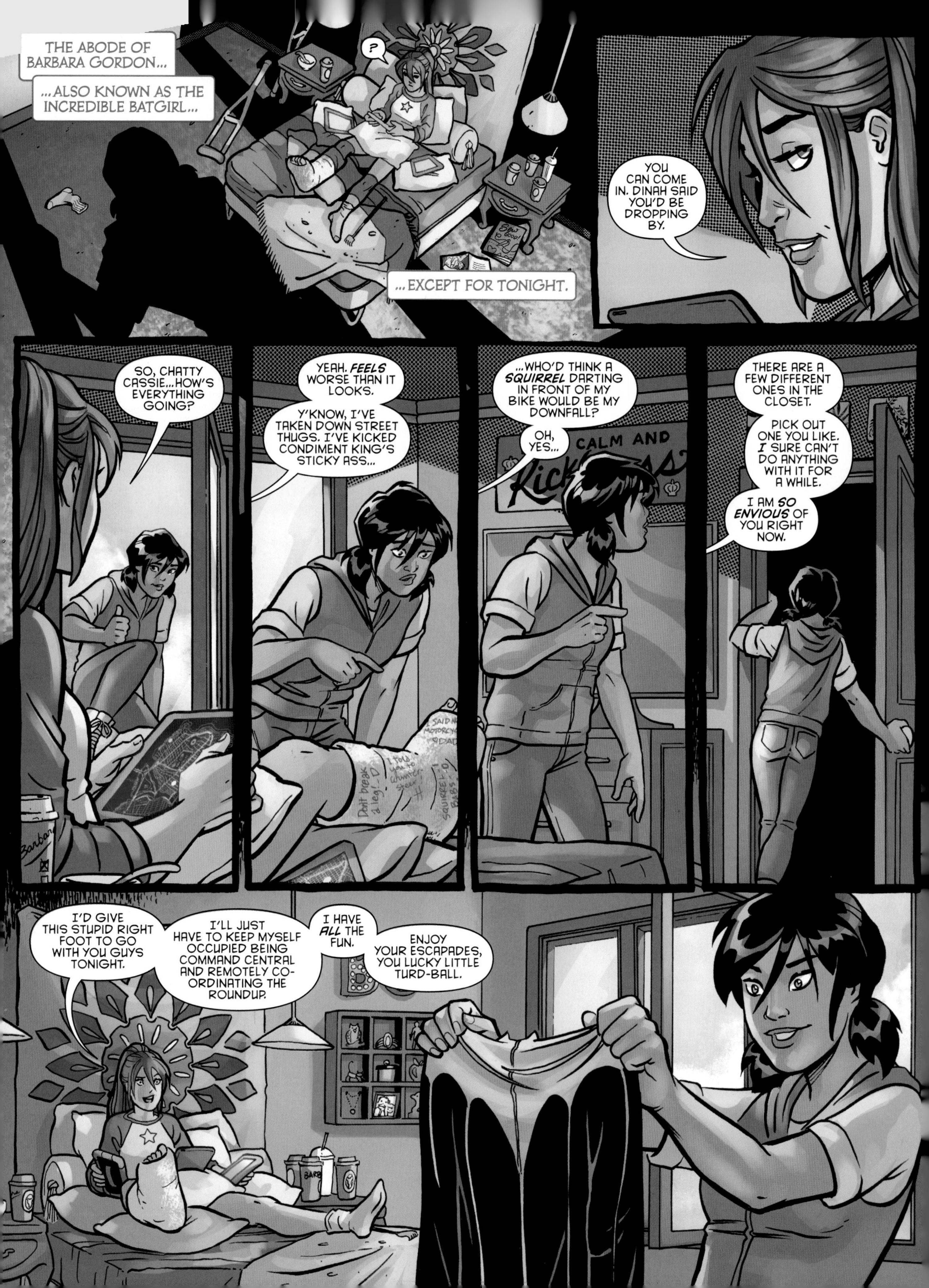
THE ABODE OF BARBARA GORDON...
...ALSO KNOWN AS THE INCREDIBLE BATGIRL...
?
...EXCEPT FOR TONIGHT.
YOU CAN COME IN. DINAH SAID YOU'D BE DROPPING BY.
SO, CHATTY CASSIE...HOW'S EVERYTHING GOING?
YEAH. FEELS WORSE THAN IT LOOKS.
Y'KNOW, I'VE TAKEN DOWN STREET THUGS. I'VE KICKED CONDIMENT KING'S STICKY ASS...
...WHO'D THINK A SQUIRREL DARTING IN FRONT OF MY BIKE WOULD BE MY DOWNFALL?
OH, YES...
THERE ARE A FEW DIFFERENT ONES IN THE CLOSET.
PICK OUT ONE YOU LIKE. I SURE CAN'T DO ANYTHING WITH IT FOR A WHILE.
I AM SO ENVIOUS OF YOU RIGHT NOW.
I'D GIVE THIS STUPID RIGHT FOOT TO GO WITH YOU GUYS TONIGHT.
I'LL JUST HAVE TO KEEP MYSELF OCCUPIED BEING COMMAND CENTRAL AND REMOTELY CO-ORDINATING THE ROUNDUP.
I HAVE ALL THE FUN.
ENJOY YOUR ESCAPADES, YOU LUCKY LITTLE TURD-BALL.

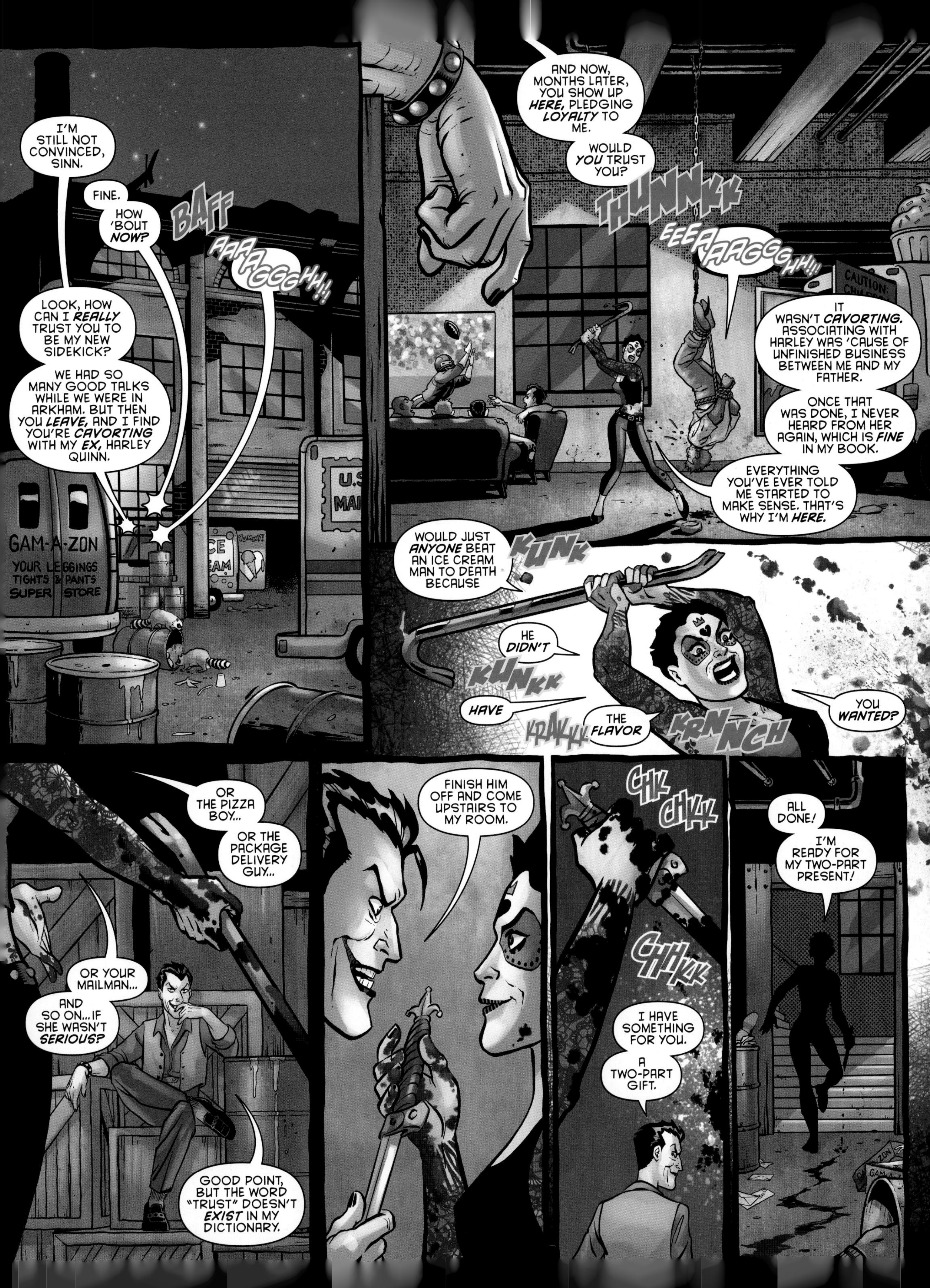
I'M STILL NOT CONVINCED, SINN.
LOOK, HOW CAN I REALLY TRUST YOU TO BE MY NEW SIDEKICK?
WE HAD SO MANY GOOD TALKS WHILE WE WERE IN ARKHAM. BUT THEN YOU LEAVE, AND I FIND YOU'RE CAVORTING WITH MY EX, HARLEY QUINN.
FINE.
HOW 'BOUT NOW?
BAFF
AAAAGGGHH!!
GAM-A-ZON
YOUR LEGGINGS TIGHTS & PANTS SUPER STORE
AND NOW, MONTHS LATER, YOU SHOW UP HERE, PLEDGING LOYALTY TO ME.
WOULD YOU TRUST YOU?
THUNNKK
EEEAAAGGGHH!!
IT WASN'T CAVORTING. ASSOCIATING WITH HARLEY WAS 'CAUSE OF UNFINISHED BUSINESS BETWEEN ME AND MY FATHER.
ONCE THAT WAS DONE, I NEVER HEARD FROM HER AGAIN, WHICH IS FINE IN MY BOOK.
EVERYTHING YOU'VE EVER TOLD ME STARTED TO MAKE SENSE. THAT'S WHY I'M HERE.
WOULD JUST ANYONE BEAT AN ICE CREAM MAN TO DEATH BECAUSE
KUNK
HE DIDN'T
KUNKK
HAVE
KRAKKK
THE FLAVOR
KRNNCH
YOU WANTED?
OR THE PIZZA BOY...
OR THE PACKAGE DELIVERY GUY...
OR YOUR MAILMAN...
AND SO ON...IF SHE WASN'T SERIOUS?
GOOD POINT, BUT THE WORD "TRUST" DOESN'T EXIST IN MY DICTIONARY.
FINISH HIM OFF AND COME UPSTAIRS TO MY ROOM.
CHK
CHKK
CHHKK
I HAVE SOMETHING FOR YOU.
A TWO-PART GIFT.
ALL DONE!
I'M READY FOR MY TWO-PART PRESENT!

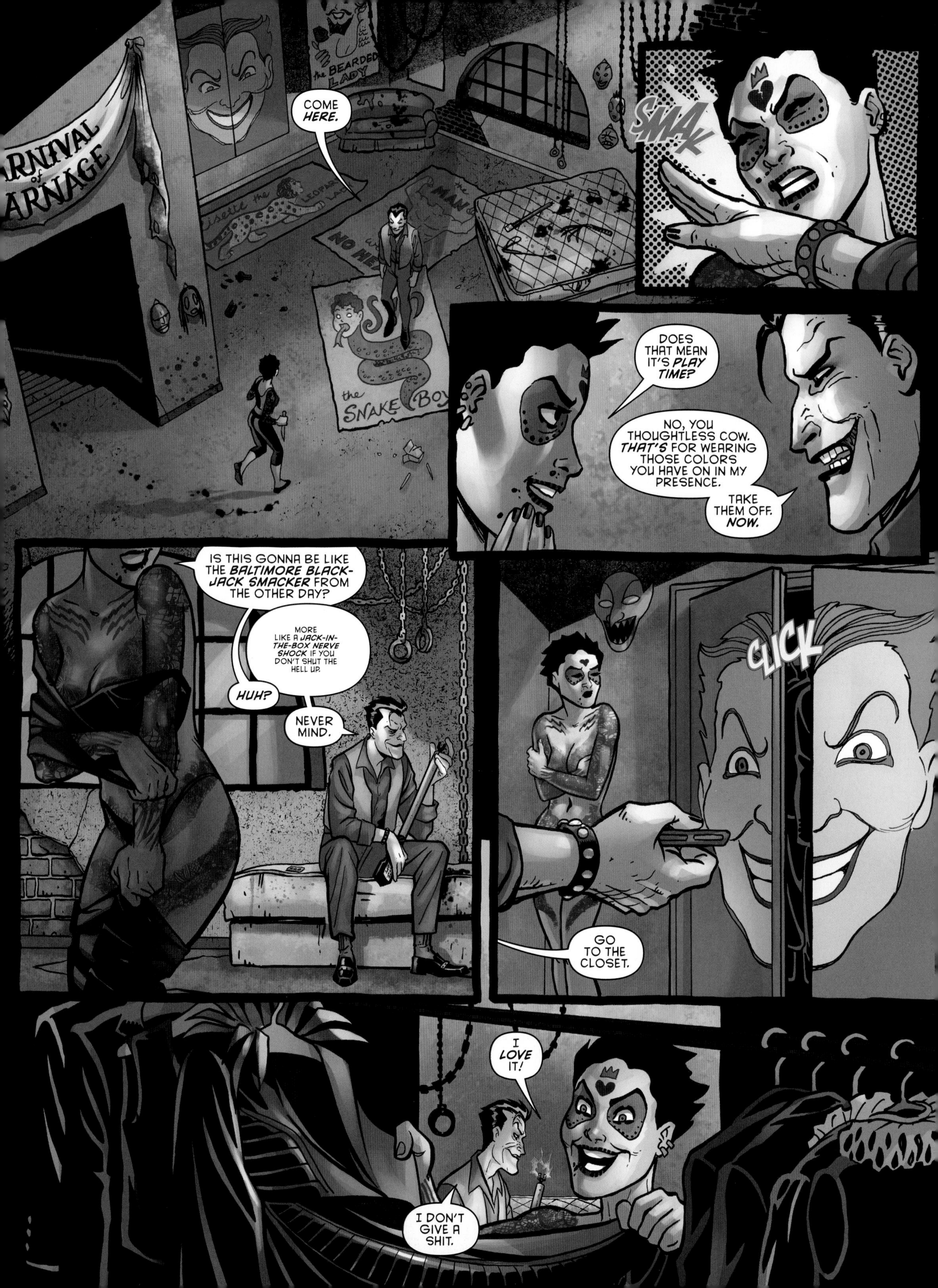

ARNIVAL of ARNAGE
the BEARDED LADY
COME HERE.
NO HE
the SNAKE BOY
SMAK
DOES THAT MEAN IT'S PLAY TIME?
NO, YOU THOUGHTLESS COW. THAT'S FOR WEARING THOSE COLORS YOU HAVE ON IN MY PRESENCE.
TAKE THEM OFF. NOW.
IS THIS GONNA BE LIKE THE BALTIMORE BLACK-JACK SMACKER FROM THE OTHER DAY?
MORE LIKE A JACK-IN-THE-BOX NERVE SHOCK IF YOU DON'T SHUT THE HELL UP.
HUH?
NEVER MIND.
CLICK
GO TO THE CLOSET.
I LOVE IT!
I DON'T GIVE A SHIT.

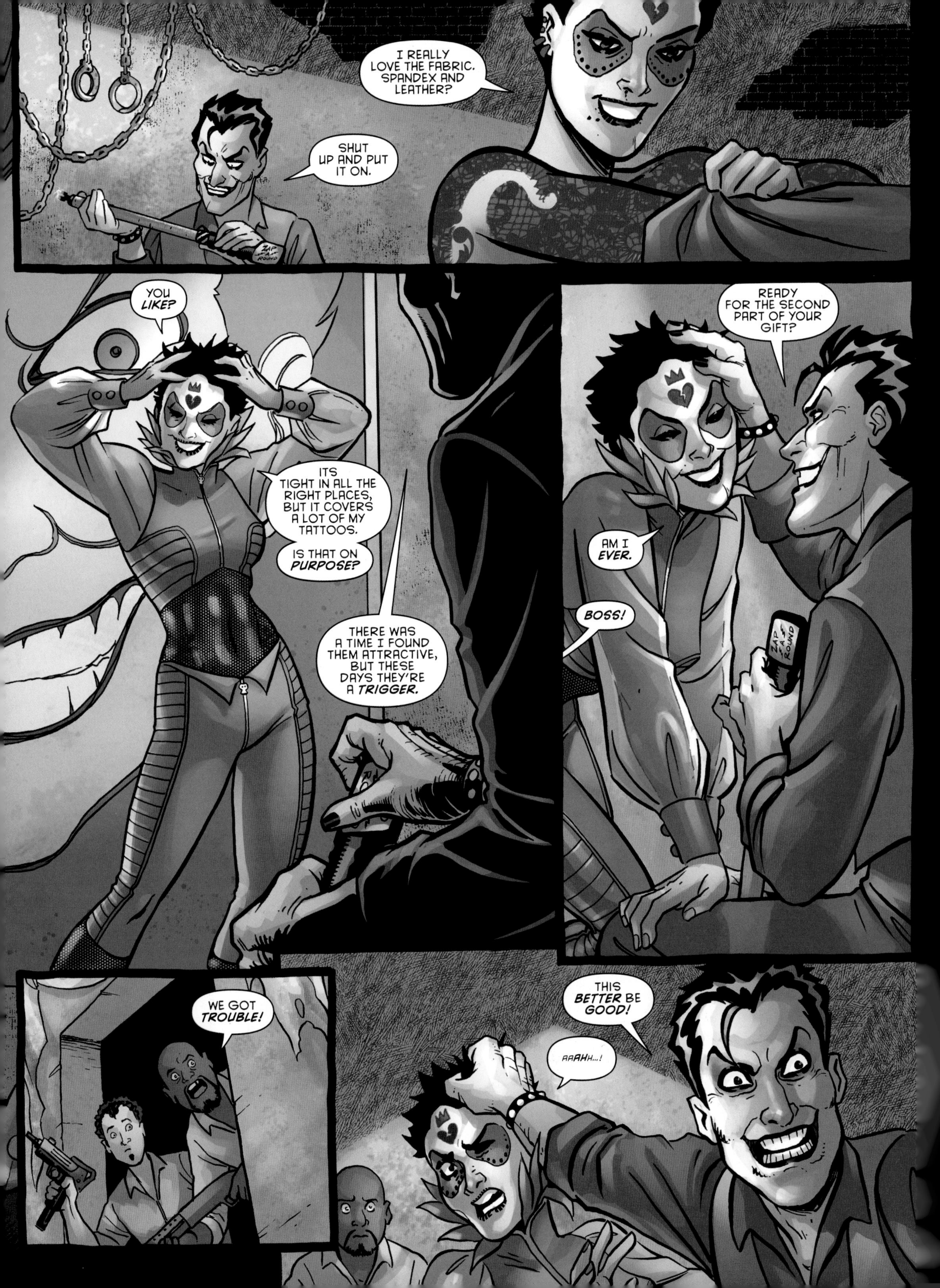

I REALLY LOVE THE FABRIC. SPANDEX AND LEATHER?
SHUT UP AND PUT IT ON.
ZAP A ROUND
YOU LIKE?
ITS TIGHT IN ALL THE RIGHT PLACES, BUT IT COVERS A LOT OF MY TATTOOS.
IS THAT ON PURPOSE?
THERE WAS A TIME I FOUND THEM ATTRACTIVE, BUT THESE DAYS THEY'RE A TRIGGER.
READY FOR THE SECOND PART OF YOUR GIFT?
AM I EVER.
BOSS!
ZAP A ROUND
WE GOT TROUBLE!
THIS BETTER BE GOOD!
AARHH...!

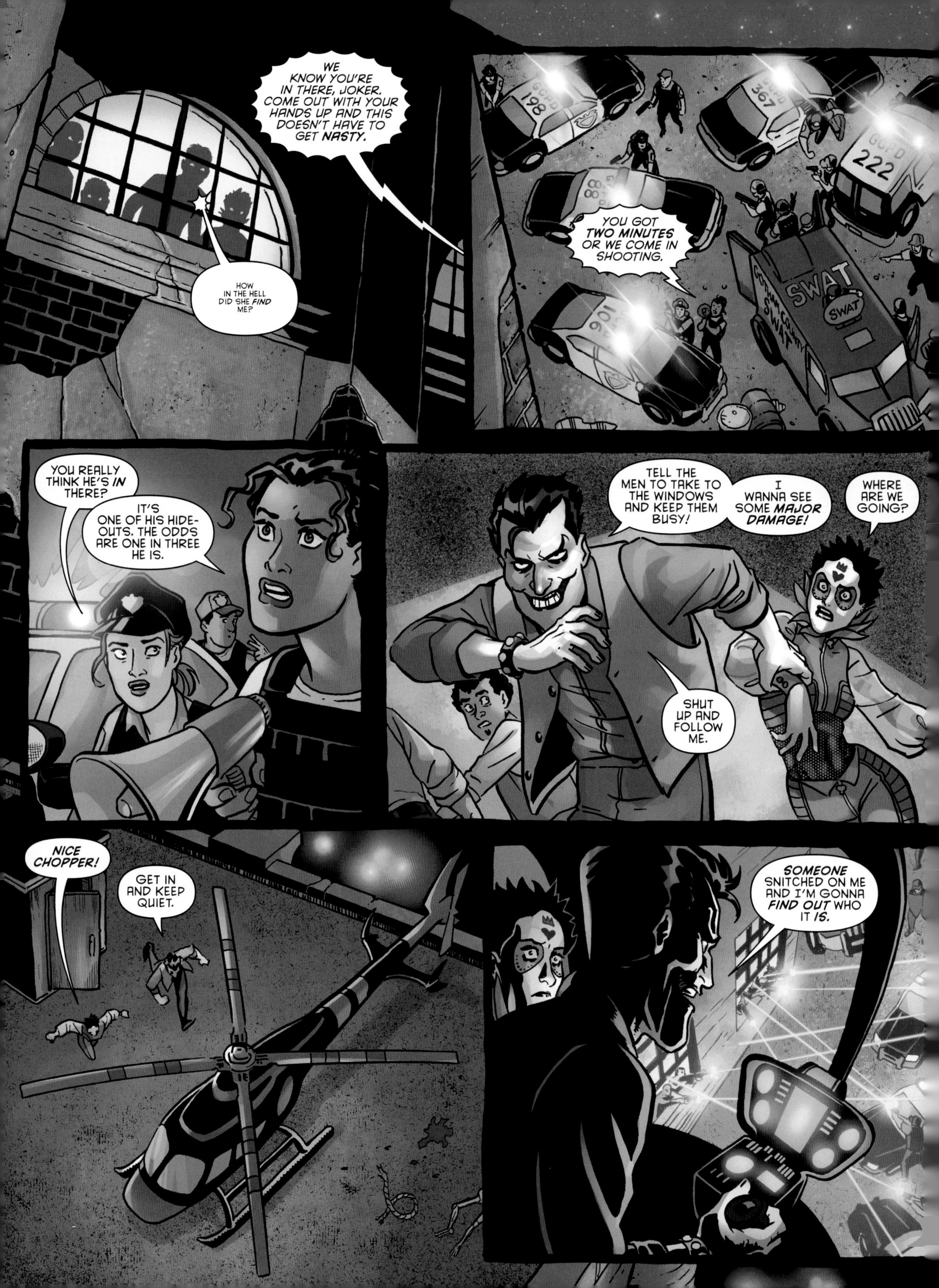
WE KNOW YOU'RE IN THERE, JOKER. COME OUT WITH YOUR HANDS UP AND THIS DOESN'T HAVE TO GET NASTY.
HOW IN THE HELL DID SHE FIND ME?
YOU GOT TWO MINUTES OR WE COME IN SHOOTING.
GCPD 198
GCPD 367
GCPD 222
GCPD 88
GCPD 106
SWAT
GOTHAM COUNTY SWAT
YOU REALLY THINK HE'S IN THERE?
IT'S ONE OF HIS HIDE-OUTS. THE ODDS ARE ONE IN THREE HE IS.
TELL THE MEN TO TAKE TO THE WINDOWS AND KEEP THEM BUSY!
I WANNA SEE SOME MAJOR DAMAGE!
WHERE ARE WE GOING?
SHUT UP AND FOLLOW ME.
NICE CHOPPER!
GET IN AND KEEP QUIET.
SOMEONE SNITCHED ON ME AND I'M GONNA FIND OUT WHO IT IS.

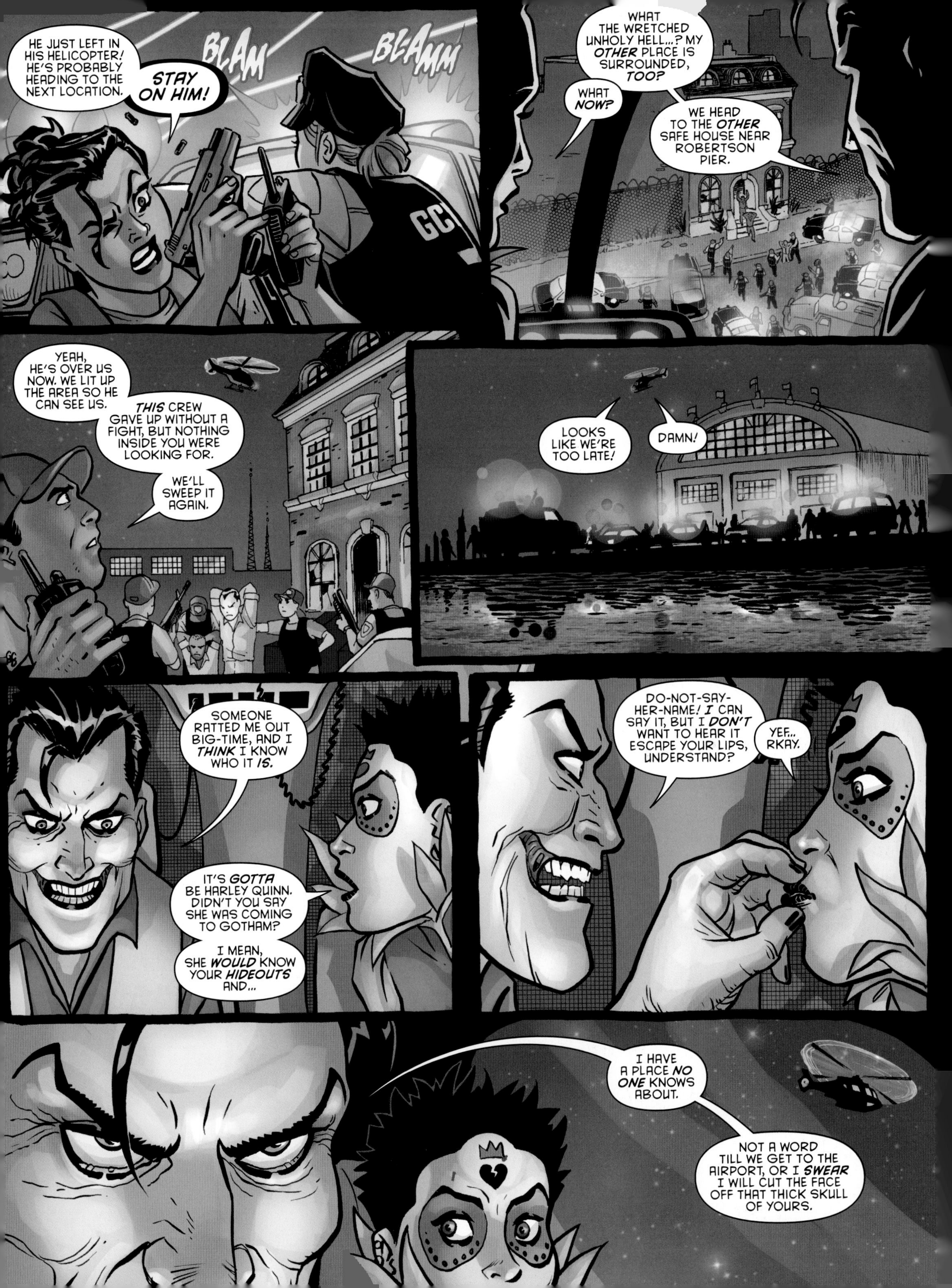
HE JUST LEFT IN HIS HELICOPTER! HE'S PROBABLY HEADING TO THE NEXT LOCATION.
STAY ON HIM!
BLAM
BLAMM
WHAT THE WRETCHED UNHOLY HELL...? MY OTHER PLACE IS SURROUNDED, TOO?
WHAT NOW?
WE HEAD TO THE OTHER SAFE HOUSE NEAR ROBERTSON PIER.
YEAH, HE'S OVER US NOW. WE LIT UP THE AREA SO HE CAN SEE US.
THIS CREW GAVE UP WITHOUT A FIGHT, BUT NOTHING INSIDE YOU WERE LOOKING FOR.
WE'LL SWEEP IT AGAIN.
LOOKS LIKE WE'RE TOO LATE!
DAMN!
SOMEONE RATTED ME OUT BIG-TIME, AND I THINK I KNOW WHO IT IS.
IT'S GOTTA BE HARLEY QUINN. DIDN'T YOU SAY SHE WAS COMING TO GOTHAM?
I MEAN, SHE WOULD KNOW YOUR HIDEOUTS AND...
DO-NOT-SAY-HER-NAME! I CAN SAY IT, BUT I DON'T WANT TO HEAR IT ESCAPE YOUR LIPS, UNDERSTAND?
YEF... RKAY.
I HAVE A PLACE NO ONE KNOWS ABOUT.
NOT A WORD TILL WE GET TO THE AIRPORT, OR I SWEAR I WILL CUT THE FACE OFF THAT THICK SKULL OF YOURS.

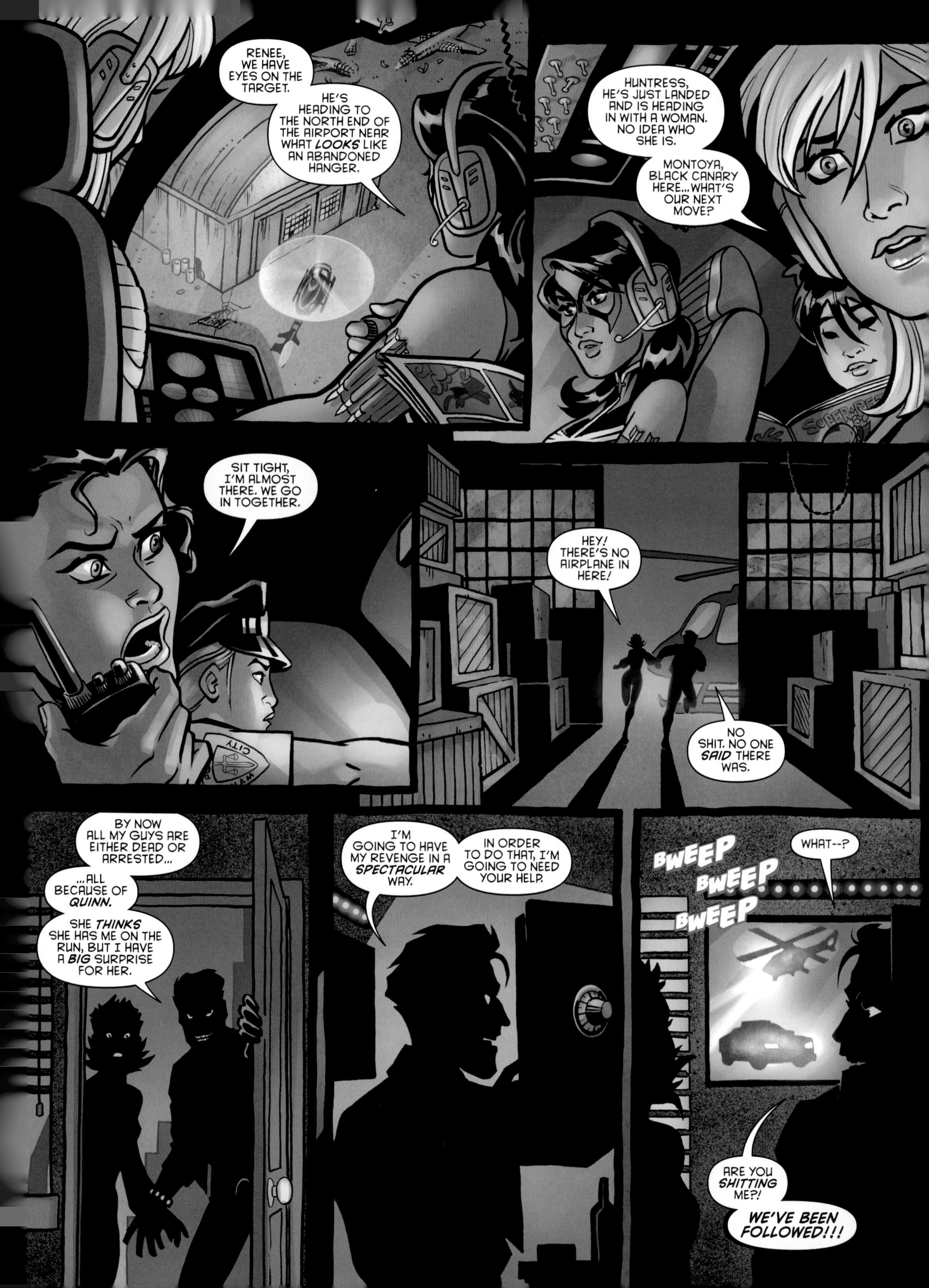
RENEE, WE HAVE EYES ON THE TARGET.
HE'S HEADING TO THE NORTH END OF THE AIRPORT NEAR WHAT *LOOKS* LIKE AN ABANDONED HANGER.
HUNTRESS, HE'S JUST LANDED AND IS HEADING IN WITH A WOMAN. NO IDEA WHO SHE IS.
MONTOYA, BLACK CANARY HERE...WHAT'S OUR NEXT MOVE?
SIT TIGHT, I'M ALMOST THERE. WE GO IN TOGETHER.
HEY! THERE'S NO AIRPLANE IN HERE!
NO SHIT. NO ONE *SAID* THERE WAS.
BY NOW ALL MY GUYS ARE EITHER DEAD OR ARRESTED...
...ALL BECAUSE OF *QUINN.*
SHE *THINKS* SHE HAS ME ON THE RUN, BUT I HAVE A *BIG* SURPRISE FOR HER.
I'M GOING TO HAVE MY REVENGE IN A *SPECTACULAR* WAY.
IN ORDER TO DO THAT, I'M GOING TO NEED YOUR HELP.
BWEEP
BWEEP
BWEEP
WHAT--?
ARE YOU *SHITTING* ME?!
WE'VE BEEN FOLLOWED!!!

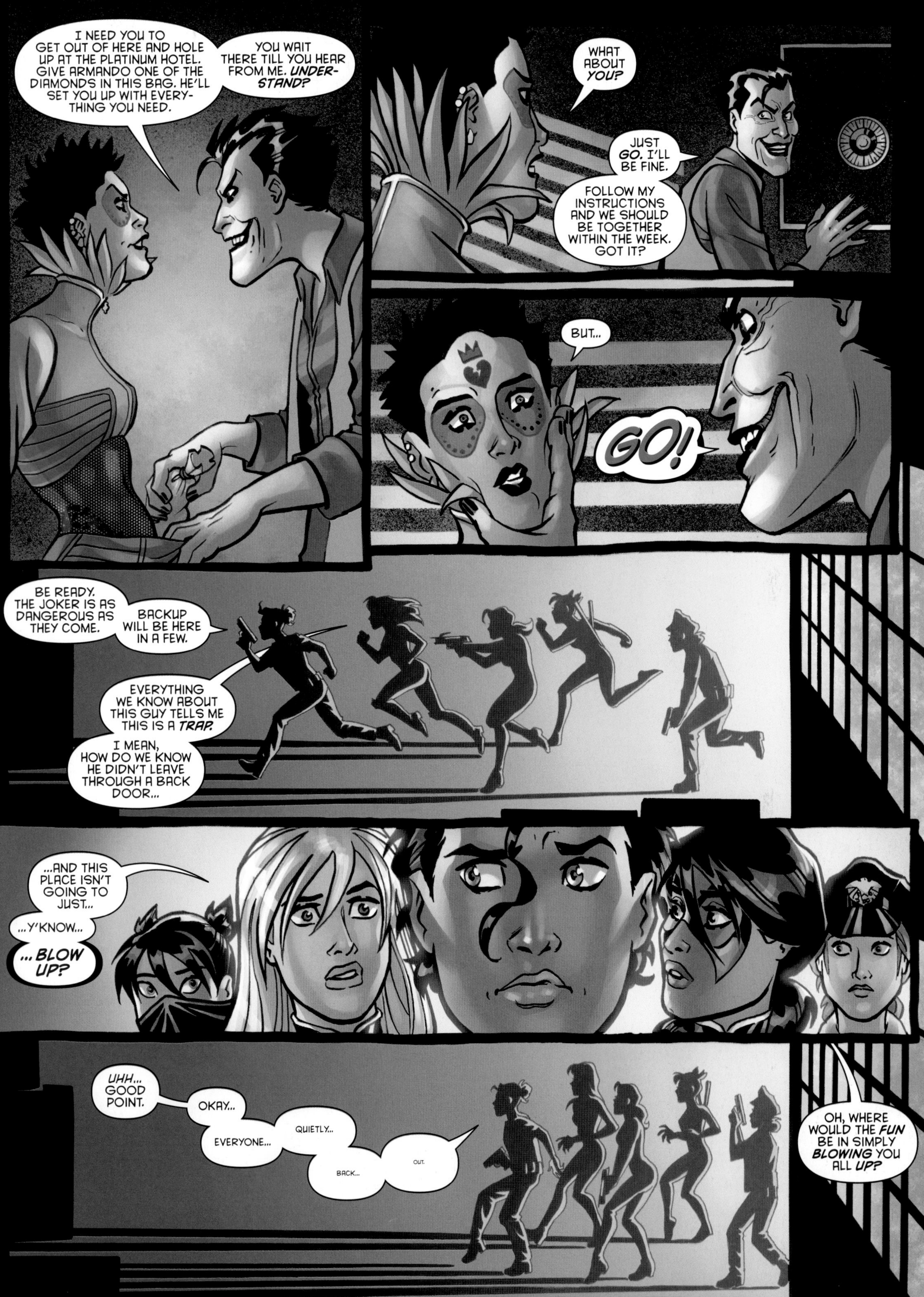
I NEED YOU TO GET OUT OF HERE AND HOLE UP AT THE PLATINUM HOTEL. GIVE ARMANDO ONE OF THE DIAMONDS IN THIS BAG. HE'LL SET YOU UP WITH EVERYTHING YOU NEED.
YOU WAIT THERE TILL YOU HEAR FROM ME. UNDERSTAND?
WHAT ABOUT YOU?
JUST GO. I'LL BE FINE.
FOLLOW MY INSTRUCTIONS AND WE SHOULD BE TOGETHER WITHIN THE WEEK. GOT IT?
BUT...
GO!
BE READY. THE JOKER IS AS DANGEROUS AS THEY COME.
BACKUP WILL BE HERE IN A FEW.
EVERYTHING WE KNOW ABOUT THIS GUY TELLS ME THIS IS A TRAP.
I MEAN, HOW DO WE KNOW HE DIDN'T LEAVE THROUGH A BACK DOOR...
...AND THIS PLACE ISN'T GOING TO JUST...
...Y'KNOW...
...BLOW UP?
UHH... GOOD POINT.
OKAY...
EVERYONE...
QUIETLY...
BACK...
OUT.
OH, WHERE WOULD THE FUN BE IN SIMPLY BLOWING YOU ALL UP?

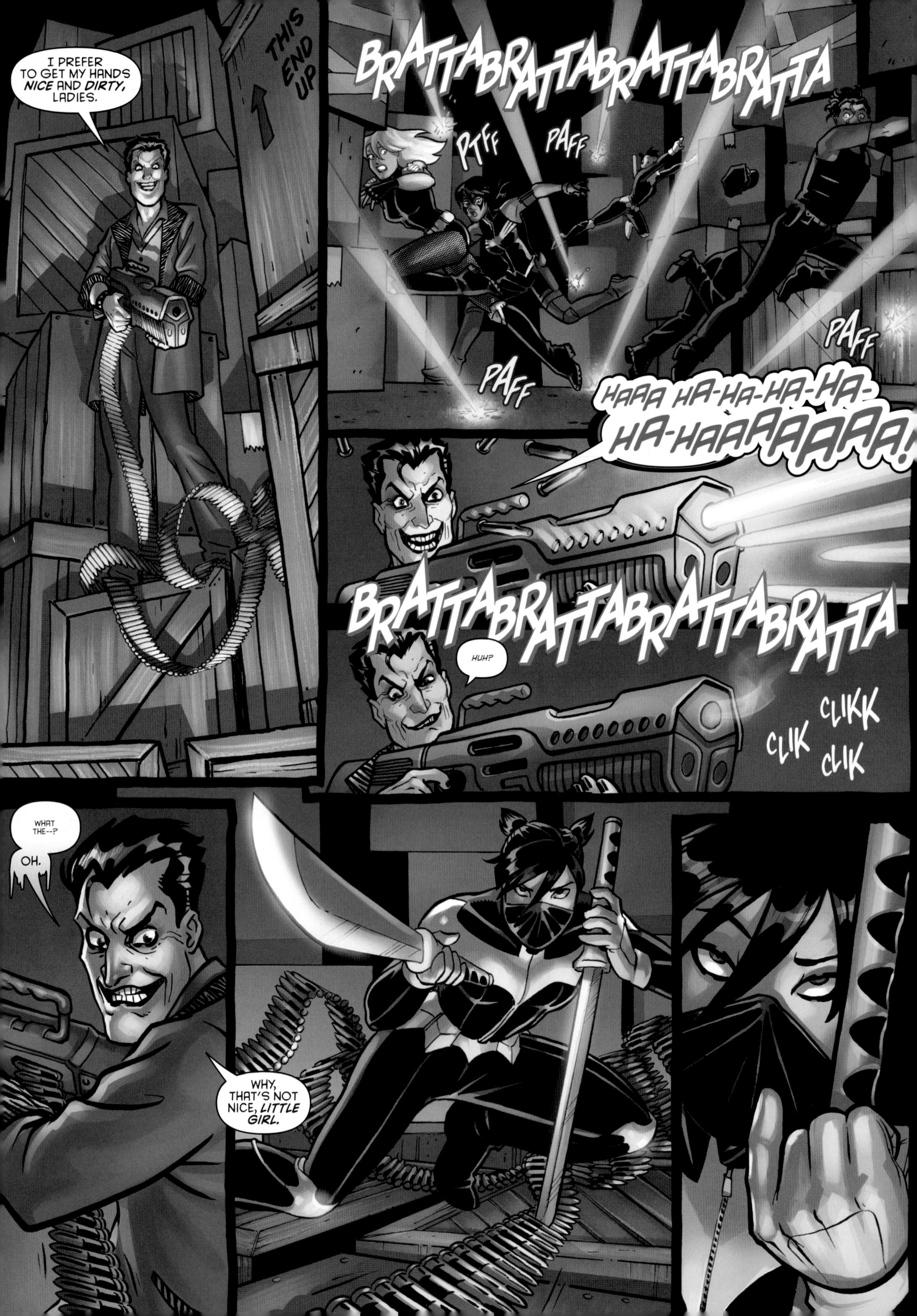
THIS END UP
I PREFER TO GET MY HANDS NICE AND DIRTY, LADIES.
BRATTABRATTABRATTABRATTA
PTFF
PAFF
PAFF
PAFF
HAAA HA-HA-HA-HA-HA-HAAAAAAAA!
BRATTABRATTABRATTABRATTA
HUH?
CLIK CLIKK CLIK
WHAT THE--?
OH.
WHY, THAT'S NOT NICE, LITTLE GIRL.

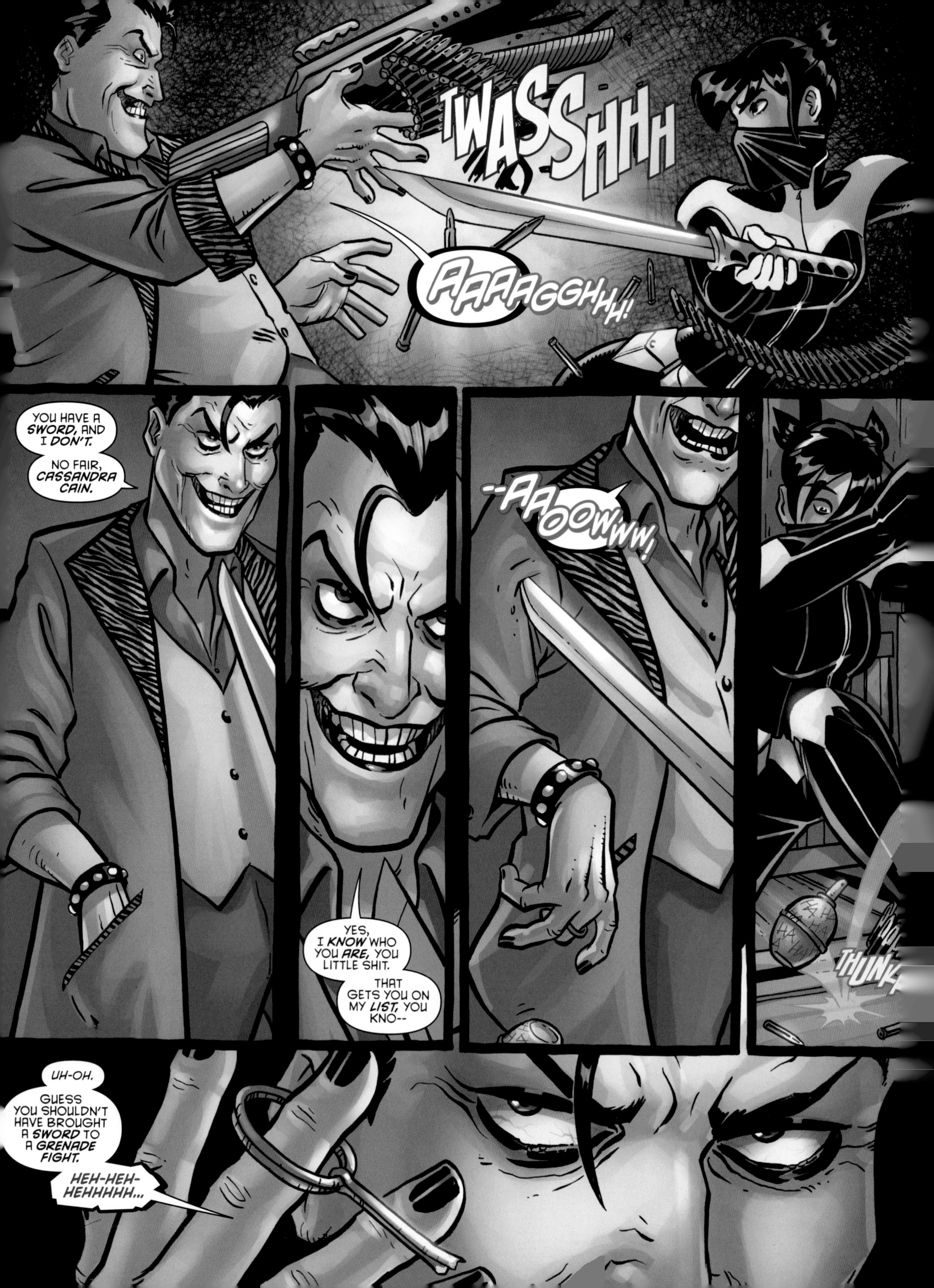
TWASSHHH
AAAAGGHHH!
YOU HAVE A *SWORD,* AND I *DON'T.*
NO FAIR, *CASSANDRA CAIN.*
YES, I *KNOW* WHO YOU *ARE,* YOU LITTLE SHIT.
THAT GETS YOU ON MY *LIST,* YOU KNO--
--AAOOWWW!
THUNK
UH-OH.
GUESS YOU SHOULDN'T HAVE BROUGHT A *SWORD* TO A *GRENADE FIGHT.*
HEH-HEH-HEHHHHH...

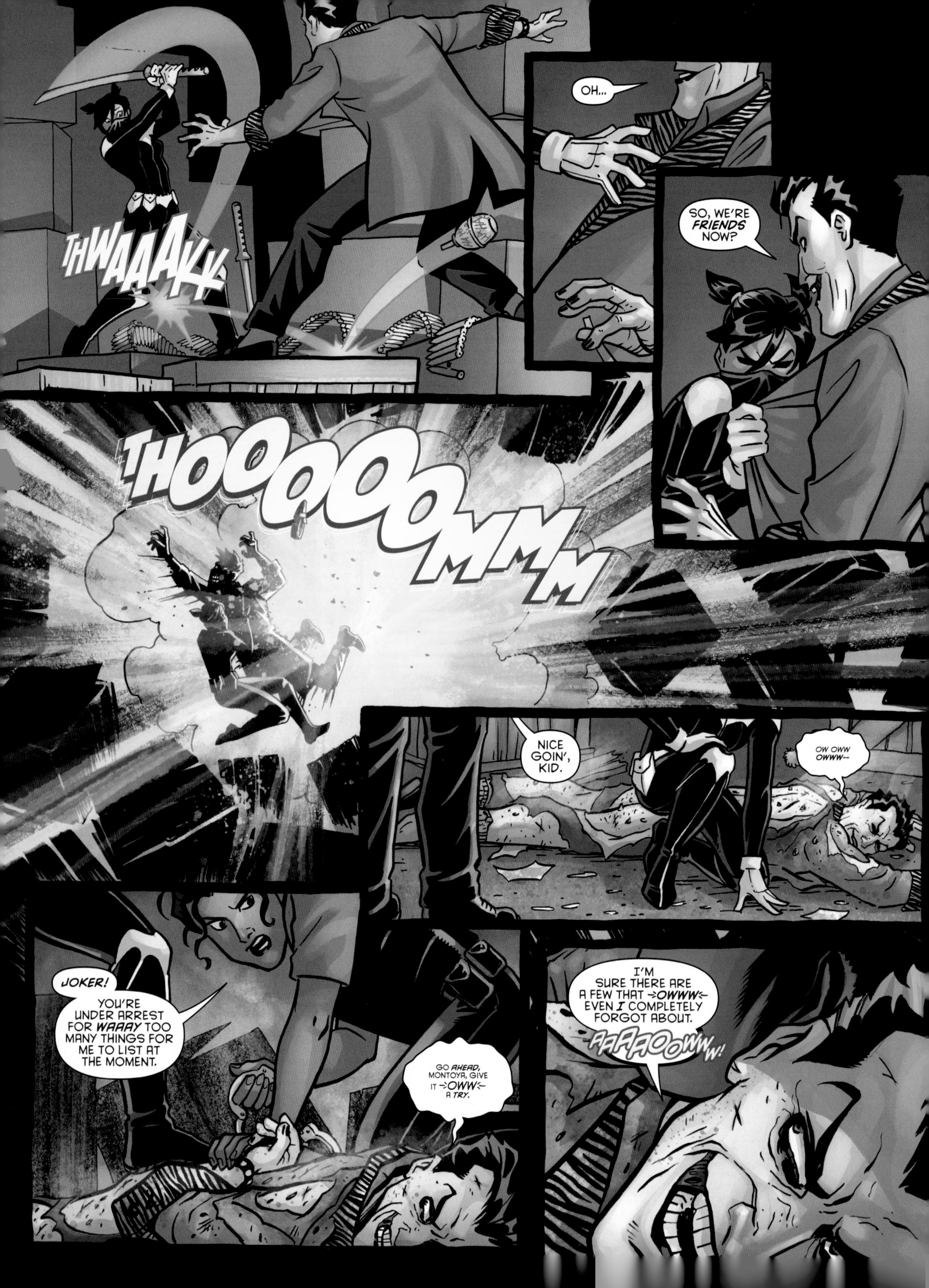
THWAAAKK
OH...
SO, WE'RE FRIENDS NOW?
THOOOOOOMMMM
NICE GOIN', KID.
OW OWW OWWW--
JOKER!
YOU'RE UNDER ARREST FOR WAAAY TOO MANY THINGS FOR ME TO LIST AT THE MOMENT.
GO AHEAD, MONTOYA, GIVE IT -OWW- A TRY.
I'M SURE THERE ARE A FEW THAT -OWWW- EVEN I COMPLETELY FORGOT ABOUT.
AAAAOOWWW!

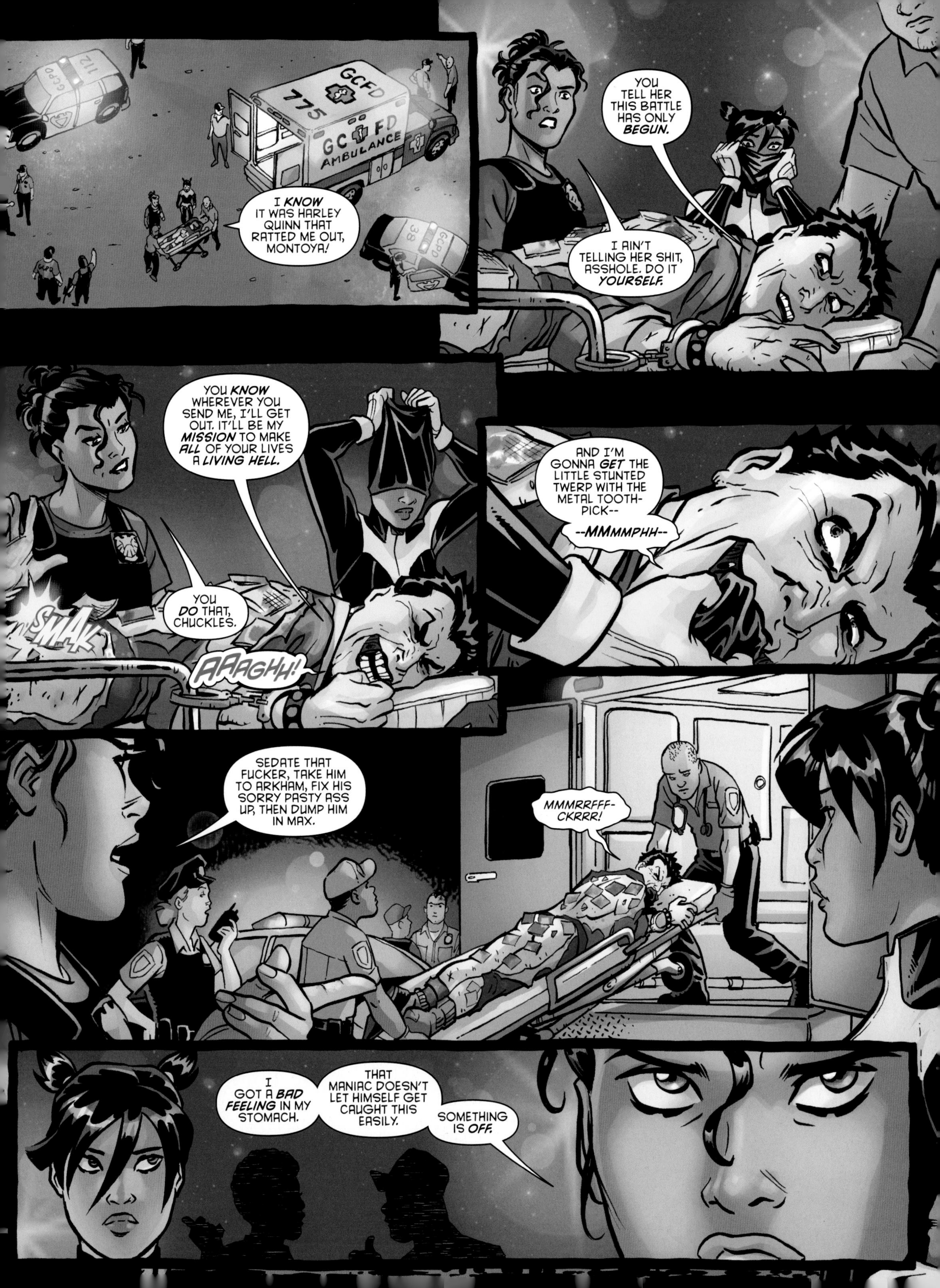
GCPD 112
GCFD 775
GC FD AMBULANCE
I KNOW IT WAS HARLEY QUINN THAT RATTED ME OUT, MONTOYA!
YOU TELL HER THIS BATTLE HAS ONLY BEGUN.
I AIN'T TELLING HER SHIT, ASSHOLE. DO IT YOURSELF.
YOU KNOW WHEREVER YOU SEND ME, I'LL GET OUT. IT'LL BE MY MISSION TO MAKE ALL OF YOUR LIVES A LIVING HELL.
YOU DO THAT, CHUCKLES.
SMAK
AAAGHH!
AND I'M GONNA GET THE LITTLE STUNTED TWERP WITH THE METAL TOOTH-PICK--
--MMMMPHH--
SEDATE THAT FUCKER, TAKE HIM TO ARKHAM, FIX HIS SORRY PASTY ASS UP, THEN DUMP HIM IN MAX.
MMMRRFFF-CKRRR!
I GOT A BAD FEELING IN MY STOMACH.
THAT MANIAC DOESN'T LET HIMSELF GET CAUGHT THIS EASILY.
SOMETHING IS OFF.

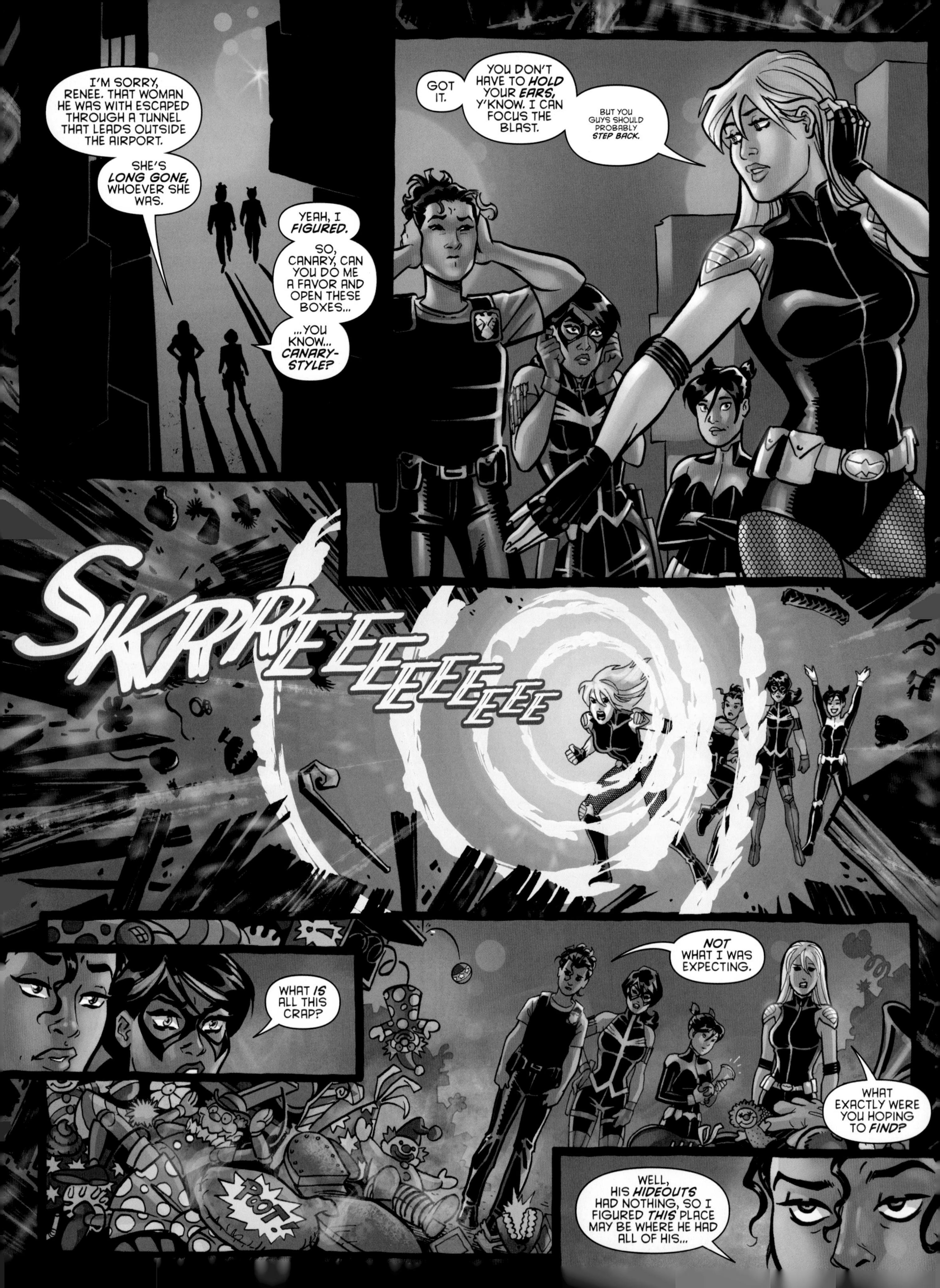
I'M SORRY, RENEE. THAT WOMAN HE WAS WITH ESCAPED THROUGH A TUNNEL THAT LEADS OUTSIDE THE AIRPORT.
SHE'S LONG GONE, WHOEVER SHE WAS.
YEAH, I FIGURED.
SO, CANARY, CAN YOU DO ME A FAVOR AND OPEN THESE BOXES...
...YOU KNOW... CANARY-STYLE?
GOT IT.
YOU DON'T HAVE TO HOLD YOUR EARS, Y'KNOW. I CAN FOCUS THE BLAST.
BUT YOU GUYS SHOULD PROBABLY STEP BACK.
SKRREEEEEEEEEE
WHAT IS ALL THIS CRAP?
NOT WHAT I WAS EXPECTING.
WHAT EXACTLY WERE YOU HOPING TO FIND?
POOT!
WELL, HIS HIDEOUTS HAD NOTHING, SO I FIGURED THIS PLACE MAY BE WHERE HE HAD ALL OF HIS...

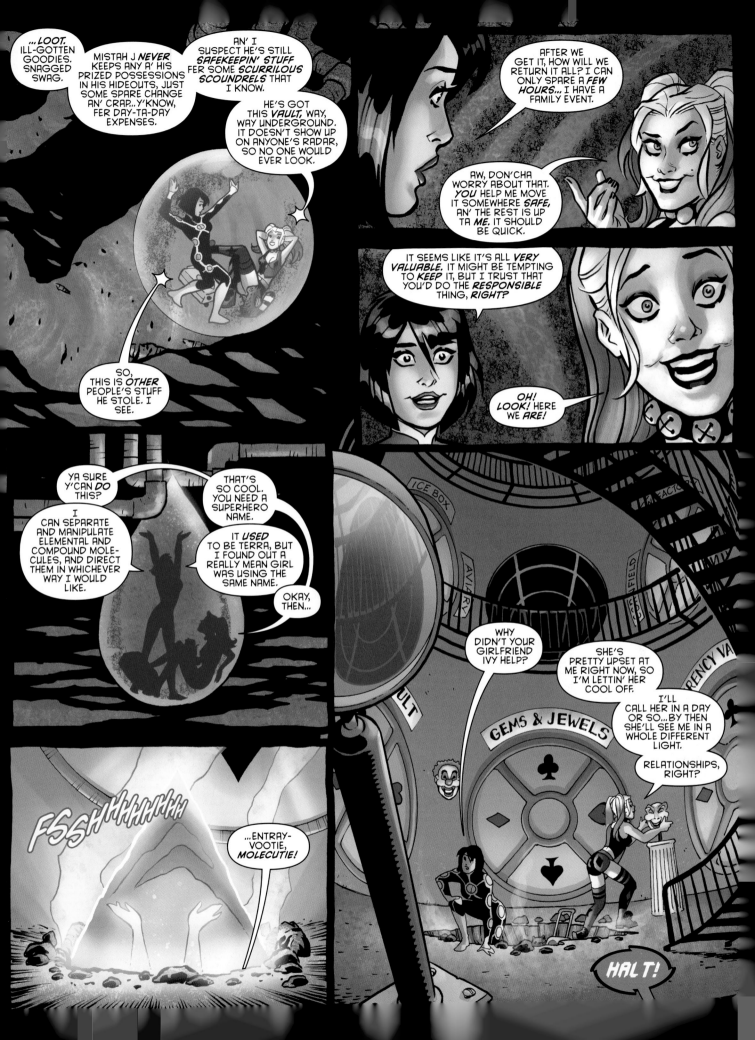

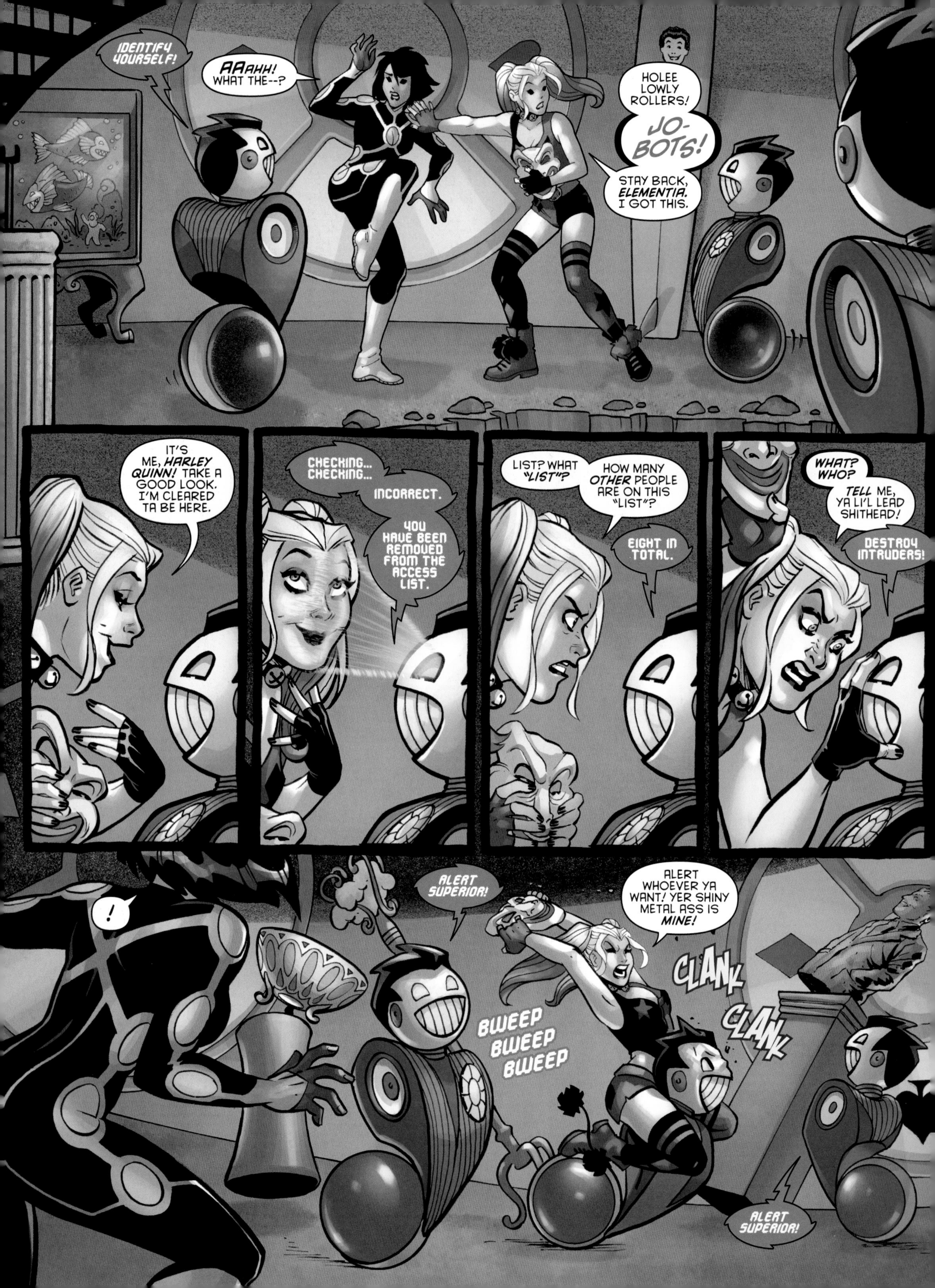
IDENTIFY YOURSELF!
AAAHH! WHAT THE--?
HOLEE LOWLY ROLLERS!
JO-BOTS!
STAY BACK, ELEMENTIA. I GOT THIS.
IT'S ME, HARLEY QUINN! TAKE A GOOD LOOK. I'M CLEARED TA BE HERE.
CHECKING... CHECKING...
INCORRECT.
YOU HAVE BEEN REMOVED FROM THE ACCESS LIST.
LIST? WHAT "LIST"?
HOW MANY OTHER PEOPLE ARE ON THIS "LIST"?
EIGHT IN TOTAL.
WHAT? WHO?
TELL ME, YA LI'L LEAD SHITHEAD!
DESTROY INTRUDERS!
!
ALERT SUPERIOR!
ALERT WHOEVER YA WANT! YER SHINY METAL ASS IS MINE!
CLANK
CLANK
BWEEP BWEEP BWEEP
ALERT SUPERIOR!

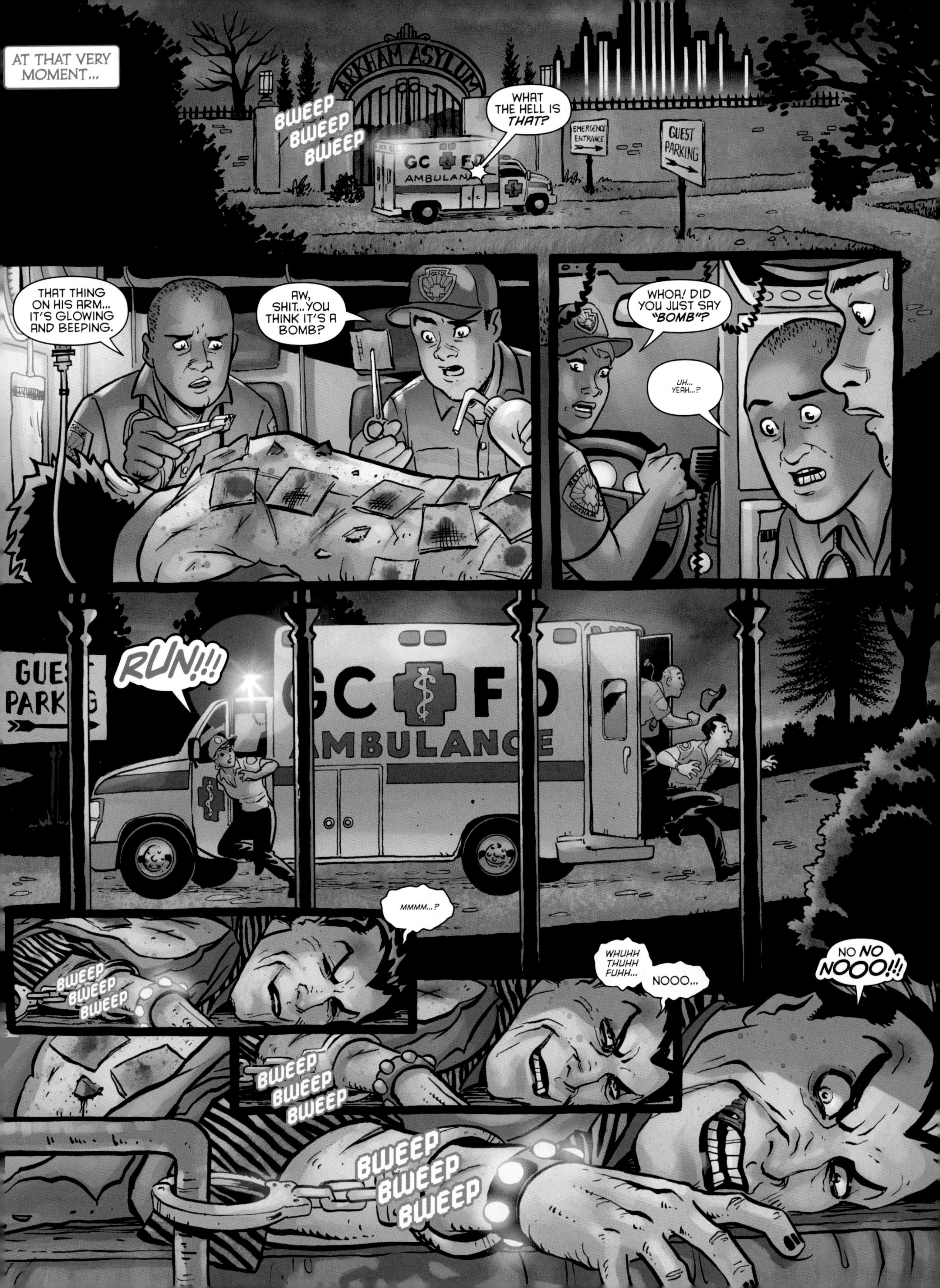
AT THAT VERY MOMENT...
ARKHAM ASYLUM
BWEEP BWEEP BWEEP
WHAT THE HELL IS THAT?
EMERGENCY ENTRANCE
GUEST PARKING
GC FD AMBULANCE
THAT THING ON HIS ARM... IT'S GLOWING AND BEEPING.
AW, SHIT...YOU THINK IT'S A BOMB?
WHOA! DID YOU JUST SAY "BOMB"?
UH... YEAH...?
GUEST PARKING
RUN!!!
GC FD AMBULANCE
MMMM...?
BWEEP BWEEP BWEEP
WHUHH THUHH FUHH...
NOOO...
NO NO NOOO!!!
BWEEP BWEEP BWEEP
BWEEP BWEEP BWEEP

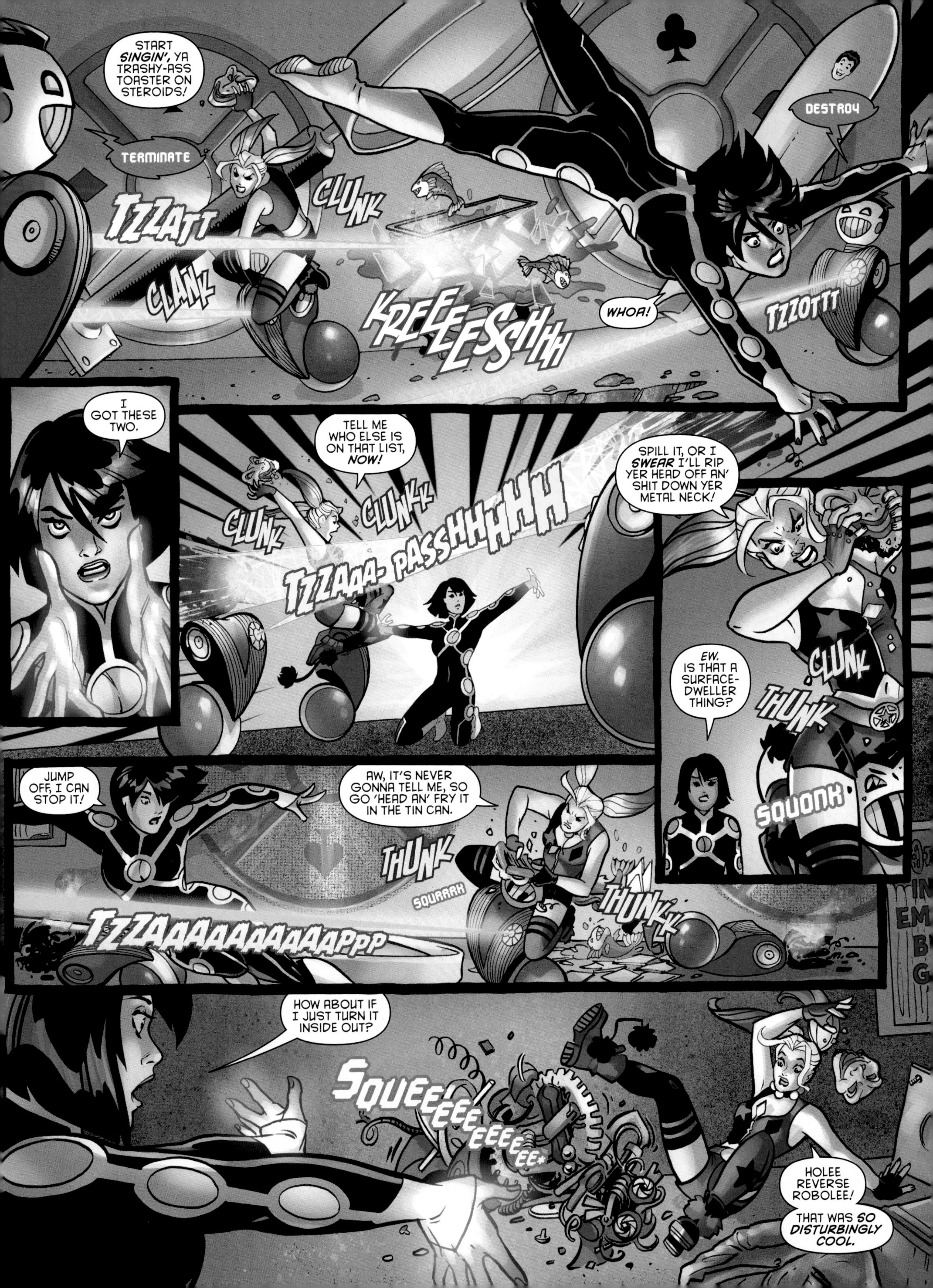
START SINGIN', YA TRASHY-ASS TOASTER ON STEROIDS!
TERMINATE
DESTROY
TZZATT
CLUNK
CLANK
KREEEEESHHH
WHOA!
TZZOTTT
I GOT THESE TWO.
TELL ME WHO ELSE IS ON THAT LIST, NOW!
CLUNK
CLUNKK
TZZAAA- PASSHHHHHH
SPILL IT, OR I SWEAR I'LL RIP YER HEAD OFF AN' SHIT DOWN YER METAL NECK!
EW. IS THAT A SURFACE-DWELLER THING?
CLUNK
THUNK
SQUONK
JUMP OFF, I CAN STOP IT!
AW, IT'S NEVER GONNA TELL ME, SO GO 'HEAD AN' FRY IT IN THE TIN CAN.
THUNK
SQURRRK
THUNKK
TZZAAAAAAAAAAAPPP
HOW ABOUT IF I JUST TURN IT INSIDE OUT?
SQUEEEEEEEEEEEEE*
HOLEE REVERSE ROBOLEE!
THAT WAS SO DISTURBINGLY COOL.

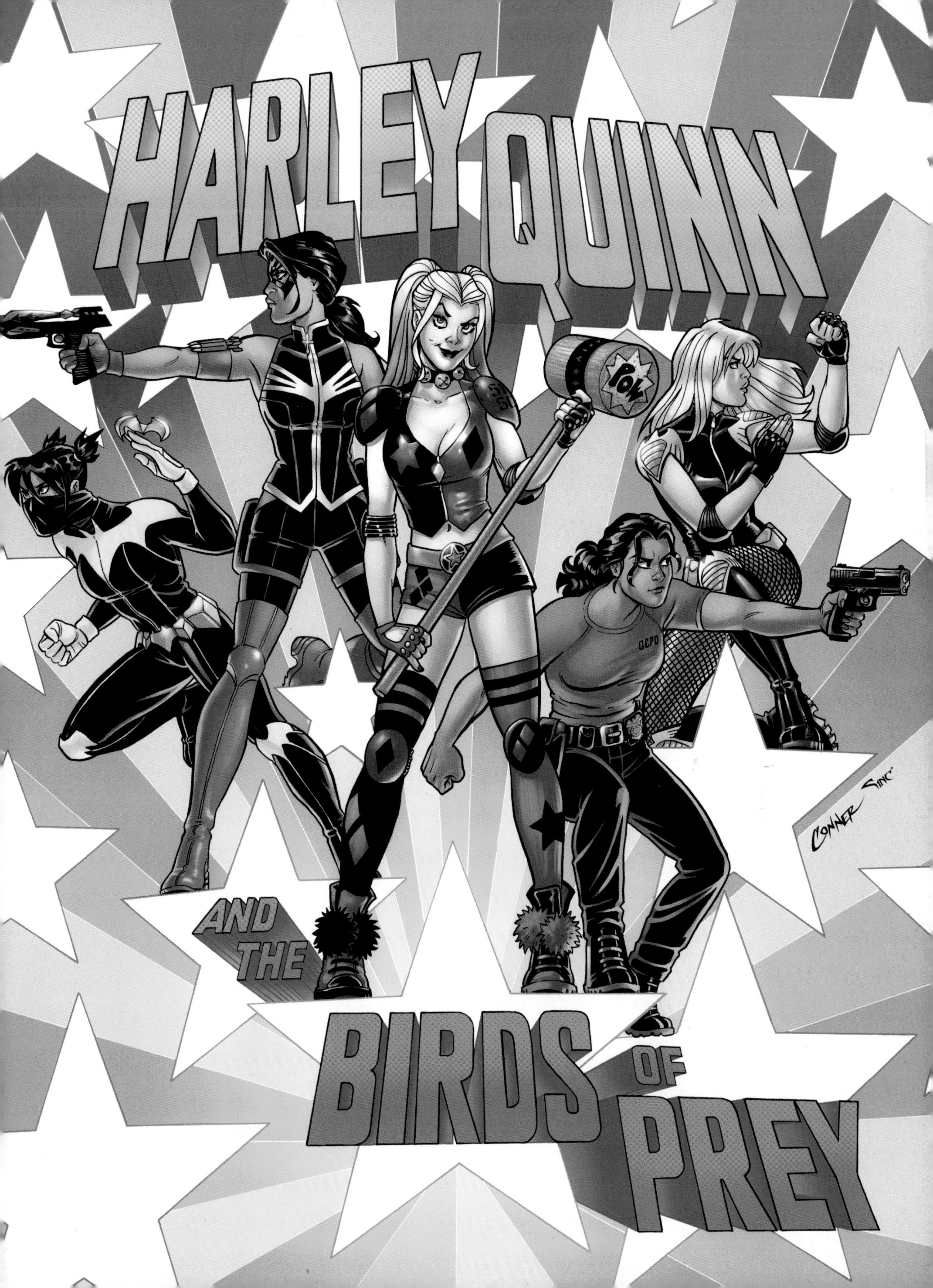
HARLEY QUINN
AND THE
BIRDS OF PREY
POW
GCPD
CONNER SINC'

BOOK THREE
GOTHAM TOWN SMACKDOWN!

"I DO have a plan that maybe ya can help me with..."

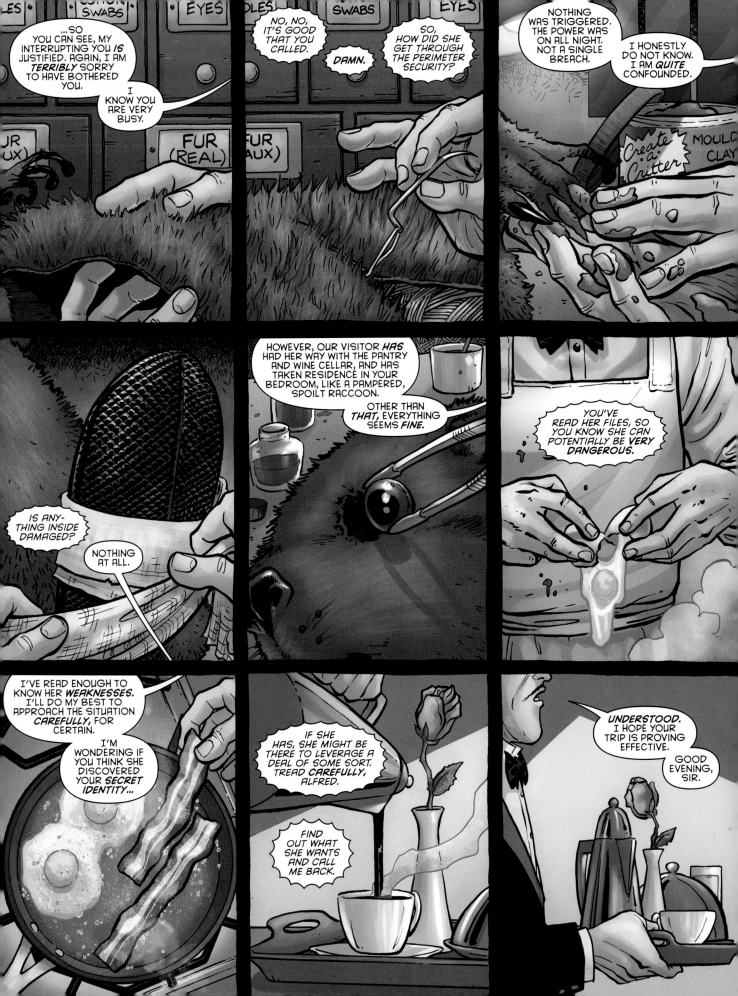

GOTHAM TOWN SMACK DOWN

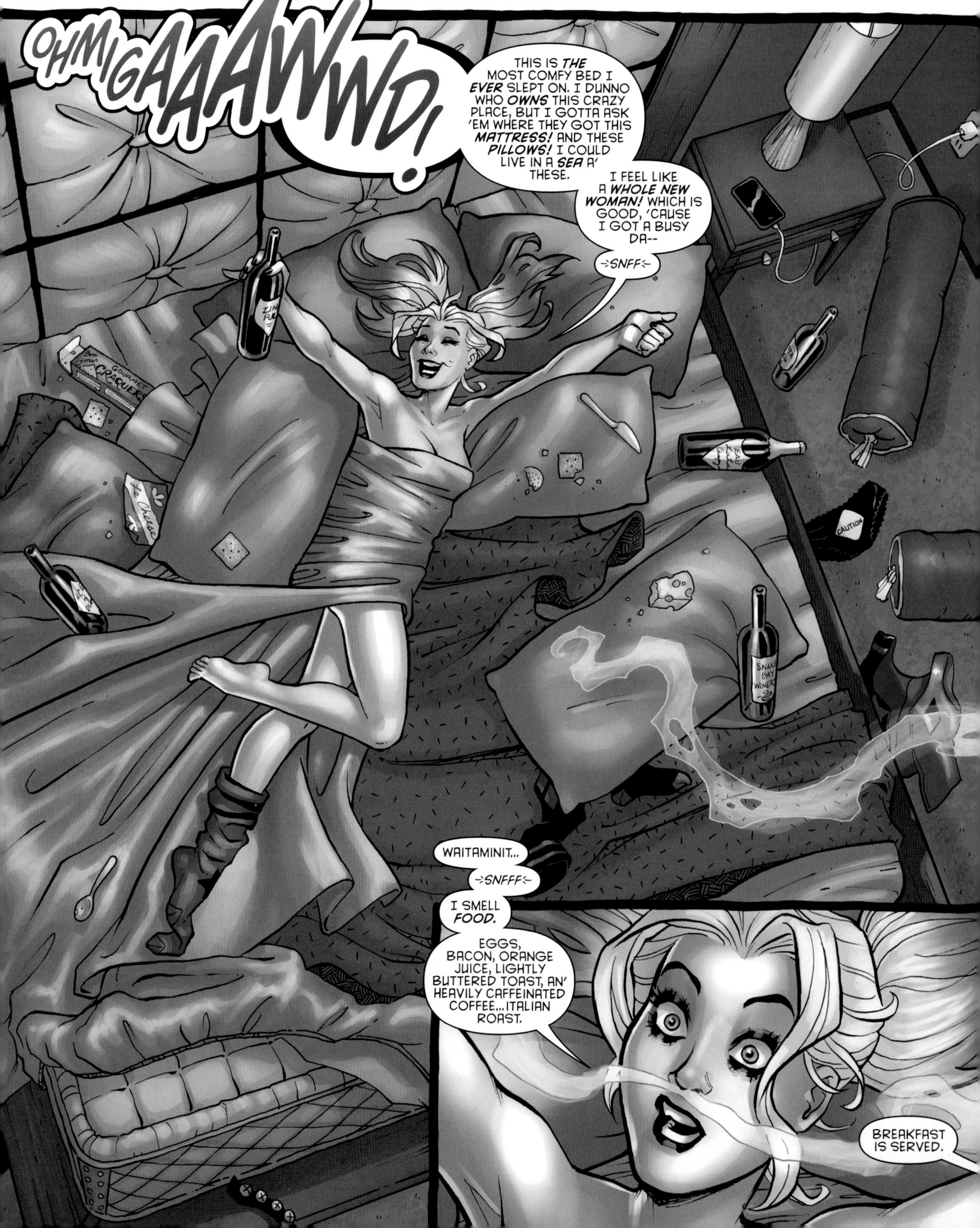
OHMIGAAAWWD!
THIS IS THE MOST COMFY BED I EVER SLEPT ON. I DUNNO WHO OWNS THIS CRAZY PLACE, BUT I GOTTA ASK 'EM WHERE THEY GOT THIS MATTRESS! AND THESE PILLOWS! I COULD LIVE IN A SEA A' THESE.
I FEEL LIKE A WHOLE NEW WOMAN! WHICH IS GOOD, 'CAUSE I GOT A BUSY DA--
SNFF
GOURMET CRAQUERS
CAUTION
SNAKE BAY WINERY
WAITAMINIT...
SNFFF
I SMELL FOOD.
EGGS, BACON, ORANGE JUICE, LIGHTLY BUTTERED TOAST, AN' HEAVILY CAFFEINATED COFFEE...ITALIAN ROAST.
BREAKFAST IS SERVED.

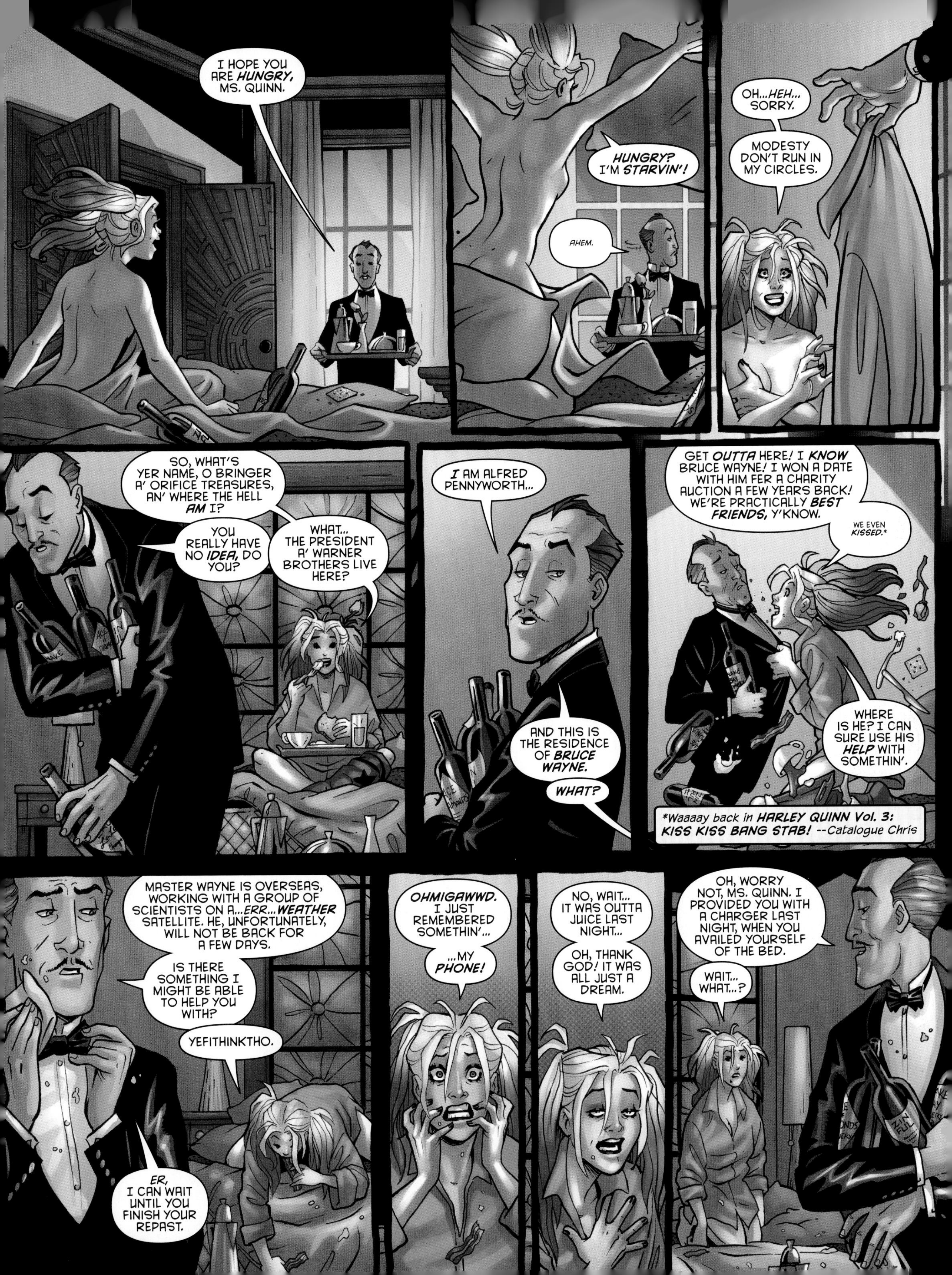
I HOPE YOU ARE *HUNGRY,* MS. QUINN.
HUNGRY? I'M *STARVIN'!*
AHEM.
OH...HEH... SORRY.
MODESTY DON'T RUN IN MY CIRCLES.
SO, WHAT'S YER NAME, O BRINGER A' ORIFICE TREASURES, AN' WHERE THE HELL *AM* I?
YOU REALLY HAVE NO *IDEA,* DO YOU?
WHAT... THE PRESIDENT A' WARNER BROTHERS LIVE HERE?
I AM ALFRED PENNYWORTH...
AND THIS IS THE RESIDENCE OF *BRUCE WAYNE.*
WHAT?
GET *OUTTA* HERE! I *KNOW* BRUCE WAYNE! I WON A DATE WITH HIM FER A CHARITY AUCTION A FEW YEARS BACK! WE'RE PRACTICALLY *BEST FRIENDS,* Y'KNOW.
WE EVEN *KISSED.**
WHERE IS HE? I CAN SURE USE HIS *HELP* WITH SOMETHIN'.
*Waaaay back in **HARLEY QUINN Vol. 3: KISS KISS BANG STAB!** --Catalogue Chris
MASTER WAYNE IS OVERSEAS, WORKING WITH A GROUP OF SCIENTISTS ON A...*ERR*...*WEATHER* SATELLITE. HE, UNFORTUNATELY, WILL NOT BE BACK FOR A FEW DAYS.
IS THERE SOMETHING I MIGHT BE ABLE TO HELP YOU WITH?
YEFITHINKTHO.
ER, I CAN WAIT UNTIL YOU FINISH YOUR REPAST.
OHMIGAWWD. I JUST REMEMBERED SOMETHIN'...
...MY *PHONE!*
NO, WAIT... IT WAS OUTTA JUICE LAST NIGHT...
OH, THANK GOD! IT WAS ALL JUST A DREAM.
OH, WORRY NOT, MS. QUINN. I PROVIDED YOU WITH A CHARGER LAST NIGHT, WHEN YOU AVAILED YOURSELF OF THE BED.
WAIT... WHAT...?

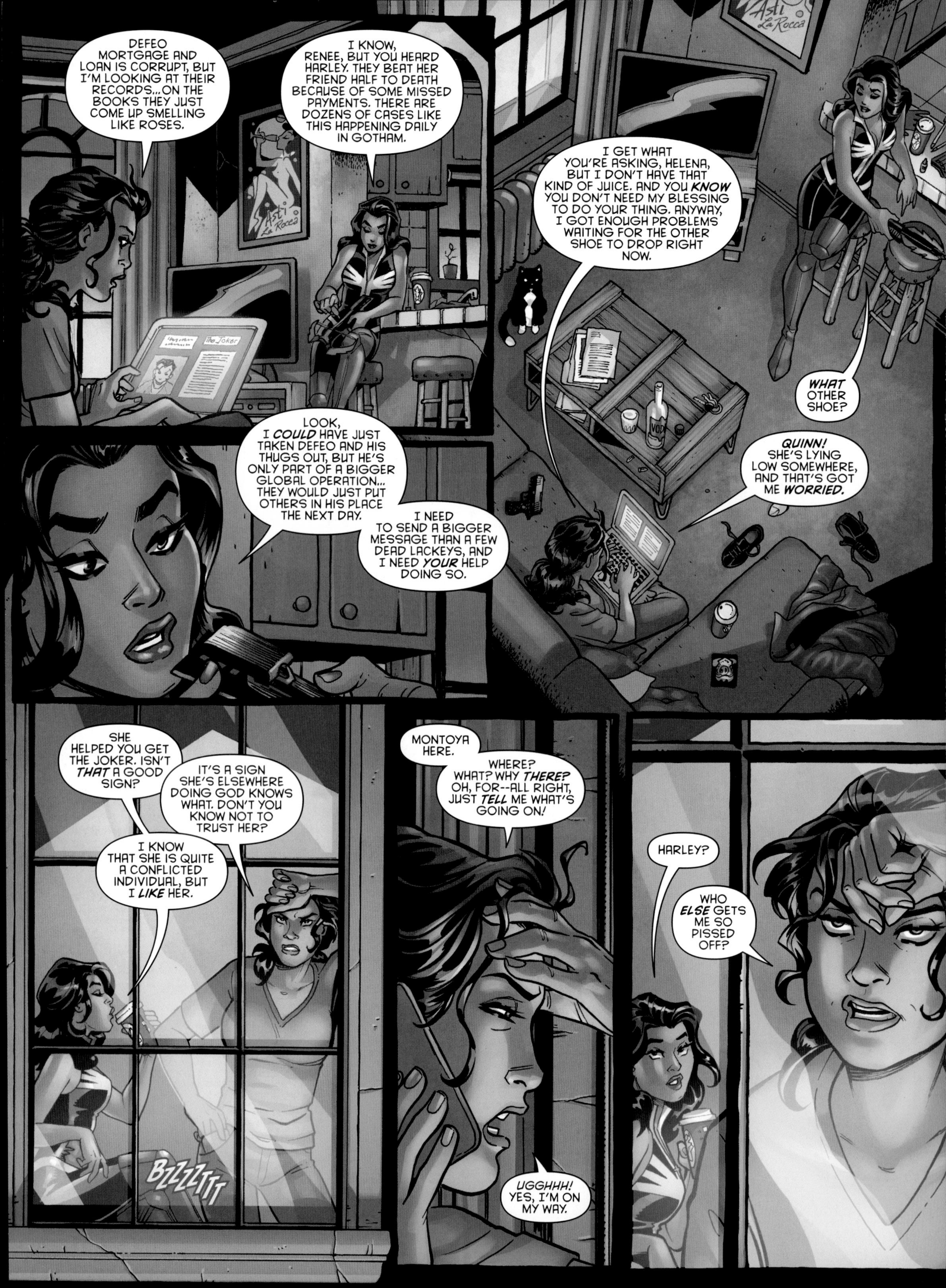
DEFEO MORTGAGE AND LOAN IS CORRUPT, BUT I'M LOOKING AT THEIR RECORDS...ON THE BOOKS THEY JUST COME UP SMELLING LIKE ROSES.
I KNOW, RENEE, BUT YOU HEARD HARLEY. THEY BEAT HER FRIEND HALF TO DEATH BECAUSE OF SOME MISSED PAYMENTS. THERE ARE DOZENS OF CASES LIKE THIS HAPPENING DAILY IN GOTHAM.
I GET WHAT YOU'RE ASKING, HELENA, BUT I DON'T HAVE THAT KIND OF JUICE. AND YOU KNOW YOU DON'T NEED MY BLESSING TO DO YOUR THING. ANYWAY, I GOT ENOUGH PROBLEMS WAITING FOR THE OTHER SHOE TO DROP RIGHT NOW.
WHAT OTHER SHOE?
LOOK, I COULD HAVE JUST TAKEN DEFEO AND HIS THUGS OUT, BUT HE'S ONLY PART OF A BIGGER GLOBAL OPERATION... THEY WOULD JUST PUT OTHERS IN HIS PLACE THE NEXT DAY.
I NEED TO SEND A BIGGER MESSAGE THAN A FEW DEAD LACKEYS, AND I NEED YOUR HELP DOING SO.
QUINN! SHE'S LYING LOW SOMEWHERE, AND THAT'S GOT ME WORRIED.
SHE HELPED YOU GET THE JOKER. ISN'T THAT A GOOD SIGN?
IT'S A SIGN SHE'S ELSEWHERE DOING GOD KNOWS WHAT. DON'T YOU KNOW NOT TO TRUST HER?
I KNOW THAT SHE IS QUITE A CONFLICTED INDIVIDUAL, BUT I LIKE HER.
BZZZZTTT
MONTOYA HERE.
WHERE? WHAT? WHY THERE? OH, FOR--ALL RIGHT, JUST TELL ME WHAT'S GOING ON!
UGGHHH! YES, I'M ON MY WAY.
HARLEY?
WHO ELSE GETS ME SO PISSED OFF?

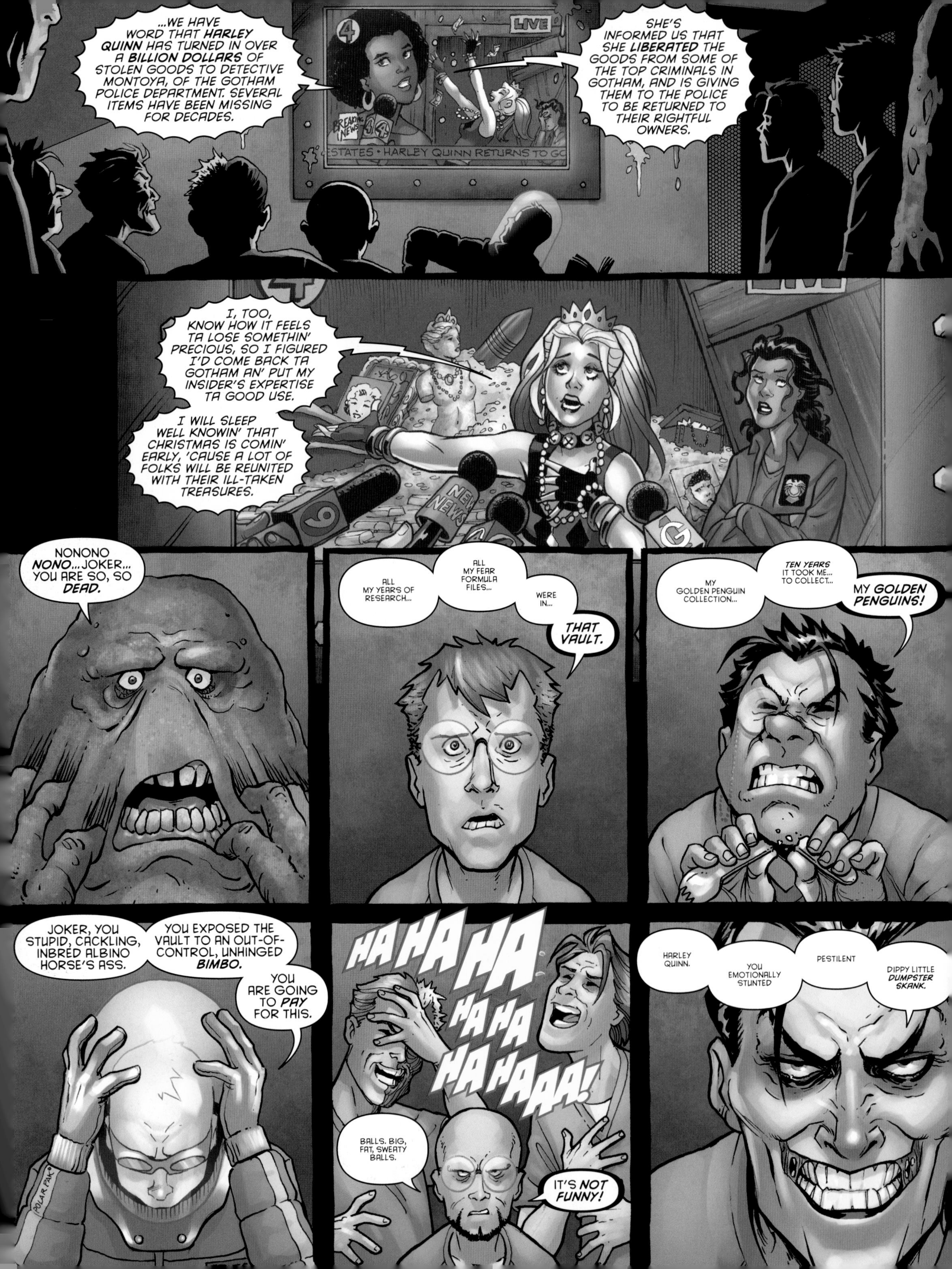

LIVE
...WE HAVE WORD THAT HARLEY QUINN HAS TURNED IN OVER A BILLION DOLLARS OF STOLEN GOODS TO DETECTIVE MONTOYA, OF THE GOTHAM POLICE DEPARTMENT. SEVERAL ITEMS HAVE BEEN MISSING FOR DECADES.
SHE'S INFORMED US THAT SHE LIBERATED THE GOODS FROM SOME OF THE TOP CRIMINALS IN GOTHAM, AND IS GIVING THEM TO THE POLICE TO BE RETURNED TO THEIR RIGHTFUL OWNERS.
BREAKING NEWS
ESTATES • HARLEY QUINN RETURNS TO G
I, TOO, KNOW HOW IT FEELS TA LOSE SOMETHIN' PRECIOUS, SO I FIGURED I'D COME BACK TA GOTHAM AN' PUT MY INSIDER'S EXPERTISE TA GOOD USE.
I WILL SLEEP WELL KNOWIN' THAT CHRISTMAS IS COMIN' EARLY, 'CAUSE A LOT OF FOLKS WILL BE REUNITED WITH THEIR ILL-TAKEN TREASURES.
NEWS
NONONO NONO... JOKER... YOU ARE SO, SO DEAD.
ALL MY YEARS OF RESEARCH...
ALL MY FEAR FORMULA FILES...
WERE IN...
THAT VAULT.
MY GOLDEN PENGUIN COLLECTION...
TEN YEARS IT TOOK ME... TO COLLECT...
MY GOLDEN PENGUINS!
JOKER, YOU STUPID, CACKLING, INBRED ALBINO HORSE'S ASS.
YOU EXPOSED THE VAULT TO AN OUT-OF-CONTROL, UNHINGED BIMBO.
YOU ARE GOING TO PAY FOR THIS.
POLAR PAK
HA HA HA HA HA HA HA HAAA!
BALLS. BIG, FAT, SWEATY BALLS.
IT'S NOT FUNNY!
HARLEY QUINN.
YOU EMOTIONALLY STUNTED
PESTILENT
DIPPY LITTLE DUMPSTER SKANK.

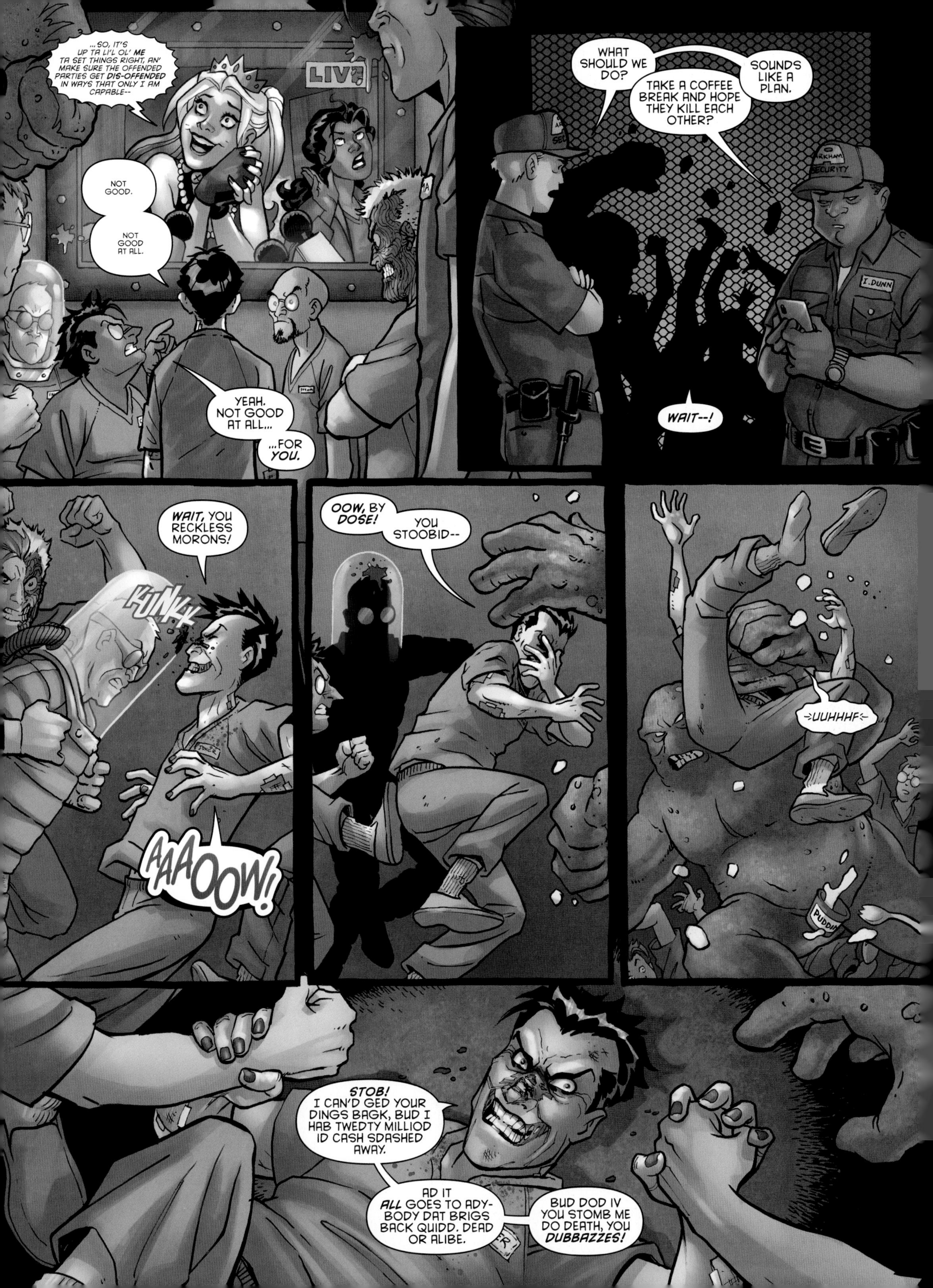
...SO, IT'S UP TA LI'L OL' ME TA SET THINGS RIGHT, AN' MAKE SURE THE OFFENDED PARTIES GET DIS-OFFENDED IN WAYS THAT ONLY I AM CAPABLE--
LIV
NOT GOOD.
NOT GOOD AT ALL.
YEAH. NOT GOOD AT ALL...
...FOR YOU.
WHAT SHOULD WE DO?
TAKE A COFFEE BREAK AND HOPE THEY KILL EACH OTHER?
SOUNDS LIKE A PLAN.
ARKHAM SECURITY
I. DUNN
WAIT--!
WAIT, YOU RECKLESS MORONS!
KLUNKK
AAAOOW!
OOW, BY DOSE!
YOU STOOBID--
UUHHHF
PUDDIN
STOB! I CAN'D GED YOUR DINGS BAGK, BUD I HAB TWEDTY MILLIOD ID CASH SDASHED AWAY.
AD IT ALL GOES TO ADY-BODY DAT BRIGS BACK QUIDD. DEAD OR ALIBE.
BUD DOD IV YOU STOMB ME DO DEATH, YOU DUBBAZZES!

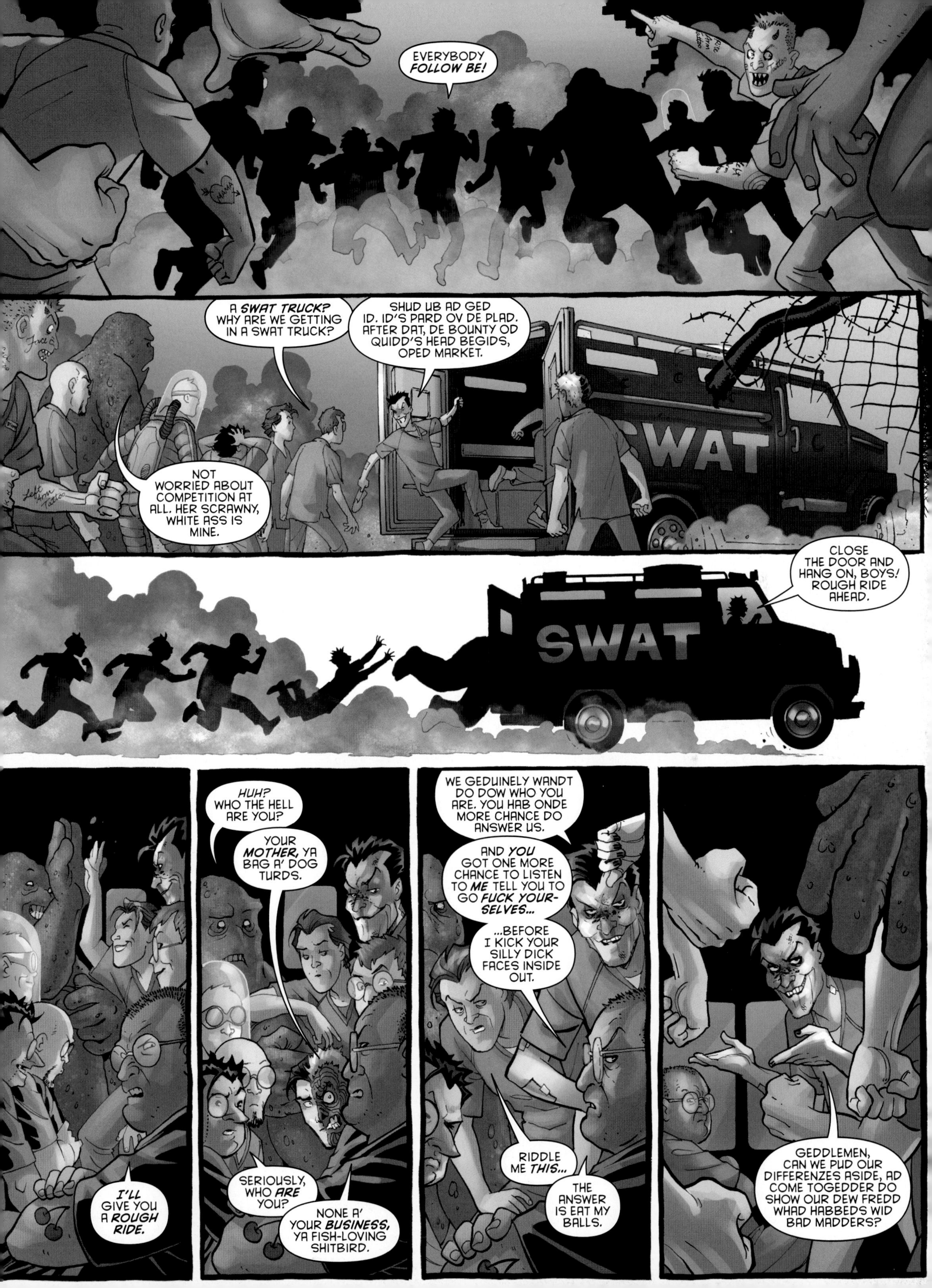

EVERYBODY FOLLOW BE!
A SWAT TRUCK? WHY ARE WE GETTING IN A SWAT TRUCK?
SHUD UB AD GED ID. ID'S PARD OV DE PLAD. AFTER DAT, DE BOUNTY OD QUIDD'S HEAD BEGIDS, OPED MARKET.
SWAT
NOT WORRIED ABOUT COMPETITION AT ALL. HER SCRAWNY, WHITE ASS IS MINE.
CLOSE THE DOOR AND HANG ON, BOYS! ROUGH RIDE AHEAD.
SWAT
I'LL GIVE YOU A ROUGH RIDE.
HUH? WHO THE HELL ARE YOU?
YOUR MOTHER, YA BAG A' DOG TURDS.
SERIOUSLY, WHO ARE YOU?
NONE A' YOUR BUSINESS, YA FISH-LOVING SHITBIRD.
WE GEDUINELY WANDT DO DOW WHO YOU ARE. YOU HAB ONDE MORE CHANCE DO ANSWER US.
AND YOU GOT ONE MORE CHANCE TO LISTEN TO ME TELL YOU TO GO FUCK YOURSELVES...
...BEFORE I KICK YOUR SILLY DICK FACES INSIDE OUT.
RIDDLE ME THIS...
THE ANSWER IS EAT MY BALLS.
GEDDLEMEN, CAN WE PUD OUR DIFFERENZES ASIDE, AD COME TOGEDDER DO SHOW OUR DEW FREDD WHAD HABBEDS WID BAD MADDERS?

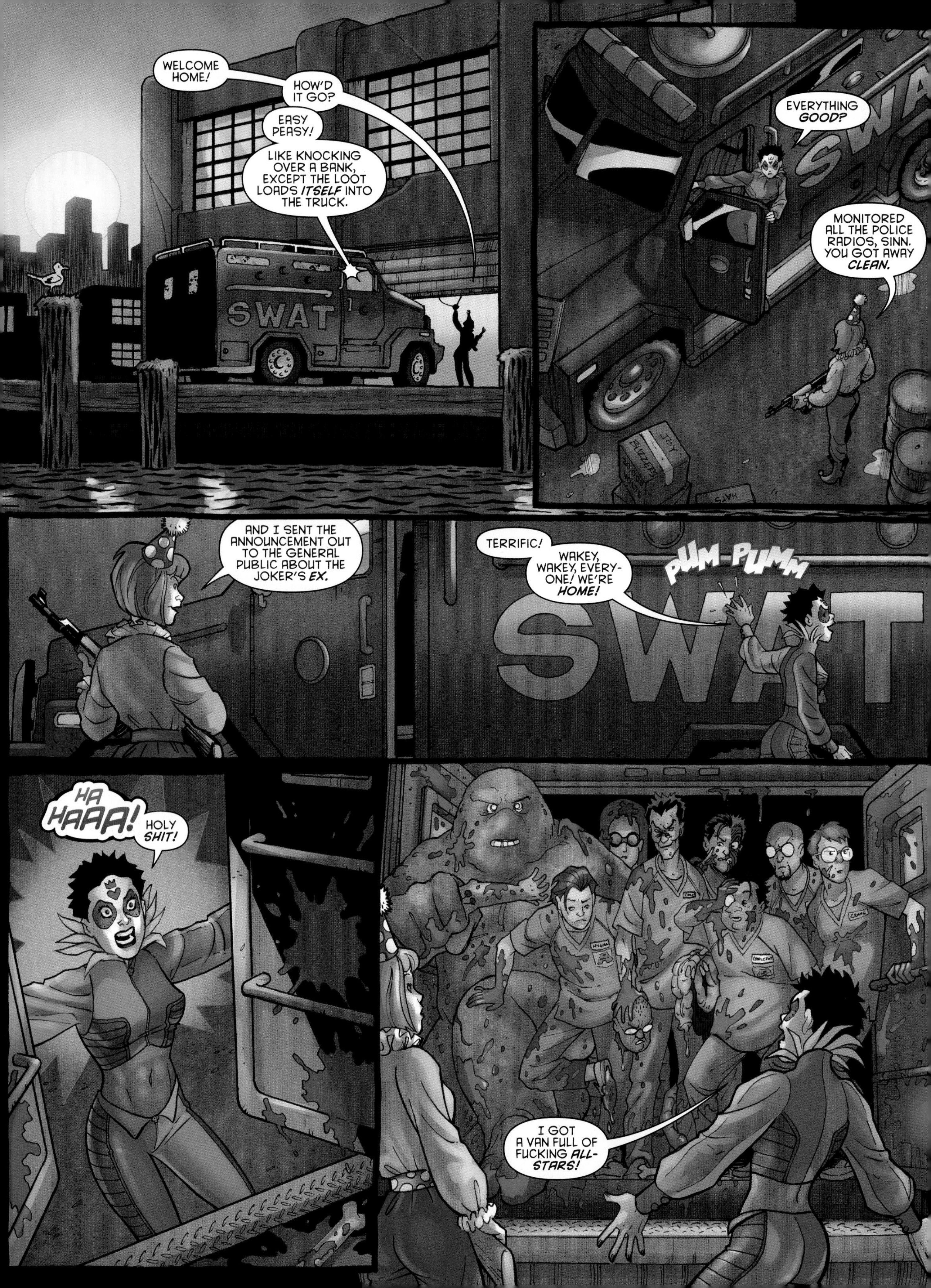
WELCOME HOME!
HOW'D IT GO?
EASY PEASY!
LIKE KNOCKING OVER A BANK, EXCEPT THE LOOT LOADS ITSELF INTO THE TRUCK.
SWAT
EVERYTHING GOOD?
MONITORED ALL THE POLICE RADIOS, SINN. YOU GOT AWAY CLEAN.
AND I SENT THE ANNOUNCEMENT OUT TO THE GENERAL PUBLIC ABOUT THE JOKER'S EX.
TERRIFIC!
WAKEY, WAKEY, EVERY-ONE! WE'RE HOME!
PUM-PUMM
HA HAAA!
HOLY SHIT!
I GOT A VAN FULL OF FUCKING ALL-STARS!

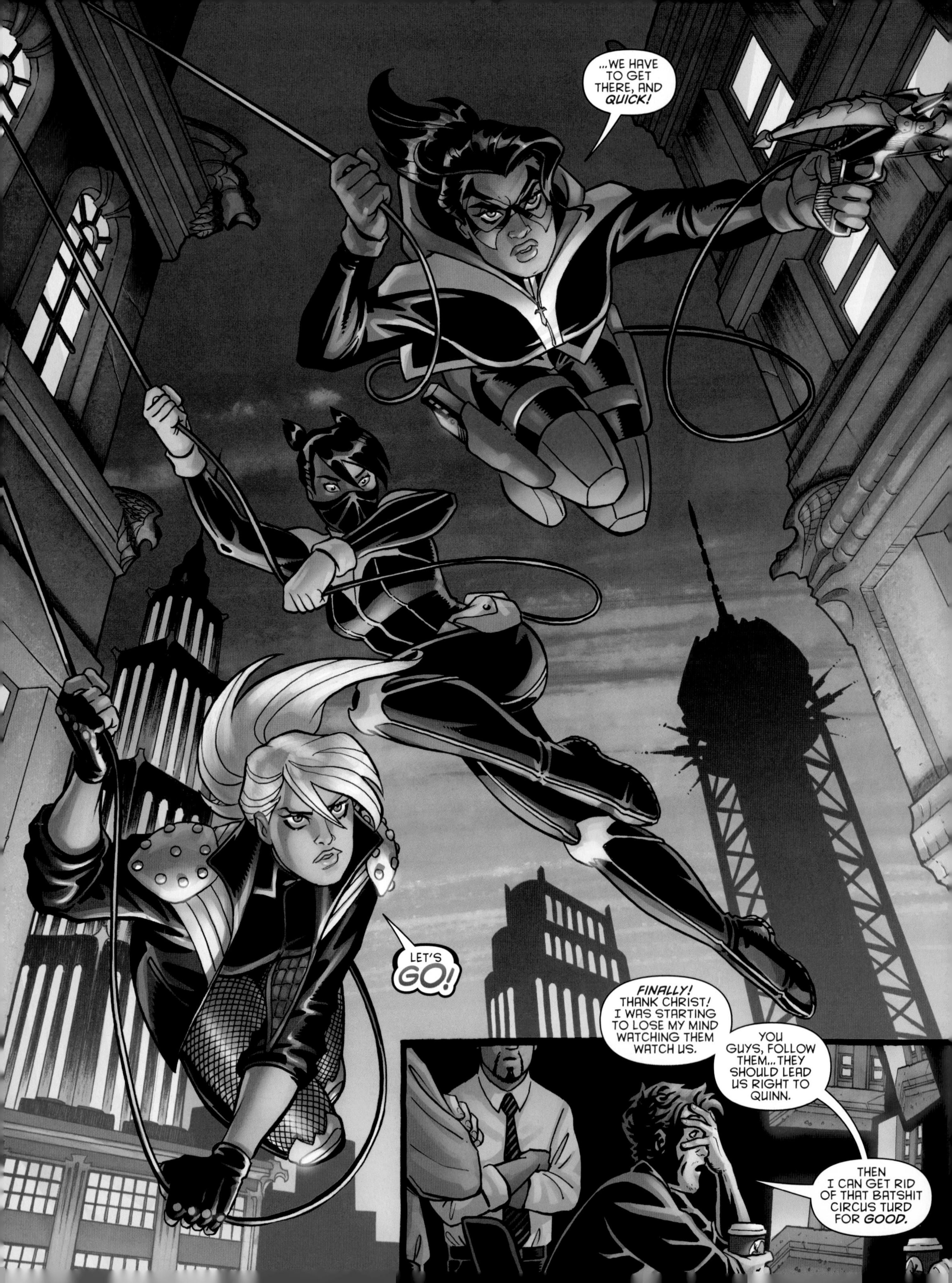
...WE HAVE TO GET THERE, AND *QUICK!*
LET'S GO!
FINALLY! THANK CHRIST! I WAS STARTING TO LOSE MY MIND WATCHING THEM WATCH US.
YOU GUYS, FOLLOW THEM... THEY SHOULD LEAD US RIGHT TO QUINN.
THEN I CAN GET RID OF THAT BATSHIT CIRCUS TURD FOR *GOOD.*

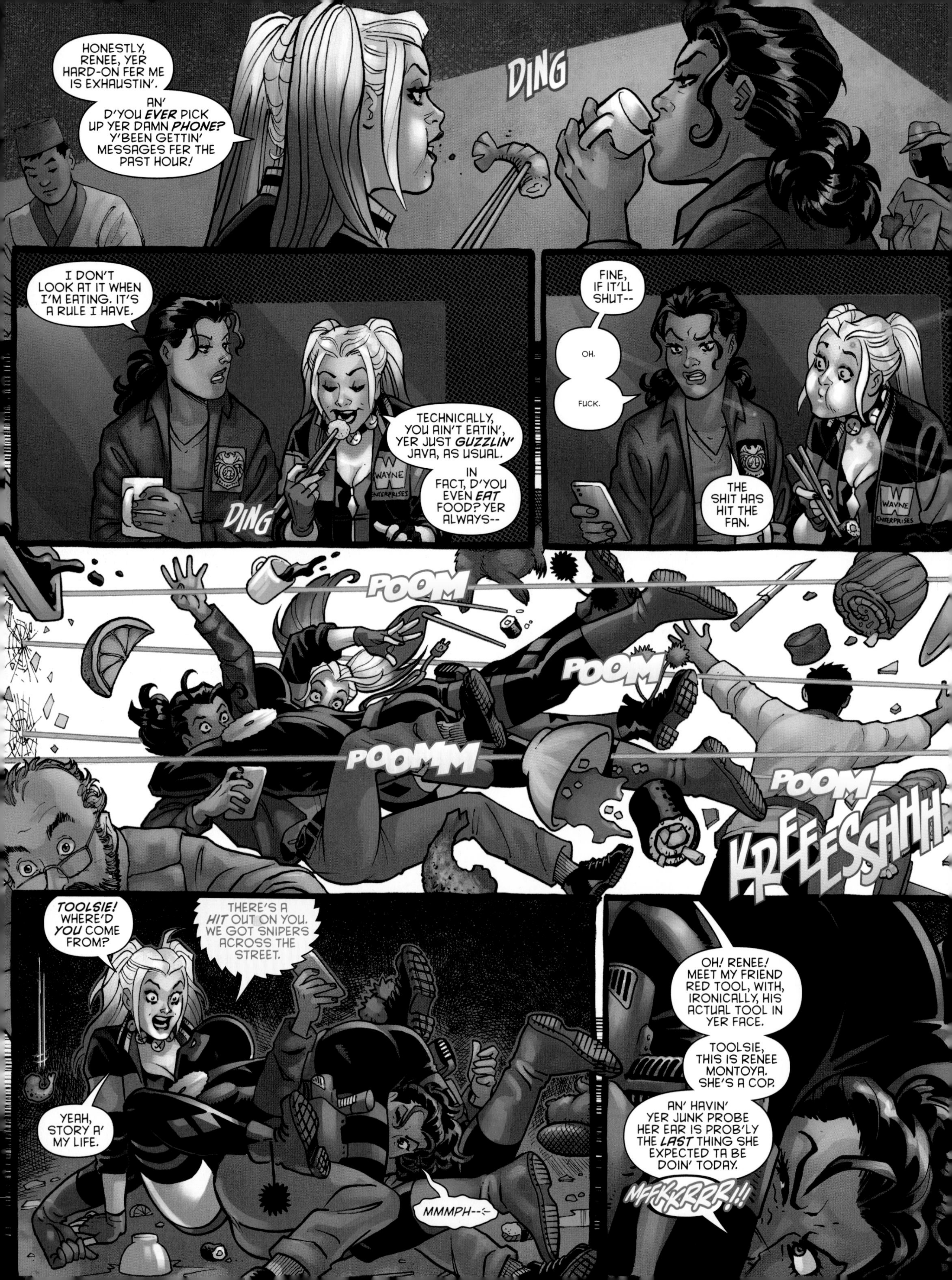
HONESTLY, RENEE, YER HARD-ON FER ME IS EXHAUSTIN'.
AN' D'YOU EVER PICK UP YER DAMN PHONE? Y'BEEN GETTIN' MESSAGES FER THE PAST HOUR!
DING
I DON'T LOOK AT IT WHEN I'M EATING. IT'S A RULE I HAVE.
TECHNICALLY, YOU AIN'T EATIN', YER JUST GUZZLIN' JAVA, AS USUAL.
IN FACT, D'YOU EVEN EAT FOOD? YER ALWAYS--
DING
FINE, IF IT'LL SHUT--
OH.
FUCK.
THE SHIT HAS HIT THE FAN.
POOM
POOM
POOMM
POOM
KREEESSHHH
TOOLSIE! WHERE'D YOU COME FROM?
THERE'S A HIT OUT ON YOU. WE GOT SNIPERS ACROSS THE STREET.
YEAH, STORY A' MY LIFE.
MMMPH--
OH! RENEE! MEET MY FRIEND RED TOOL, WITH, IRONICALLY, HIS ACTUAL TOOL IN YER FACE.
TOOLSIE, THIS IS RENEE MONTOYA. SHE'S A COP.
AN' HAVIN' YER JUNK PROBE HER EAR IS PROB'LY THE LAST THING SHE EXPECTED TA BE DOIN' TODAY.
MFFKRRRR!!!

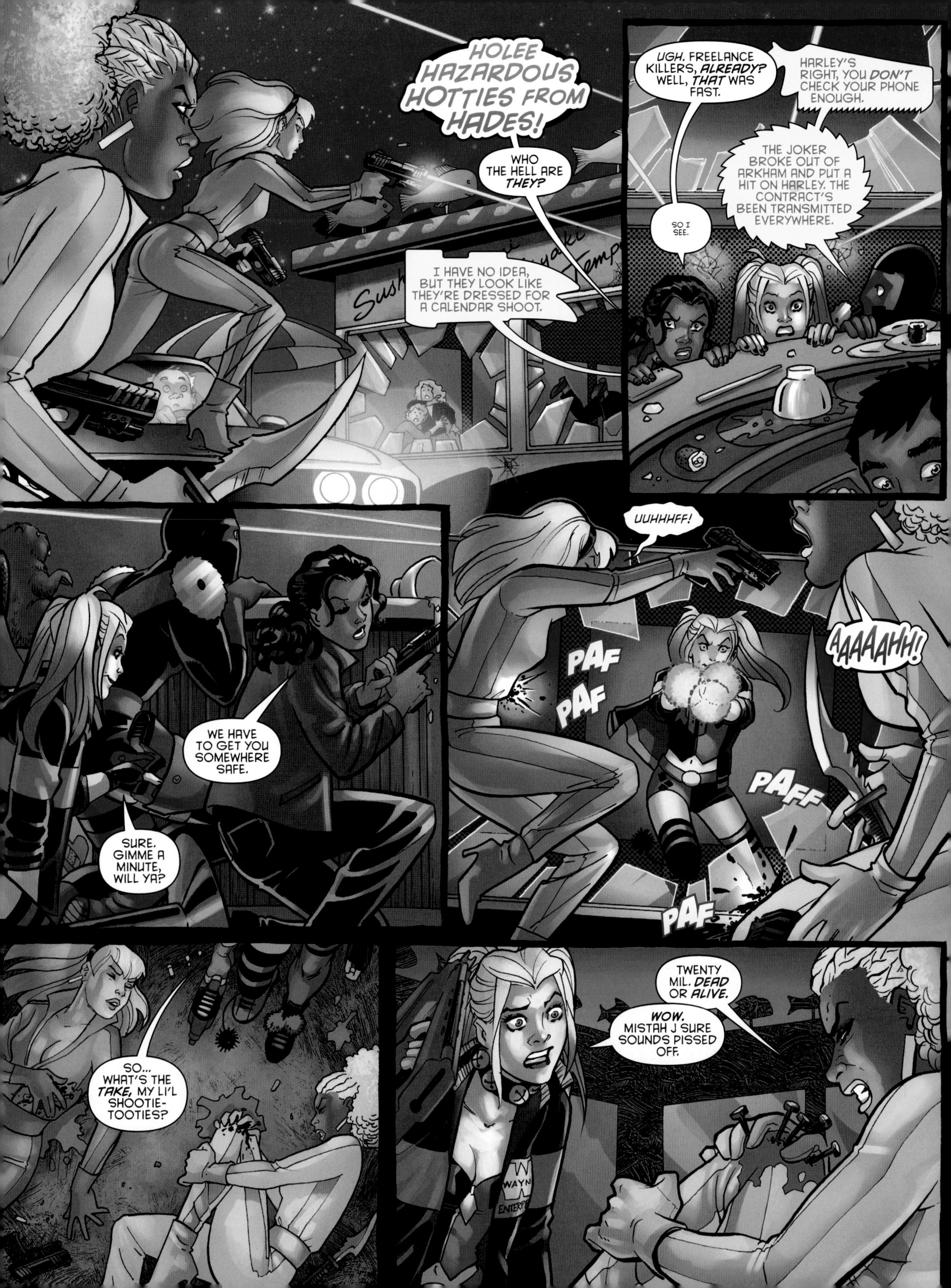
HOLEE HAZARDOUS HOTTIES FROM HADES!
WHO THE HELL ARE THEY?
I HAVE NO IDEA, BUT THEY LOOK LIKE THEY'RE DRESSED FOR A CALENDAR SHOOT.
Sushi
UGH. FREELANCE KILLERS, ALREADY? WELL, THAT WAS FAST.
HARLEY'S RIGHT, YOU DON'T CHECK YOUR PHONE ENOUGH.
THE JOKER BROKE OUT OF ARKHAM AND PUT A HIT ON HARLEY. THE CONTRACT'S BEEN TRANSMITTED EVERYWHERE.
SO I SEE.
WE HAVE TO GET YOU SOMEWHERE SAFE.
SURE. GIMME A MINUTE, WILL YA?
UUHHHFF!
PAF
PAF
AAAAAHH!
PAFF
PAF
SO... WHAT'S THE TAKE, MY LI'L SHOOTIE-TOOTIES?
TWENTY MIL. DEAD OR ALIVE.
WOW. MISTAH J SURE SOUNDS PISSED OFF.

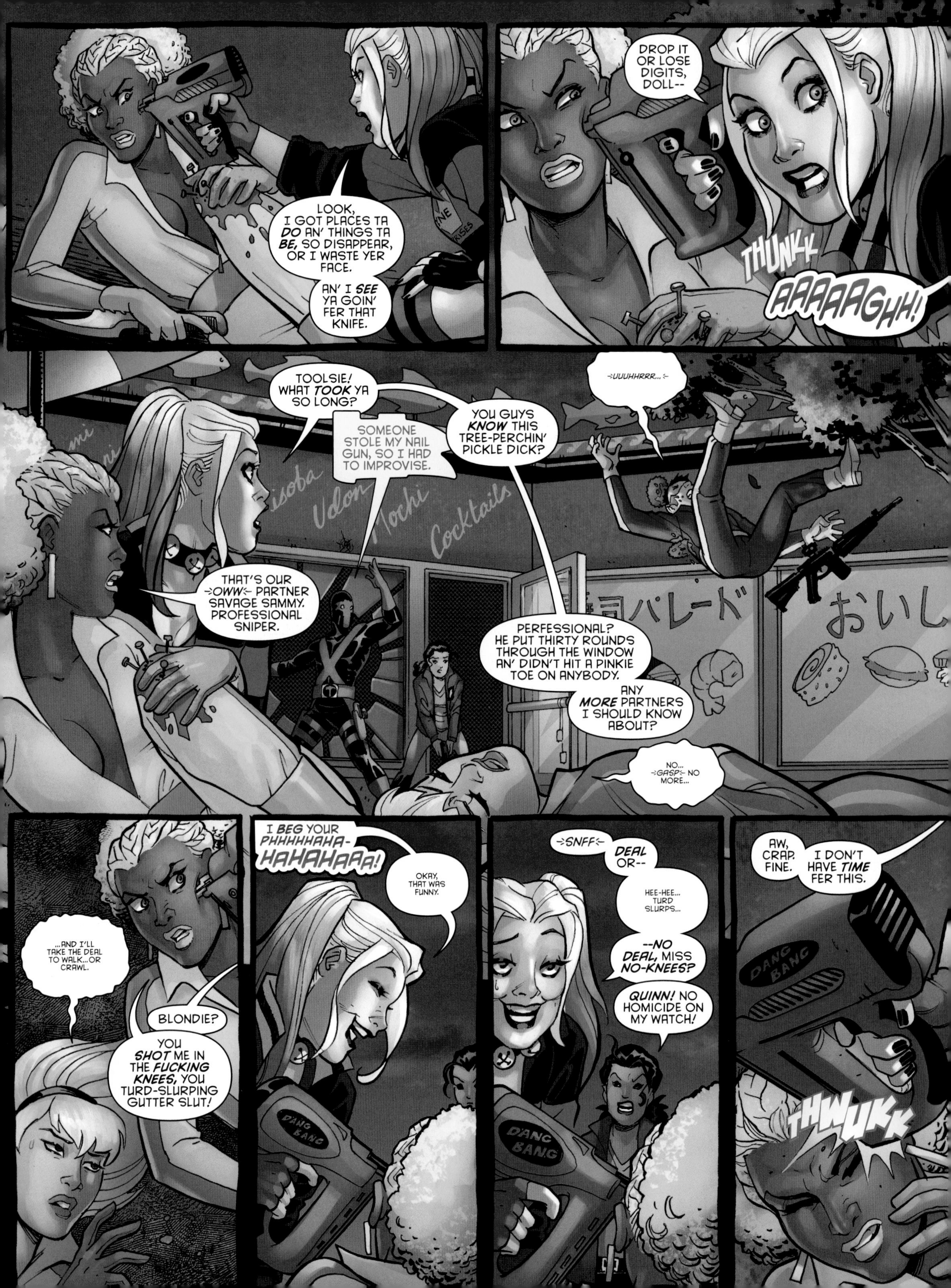

LOOK, I GOT PLACES TA DO AN' THINGS TA BE, SO DISAPPEAR, OR I WASTE YER FACE.
AN' I SEE YA GOIN' FER THAT KNIFE.
DROP IT OR LOSE DIGITS, DOLL--
THUNKK
AAAAAGHH!
TOOLSIE! WHAT TOOK YA SO LONG?
SOMEONE STOLE MY NAIL GUN, SO I HAD TO IMPROVISE.
YOU GUYS KNOW THIS TREE-PERCHIN' PICKLE DICK?
UUUHHRRR...
Udon
Mochi
Cocktails
パレード
THAT'S OUR OWW PARTNER SAVAGE SAMMY. PROFESSIONAL SNIPER.
PERFESSIONAL? HE PUT THIRTY ROUNDS THROUGH THE WINDOW AN' DIDN'T HIT A PINKIE TOE ON ANYBODY.
ANY MORE PARTNERS I SHOULD KNOW ABOUT?
NO... GASP NO MORE...
...AND I'LL TAKE THE DEAL TO WALK...OR CRAWL.
BLONDIE?
YOU SHOT ME IN THE FUCKING KNEES, YOU TURD-SLURPING GUTTER SLUT!
I BEG YOUR PHHHHHAHA-HAHAHAAA!
OKAY, THAT WAS FUNNY.
DANG BANG
SNFF
DEAL OR--
HEE-HEE... TURD SLURPS...
--NO DEAL, MISS NO-KNEES?
QUINN! NO HOMICIDE ON MY WATCH!
DANG BANG
AW, CRAP. FINE.
I DON'T HAVE TIME FER THIS.
DANG BANG
THWUKK

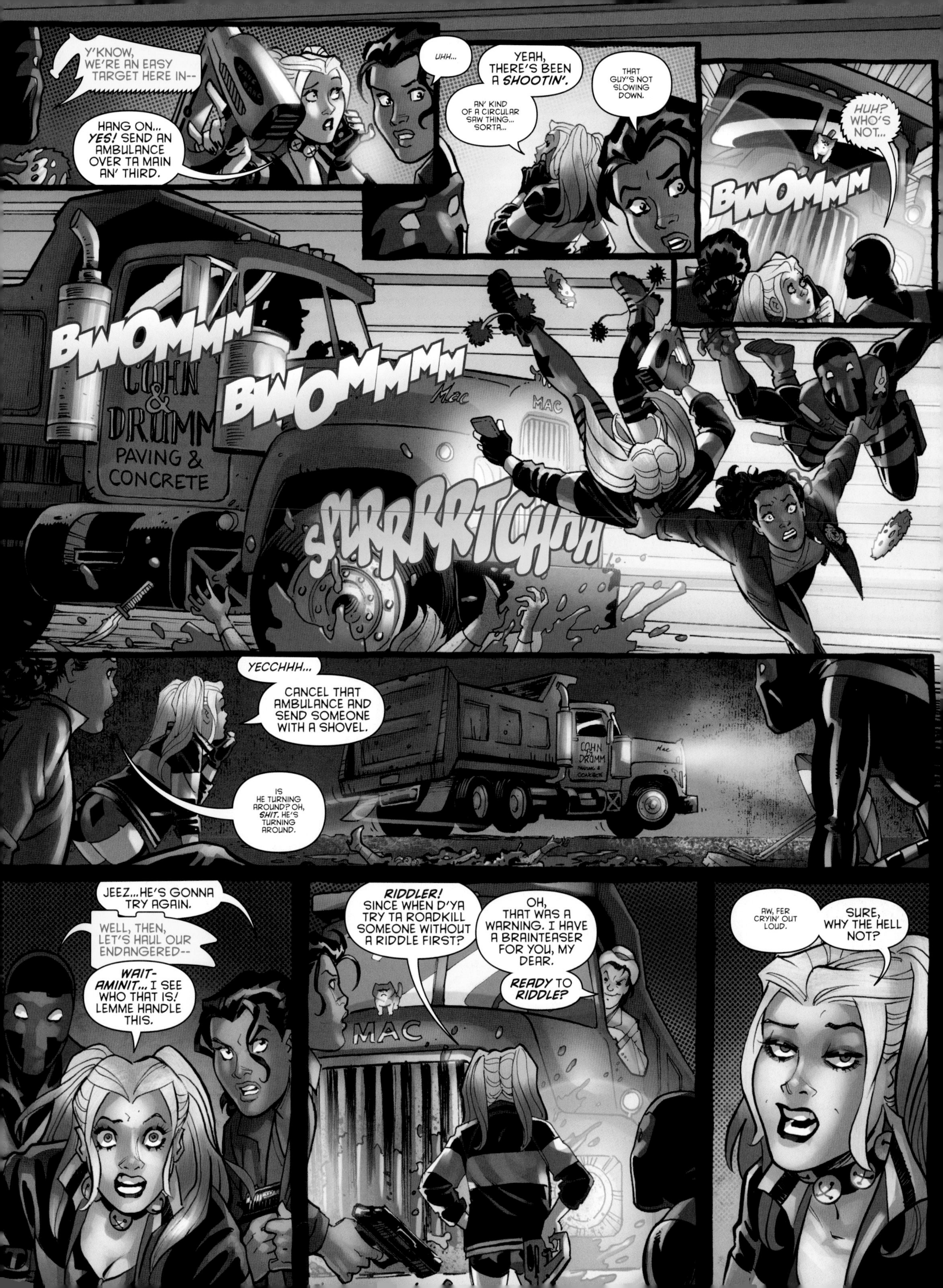

Y'KNOW, WE'RE AN EASY TARGET HERE IN--
HANG ON... YES! SEND AN AMBULANCE OVER TA MAIN AN' THIRD.
UHH...
YEAH, THERE'S BEEN A SHOOTIN'.
AN' KIND OF A CIRCULAR SAW THING... SORTA...
THAT GUY'S NOT SLOWING DOWN.
HUH? WHO'S NOT...
BWOMMM
BWOMMM
COHN & DRUMM PAVING & CONCRETE
BWOMMMM
MAC
SPLRRRRTCHHH
YECCHHH...
CANCEL THAT AMBULANCE AND SEND SOMEONE WITH A SHOVEL.
IS HE TURNING AROUND? OH, SHIT. HE'S TURNING AROUND.
JEEZ...HE'S GONNA TRY AGAIN.
WELL, THEN, LET'S HAUL OUR ENDANGERED--
WAIT-AMINIT... I SEE WHO THAT IS! LEMME HANDLE THIS.
RIDDLER! SINCE WHEN D'YA TRY TA ROADKILL SOMEONE WITHOUT A RIDDLE FIRST?
OH, THAT WAS A WARNING. I HAVE A BRAINTEASER FOR YOU, MY DEAR.
READY TO RIDDLE?
MAC
AW, FER CRYIN' OUT LOUD.
SURE, WHY THE HELL NOT?

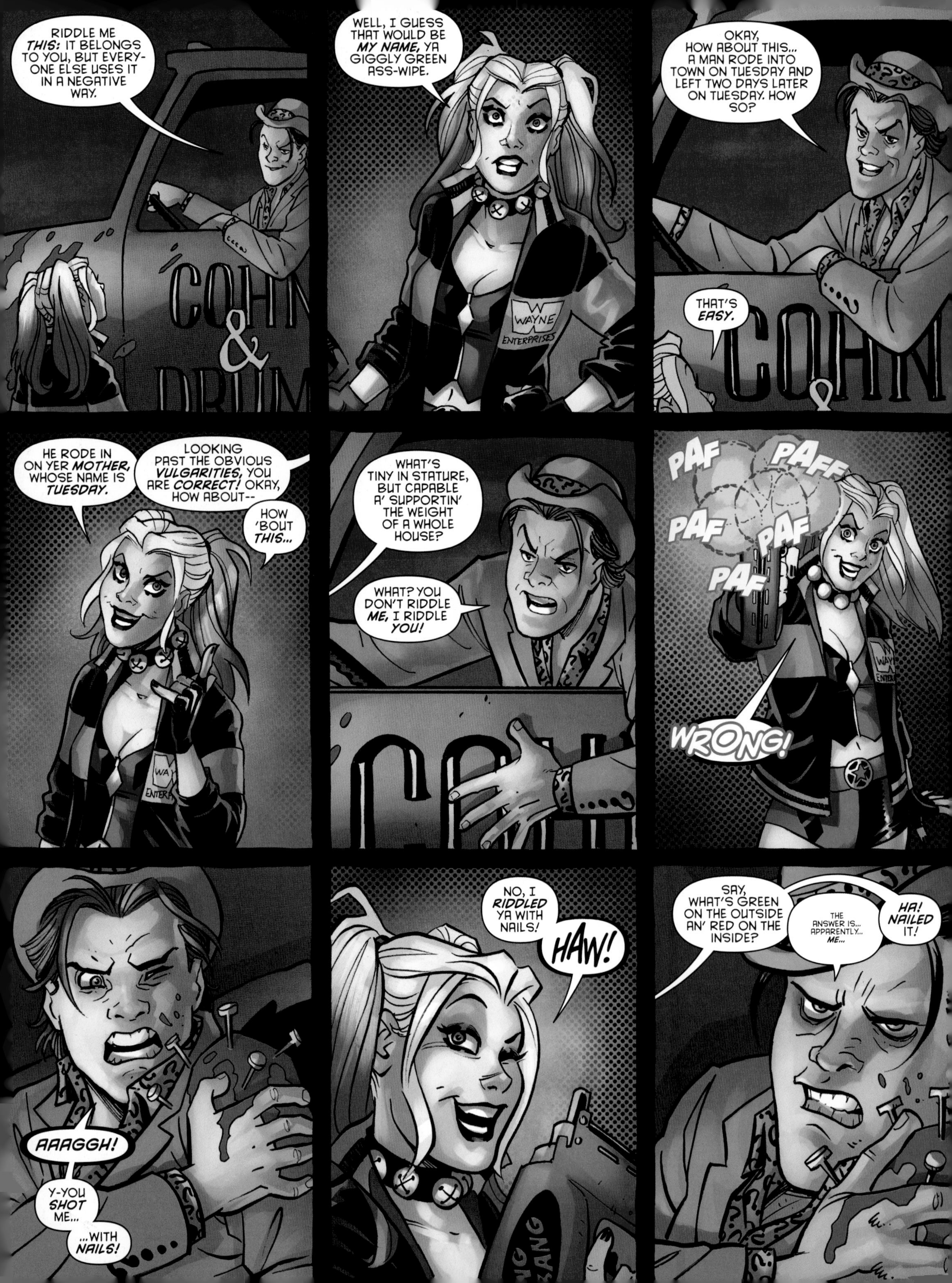
RIDDLE ME THIS: IT BELONGS TO YOU, BUT EVERY-ONE ELSE USES IT IN A NEGATIVE WAY.
COHN & DRUM
WELL, I GUESS THAT WOULD BE MY NAME, YA GIGGLY GREEN ASS-WIPE.
WAYNE ENTERPRISES
OKAY, HOW ABOUT THIS... A MAN RODE INTO TOWN ON TUESDAY AND LEFT TWO DAYS LATER ON TUESDAY. HOW SO?
THAT'S EASY.
COHN &
HE RODE IN ON YER MOTHER, WHOSE NAME IS TUESDAY.
LOOKING PAST THE OBVIOUS VULGARITIES, YOU ARE CORRECT! OKAY, HOW ABOUT--
HOW 'BOUT THIS...
WHAT'S TINY IN STATURE, BUT CAPABLE A' SUPPORTIN' THE WEIGHT OF A WHOLE HOUSE?
WHAT? YOU DON'T RIDDLE ME, I RIDDLE YOU!
PAF
PAFF
PAF
PAF
PAF
WRONG!
AAAGGH!
Y-YOU SHOT ME...
...WITH NAILS!
NO, I RIDDLED YA WITH NAILS!
HAW!
SAY, WHAT'S GREEN ON THE OUTSIDE AN' RED ON THE INSIDE?
THE ANSWER IS... APPARENTLY... ME...
HA! NAILED IT!

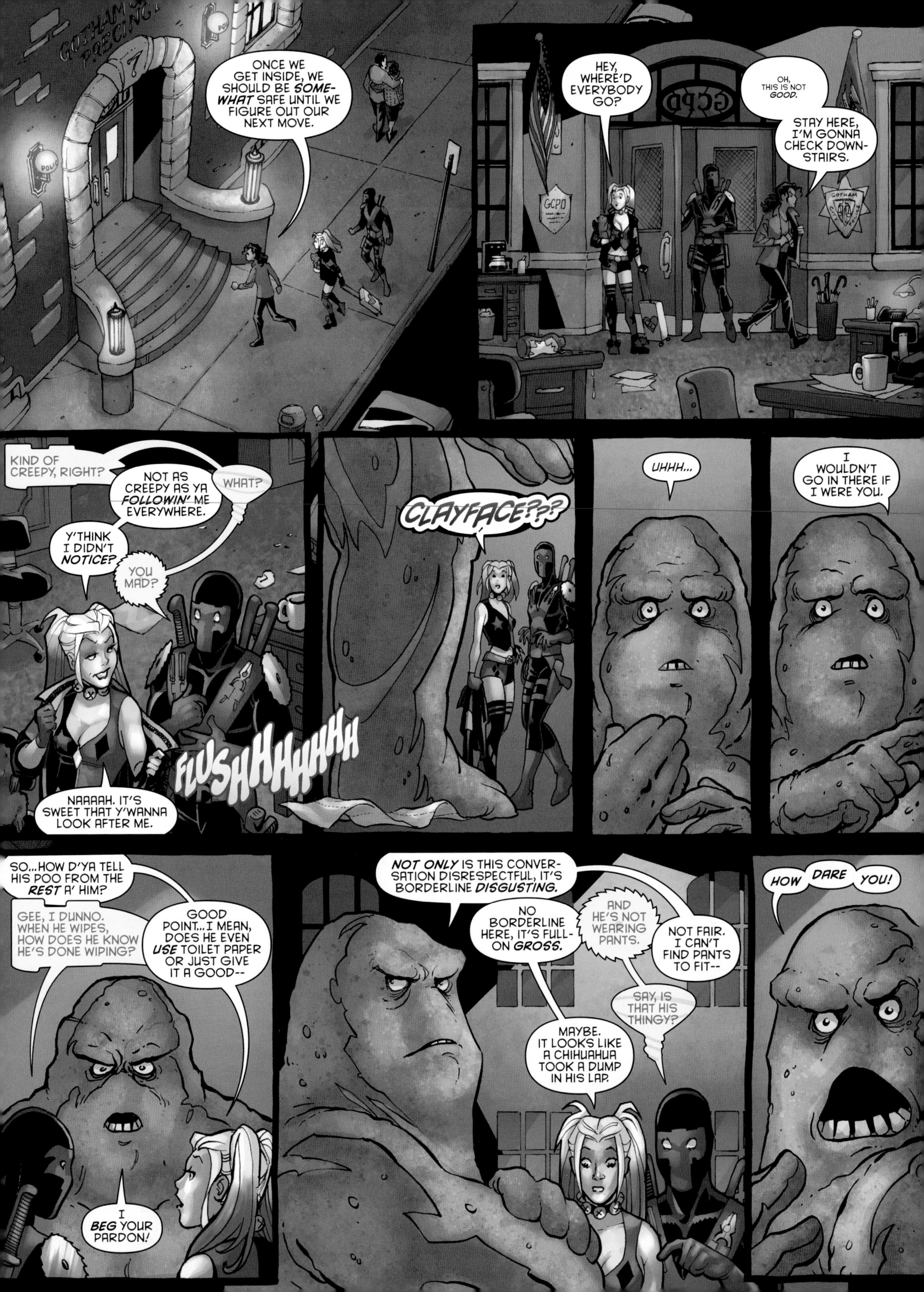
GOTHAM CITY PRECINCT 7
ONCE WE GET INSIDE, WE SHOULD BE SOME-WHAT SAFE UNTIL WE FIGURE OUT OUR NEXT MOVE.
HEY, WHERE'D EVERYBODY GO?
GCPD
OH, THIS IS NOT GOOD.
STAY HERE, I'M GONNA CHECK DOWN-STAIRS.
KIND OF CREEPY, RIGHT?
NOT AS CREEPY AS YA FOLLOWIN' ME EVERYWHERE.
WHAT?
Y'THINK I DIDN'T NOTICE?
YOU MAD?
NAAAAH. IT'S SWEET THAT Y'WANNA LOOK AFTER ME.
FLUSHHHHHHH
CLAYFACE???
UHHH...
I WOULDN'T GO IN THERE IF I WERE YOU.
SO...HOW D'YA TELL HIS POO FROM THE REST A' HIM?
GEE, I DUNNO. WHEN HE WIPES, HOW DOES HE KNOW HE'S DONE WIPING?
GOOD POINT...I MEAN, DOES HE EVEN USE TOILET PAPER OR JUST GIVE IT A GOOD--
I BEG YOUR PARDON!
NOT ONLY IS THIS CONVER-SATION DISRESPECTFUL, IT'S BORDERLINE DISGUSTING.
NO BORDERLINE HERE, IT'S FULL-ON GROSS.
AND HE'S NOT WEARING PANTS.
NOT FAIR. I CAN'T FIND PANTS TO FIT--
SAY, IS THAT HIS THINGY?
MAYBE. IT LOOKS LIKE A CHIHUAHUA TOOK A DUMP IN HIS LAP.
HOW DARE YOU!

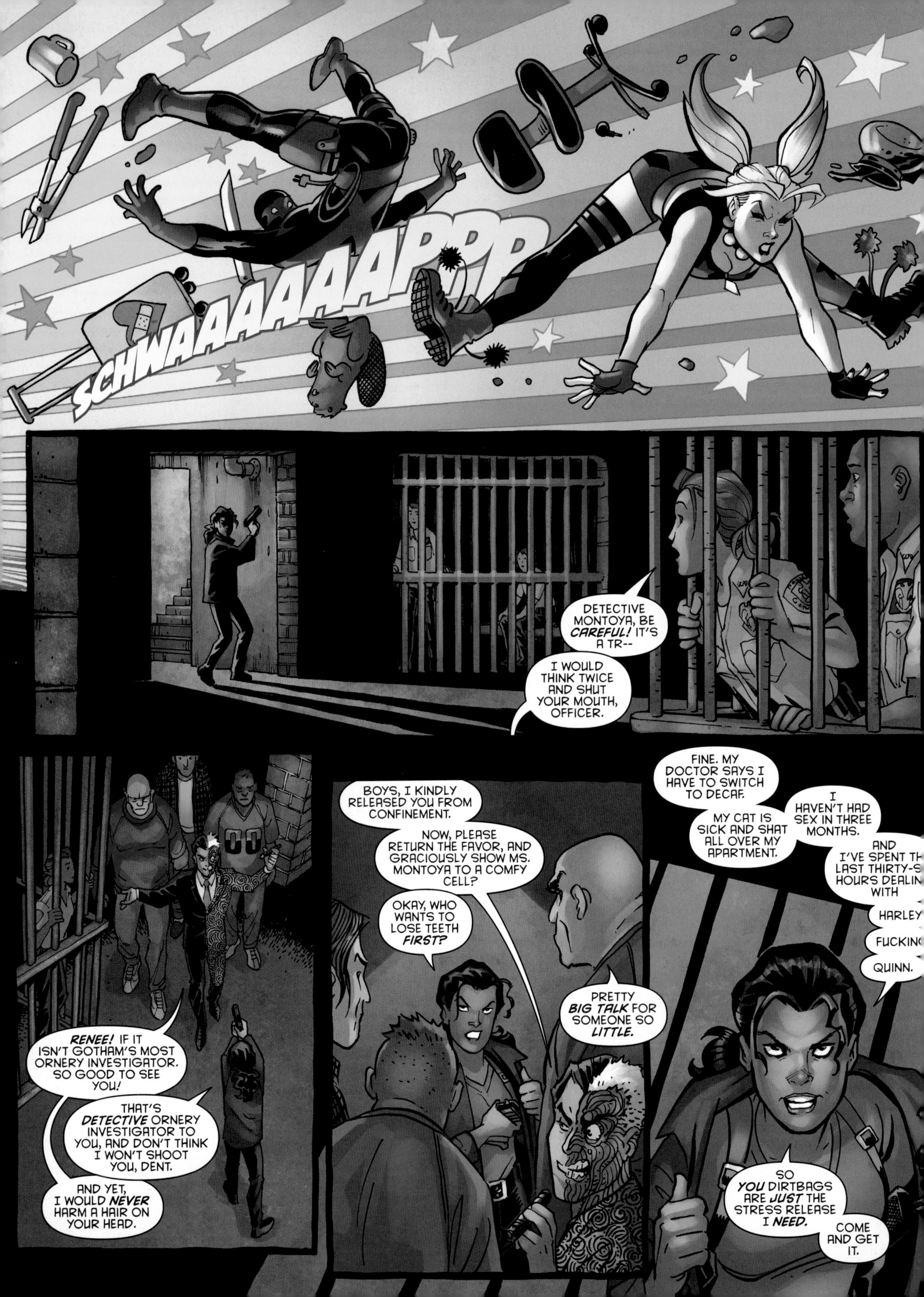
SCHWAAAAAAAPPP
DETECTIVE MONTOYA, BE CAREFUL! IT'S A TR--
I WOULD THINK TWICE AND SHUT YOUR MOUTH, OFFICER.
RENEE! IF IT ISN'T GOTHAM'S MOST ORNERY INVESTIGATOR. SO GOOD TO SEE YOU!
THAT'S DETECTIVE ORNERY INVESTIGATOR TO YOU, AND DON'T THINK I WON'T SHOOT YOU, DENT.
AND YET, I WOULD NEVER HARM A HAIR ON YOUR HEAD.
BOYS, I KINDLY RELEASED YOU FROM CONFINEMENT.
NOW, PLEASE RETURN THE FAVOR, AND GRACIOUSLY SHOW MS. MONTOYA TO A COMFY CELL?
OKAY, WHO WANTS TO LOSE TEETH FIRST?
PRETTY BIG TALK FOR SOMEONE SO LITTLE.
FINE. MY DOCTOR SAYS I HAVE TO SWITCH TO DECAF.
MY CAT IS SICK AND SHAT ALL OVER MY APARTMENT.
I HAVEN'T HAD SEX IN THREE MONTHS.
AND I'VE SPENT TH LAST THIRTY-S HOURS DEALIN WITH
HARLEY
FUCKIN
QUINN.
SO YOU DIRTBAGS ARE JUST THE STRESS RELEASE I NEED.
COME AND GET IT.

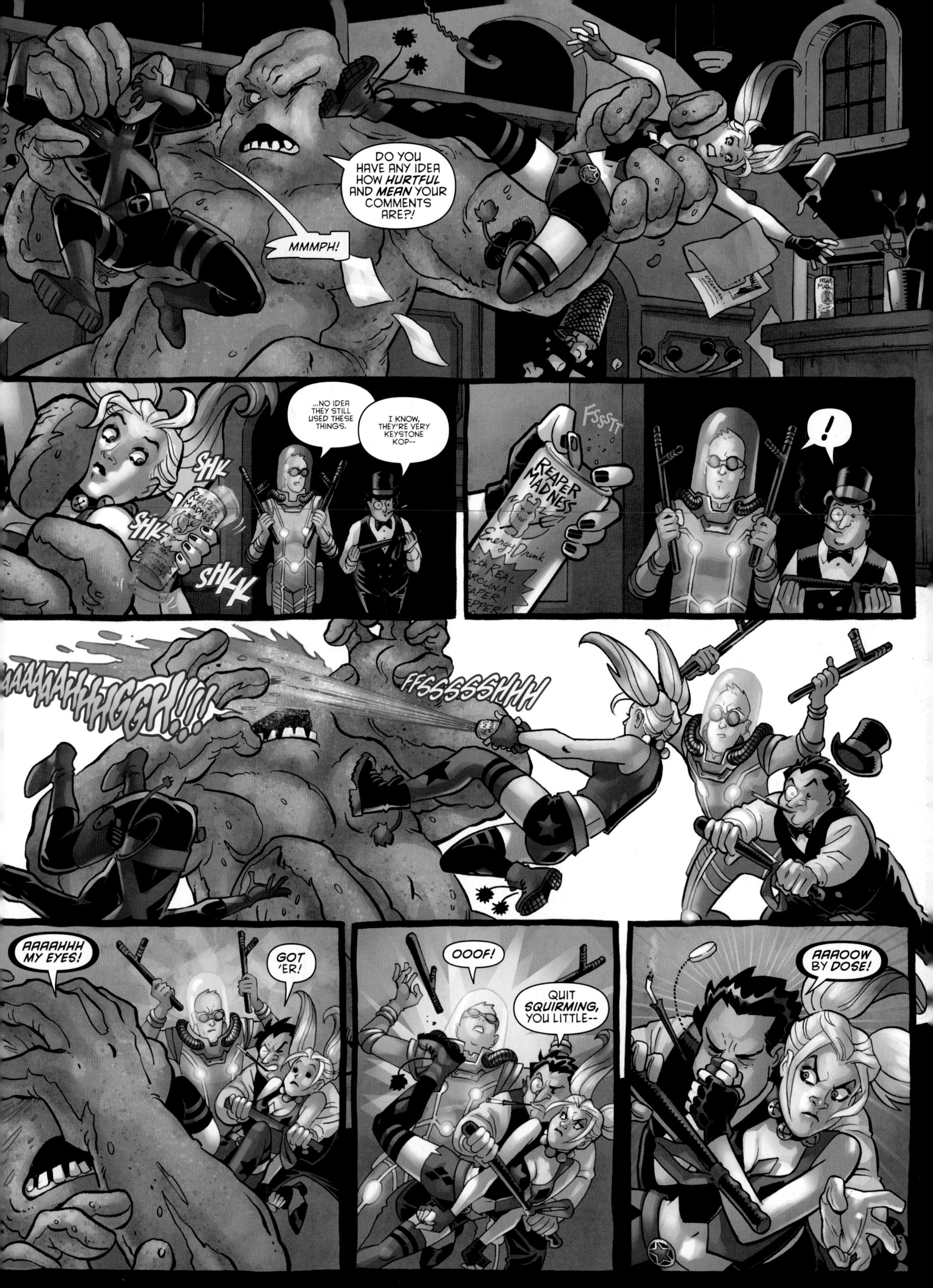
DO YOU HAVE ANY IDEA HOW HURTFUL AND MEAN YOUR COMMENTS ARE?!
MMMPH!
...NO IDEA THEY STILL USED THESE THINGS.
I KNOW, THEY'RE VERY KEYSTONE KOP--
SHK
SHK
SHKK
FSSSTT
REAPER MADNESS Energy Drink with REAL CAROLINA REAPER PEPPER!
!
AAAAAAHHHGGH!!!!
FFSSSSSSHHH
AAAAHHH MY EYES!
GOT 'ER!
OOOF!
QUIT SQUIRMING, YOU LITTLE--
AAAOOW BY DOSE!

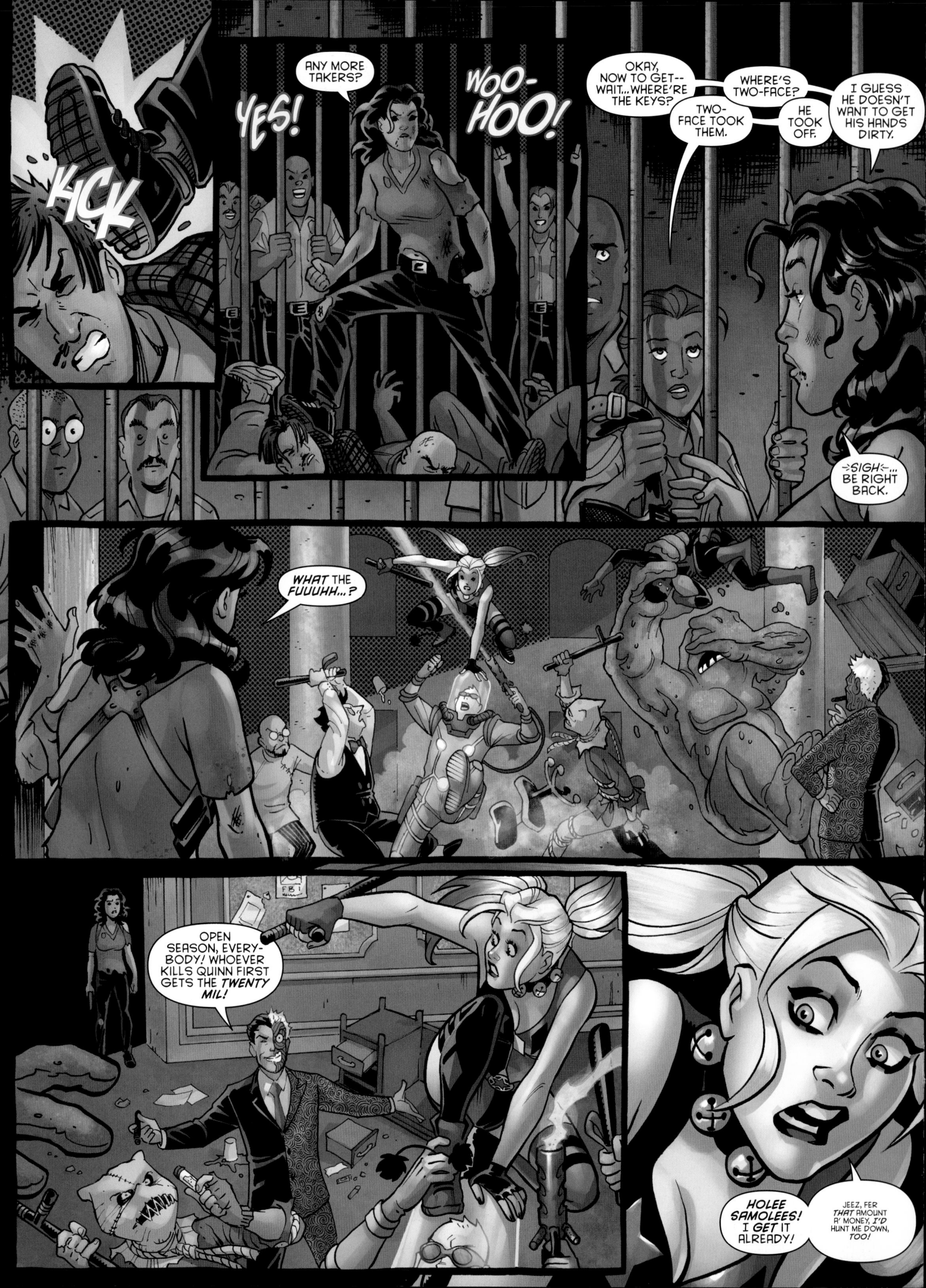
KICK
ANY MORE TAKERS?
YES!
WOO-HOO!
OKAY, NOW TO GET-- WAIT... WHERE'RE THE KEYS?
TWO-FACE TOOK THEM.
WHERE'S TWO-FACE?
HE TOOK OFF.
I GUESS HE DOESN'T WANT TO GET HIS HANDS DIRTY.
-SIGH-... BE RIGHT BACK.
WHAT THE FUUUHH...?
OPEN SEASON, EVERY-BODY! WHOEVER KILLS QUINN FIRST GETS THE TWENTY MIL!
HOLEE SAMOLEES! I GET IT ALREADY!
JEEZ, FER THAT AMOUNT A' MONEY, I'D HUNT ME DOWN, TOO!

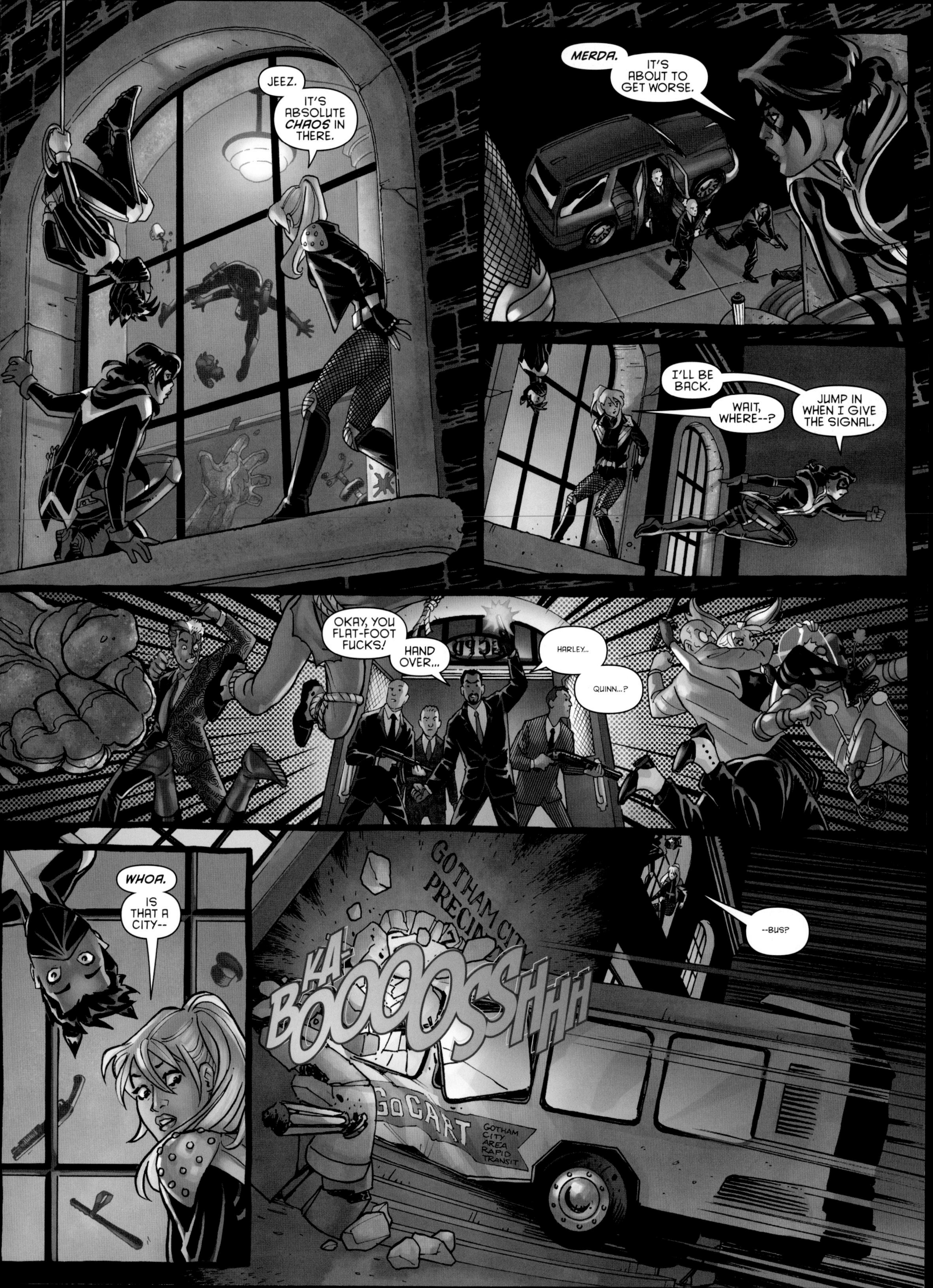
JEEZ.
IT'S ABSOLUTE CHAOS IN THERE.
MERDA.
IT'S ABOUT TO GET WORSE.
I'LL BE BACK.
WAIT, WHERE--?
JUMP IN WHEN I GIVE THE SIGNAL.
OKAY, YOU FLAT-FOOT FUCKS!
HAND OVER...
HARLEY...
QUINN...?
WHOA.
IS THAT A CITY--
--BUS?
GOTHAM CITY PRECINCT
KA-BOOOOSHHH
GOCART
GOTHAM CITY AREA RAPID TRANSIT

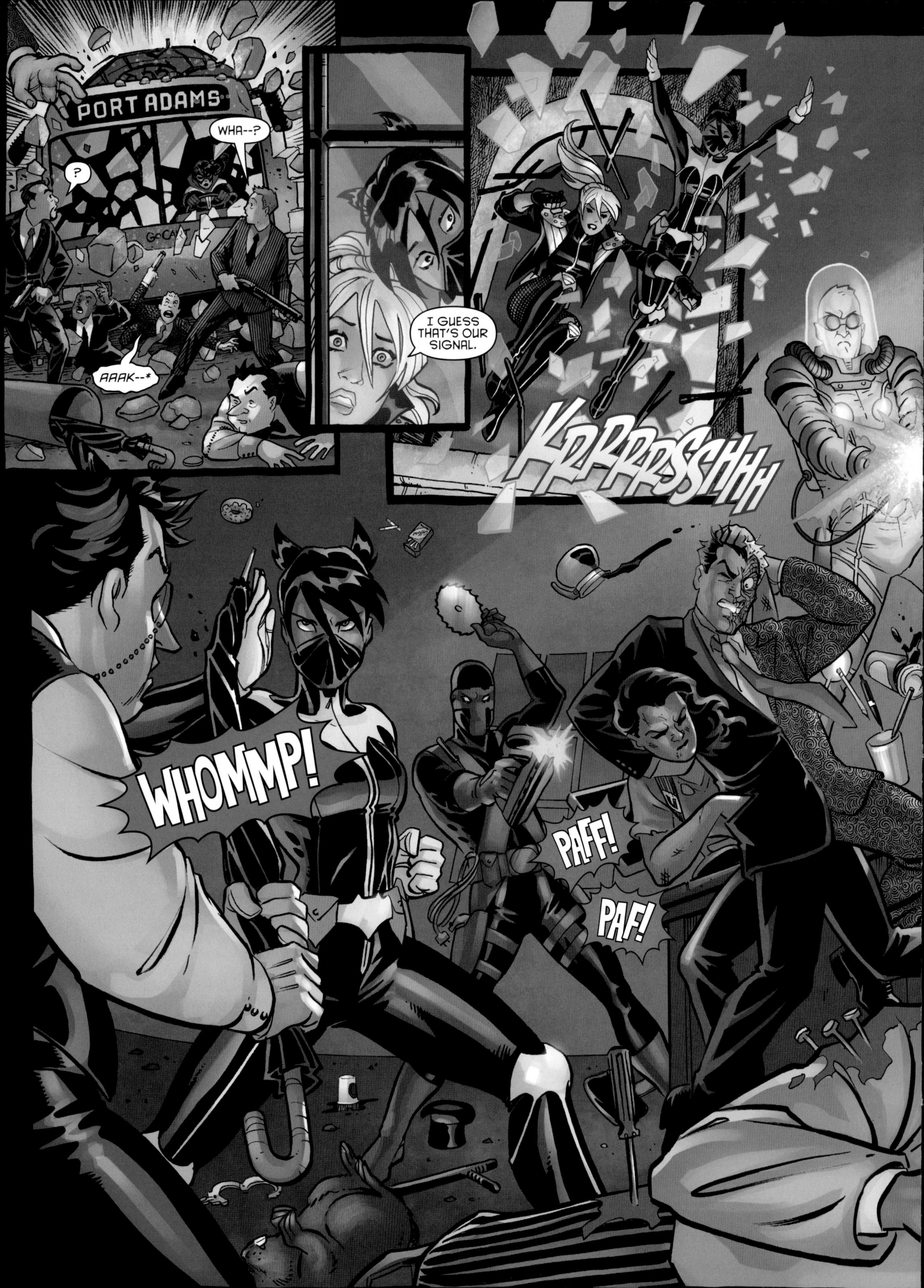

PORT ADAMS
?
WHA--?
AAAK--*
I GUESS THAT'S OUR SIGNAL.
KRRRRSSHHH
WHOMMP!
PAFF!
PAF!

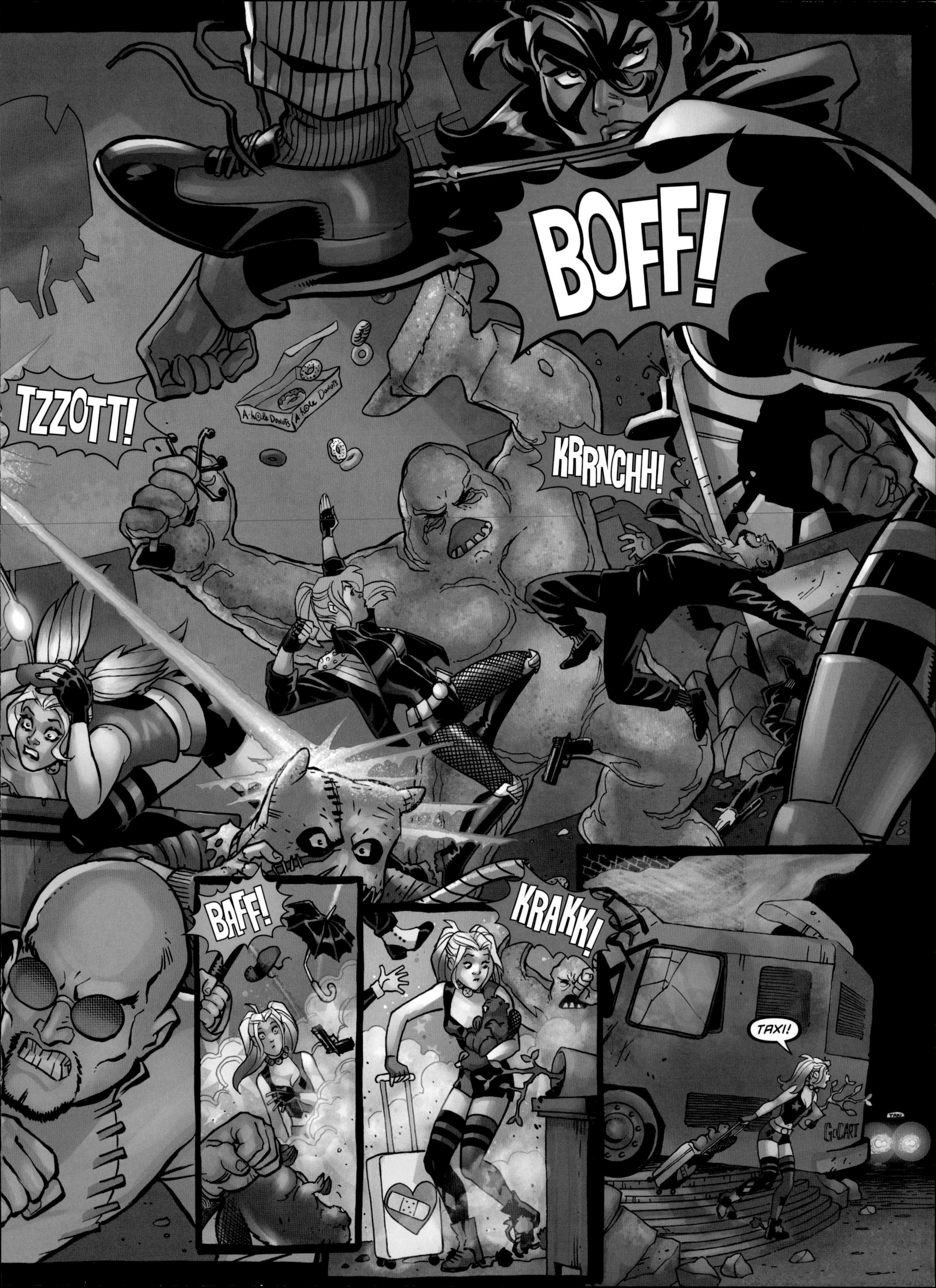
BOFF!
TZZOTT!
KRRNCHH!
BAFF!
KRAKK!
TAXI!

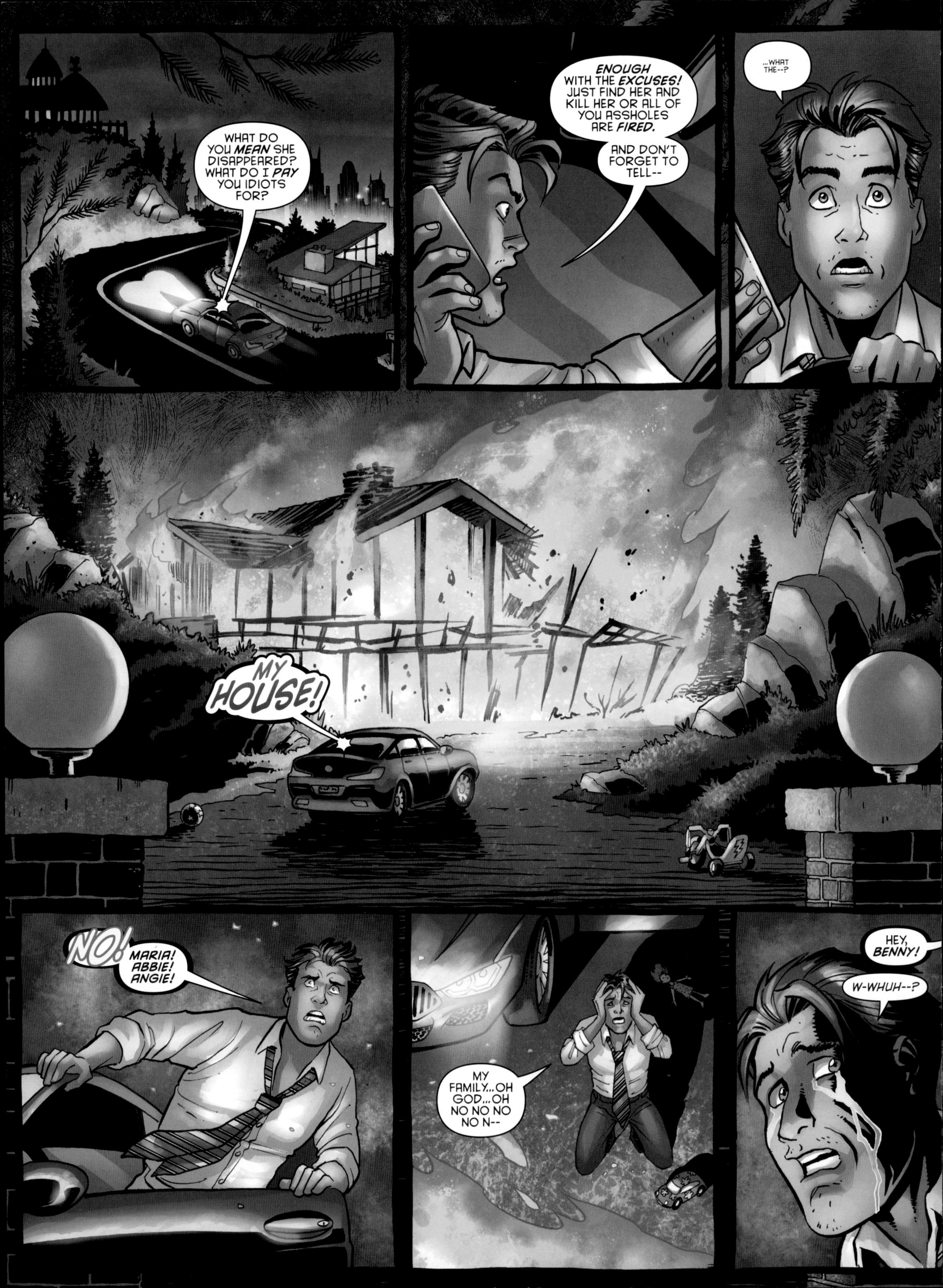
WHAT DO YOU MEAN SHE DISAPPEARED? WHAT DO I PAY YOU IDIOTS FOR?
ENOUGH WITH THE EXCUSES! JUST FIND HER AND KILL HER OR ALL OF YOU ASSHOLES ARE FIRED.
AND DON'T FORGET TO TELL--
...WHAT THE--?
MY HOUSE!
NO!
MARIA! ABBIE! ANGIE!
MY FAMILY... OH GOD... OH NO NO NO NO N--
HEY, BENNY!
W-WHUH--?

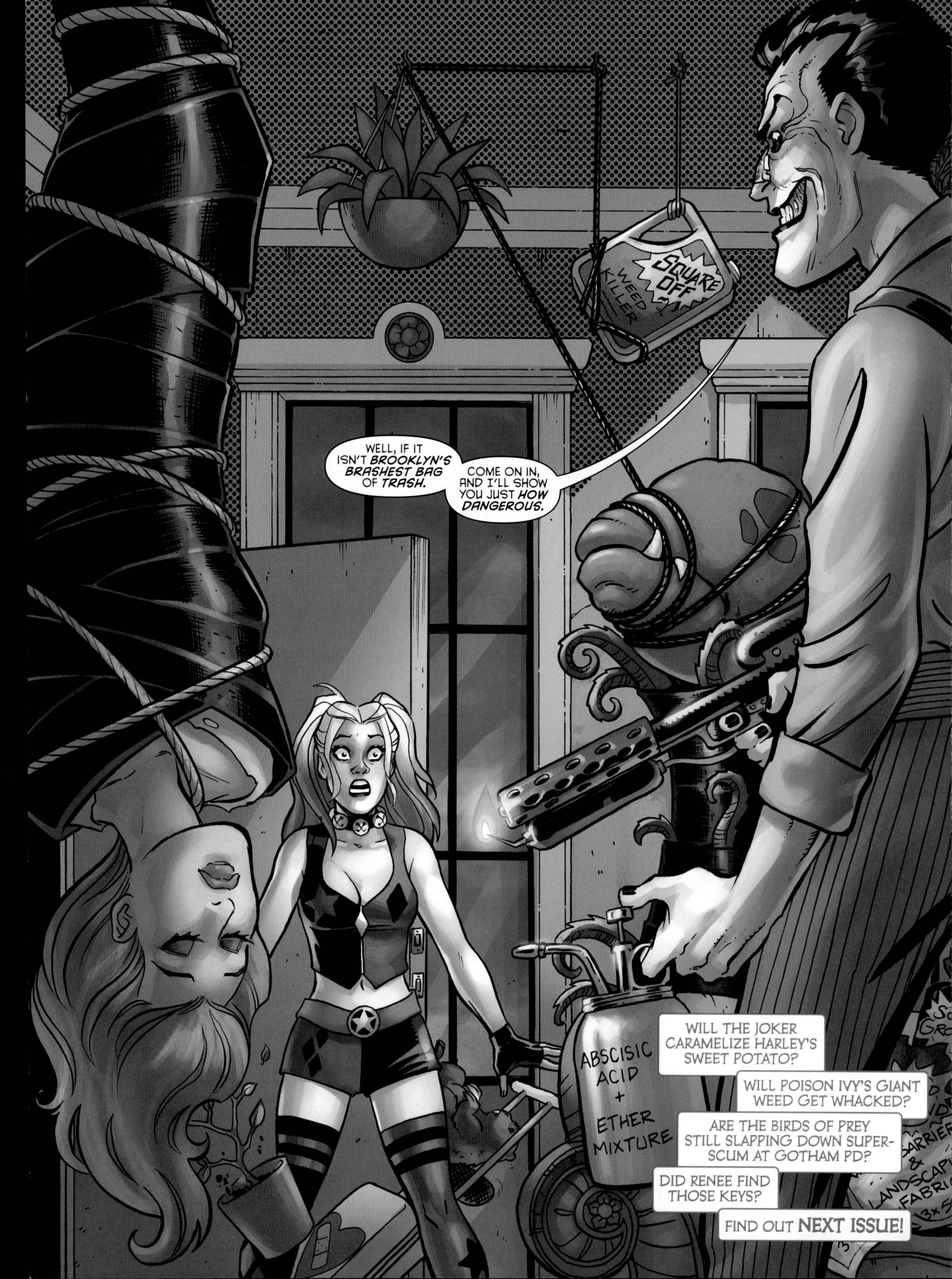
SQUARE OFF
WEED KILLER
WELL, IF IT ISN'T BROOKLYN'S BRASHEST BAG OF TRASH.
COME ON IN, AND I'LL SHOW YOU JUST HOW DANGEROUS.
ABSCISIC ACID + ETHER MIXTURE
WILL THE JOKER CARAMELIZE HARLEY'S SWEET POTATO?
WILL POISON IVY'S GIANT WEED GET WHACKED?
ARE THE BIRDS OF PREY STILL SLAPPING DOWN SUPER-SCUM AT GOTHAM PD?
DID RENEE FIND THOSE KEYS?
FIND OUT NEXT ISSUE!

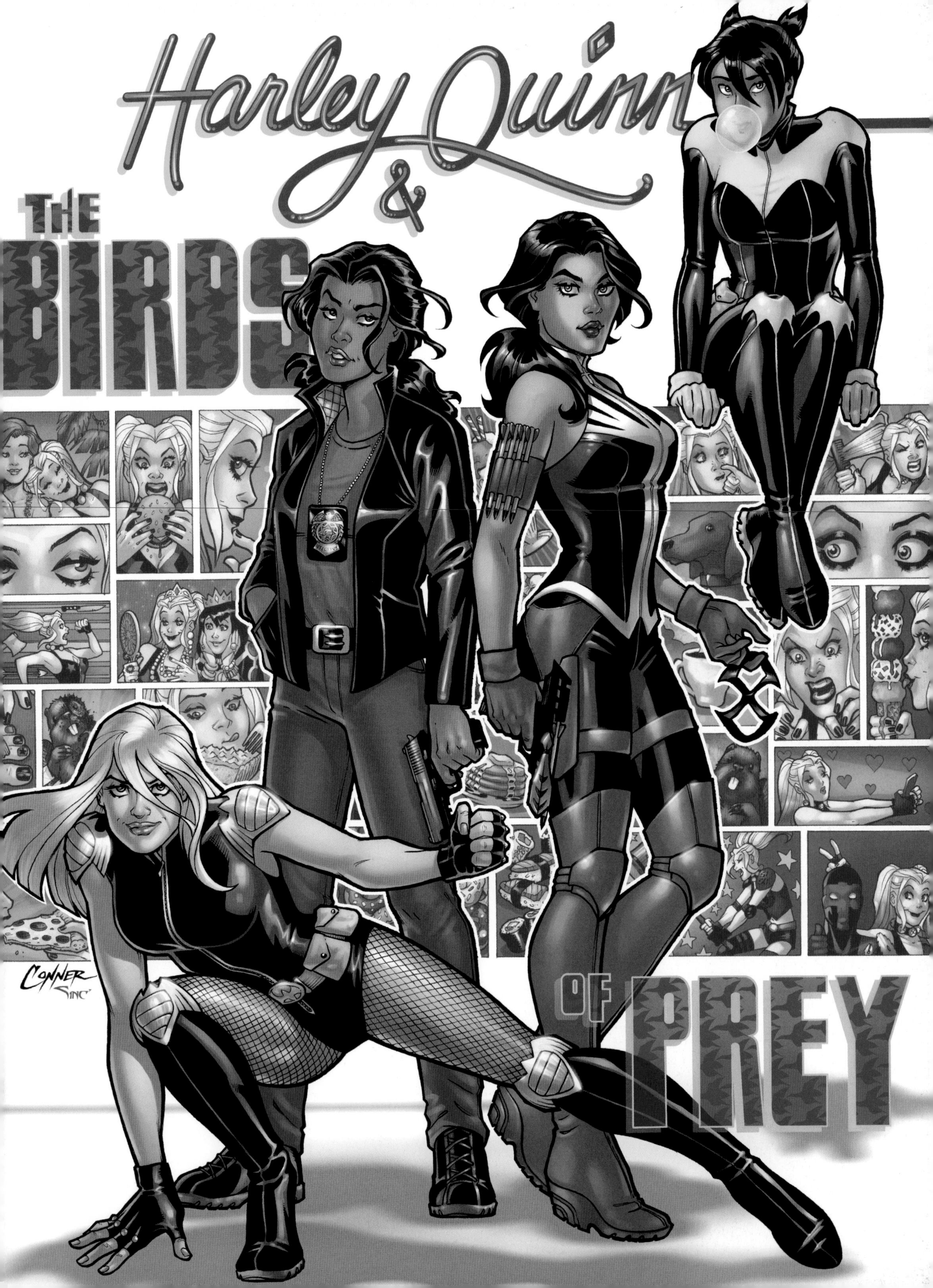
Harley Quinn
&
THE BIRDS
OF PREY
CONNER SINC'

BOOK FOUR
FLOWERING INFERNO

"It's MY turn now."

THWOKK

IT BURNS!

UHFF!

OOOFF!

WHAT?! WHO--?

WHAT'S GOING ON BACK--

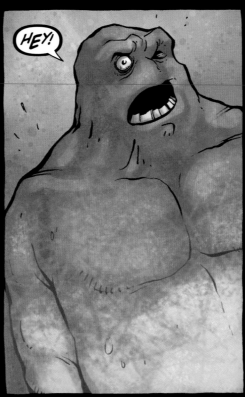

HEY!

--*

OH! THAT WASN'T NICE.

SHE COULD'VE POINTED THAT THING ANYWHERE ELSE.

YOW. ICE ENEMA'S GOTTA BE UNCOMFORT-ABLE.

MAYBE NOT, DOLL. IT DEPENDS...

...IF HE DRANK ANY OF THIS, THEN IT'S PROBABLY COOL AND REFRESHING.

NOBODY ASKED, HARVEY.

AND CALL ME "DOLL" AGAIN IF YOU HATE YOUR OTHER EYE.

BAFF

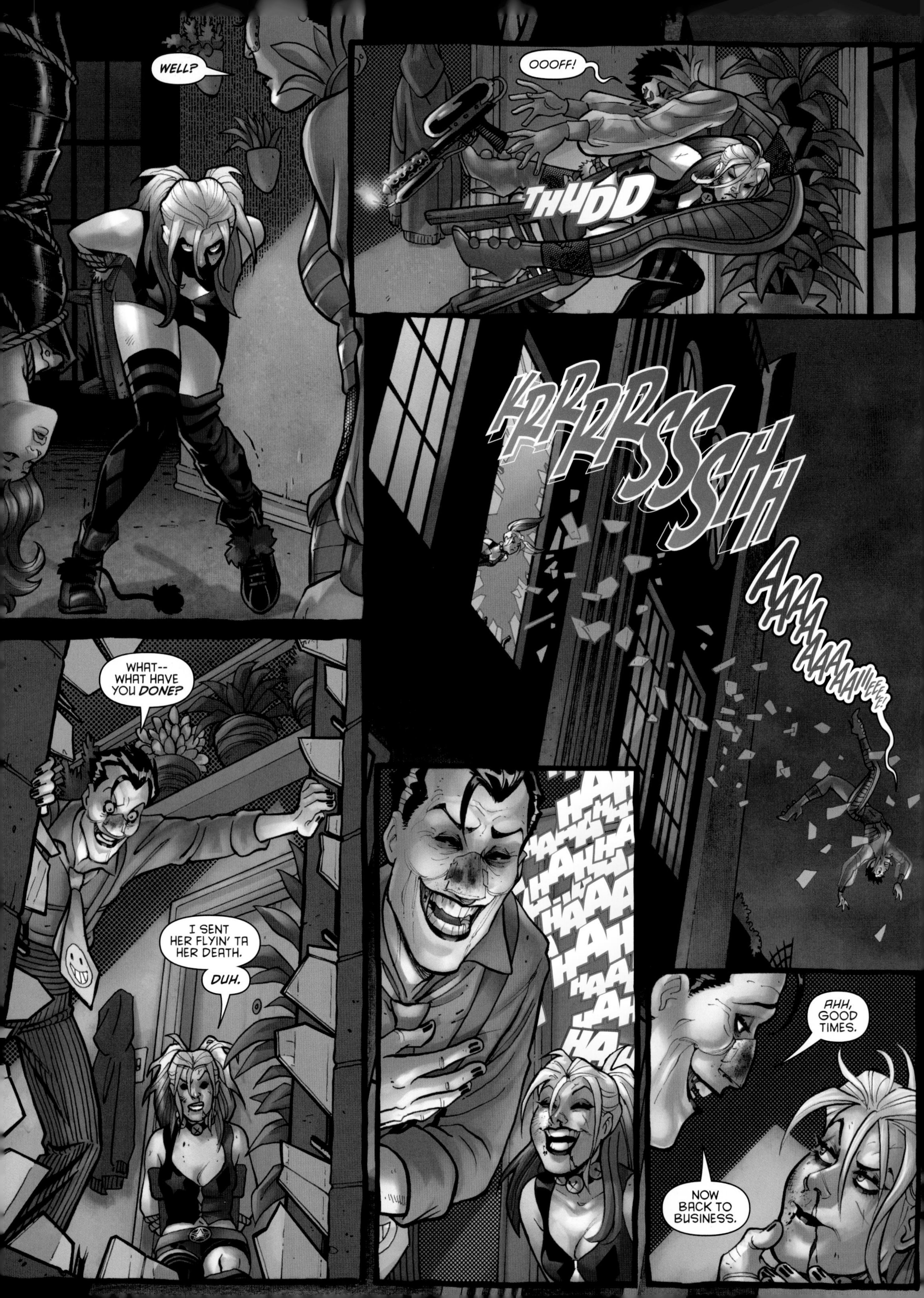
WELL?
OOOFF!
THUDD
KRRRRSSSHH
AAAAAAAAIIIEEEE!
WHAT-- WHAT HAVE YOU DONE?
I SENT HER FLYIN' TA HER DEATH.
DUH.
AHH, GOOD TIMES.
NOW BACK TO BUSINESS.

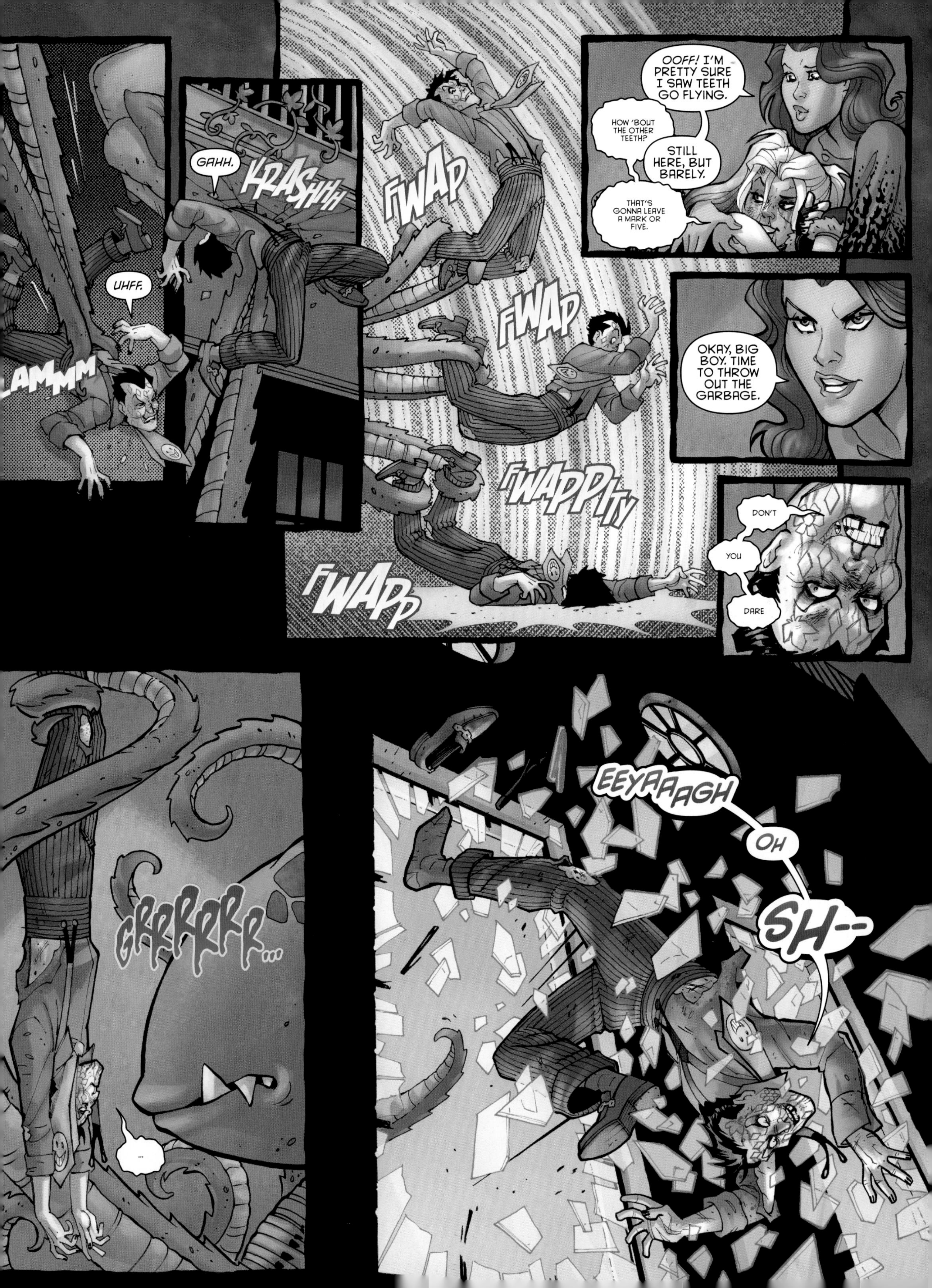

GAHH.
KRASHHH
UHFF.
LAMMM
FWAP
FWAP
FWAPPITY
FWAPP
OOFF! I'M PRETTY SURE I SAW TEETH GO FLYING.
HOW 'BOUT THE OTHER TEETH?
STILL HERE, BUT BARELY.
THAT'S GONNA LEAVE A MARK OR FIVE.
OKAY, BIG BOY. TIME TO THROW OUT THE GARBAGE.
DON'T
YOU
DARE
GRRRRRR...
...
EEYAAAAGH
OH
SH--

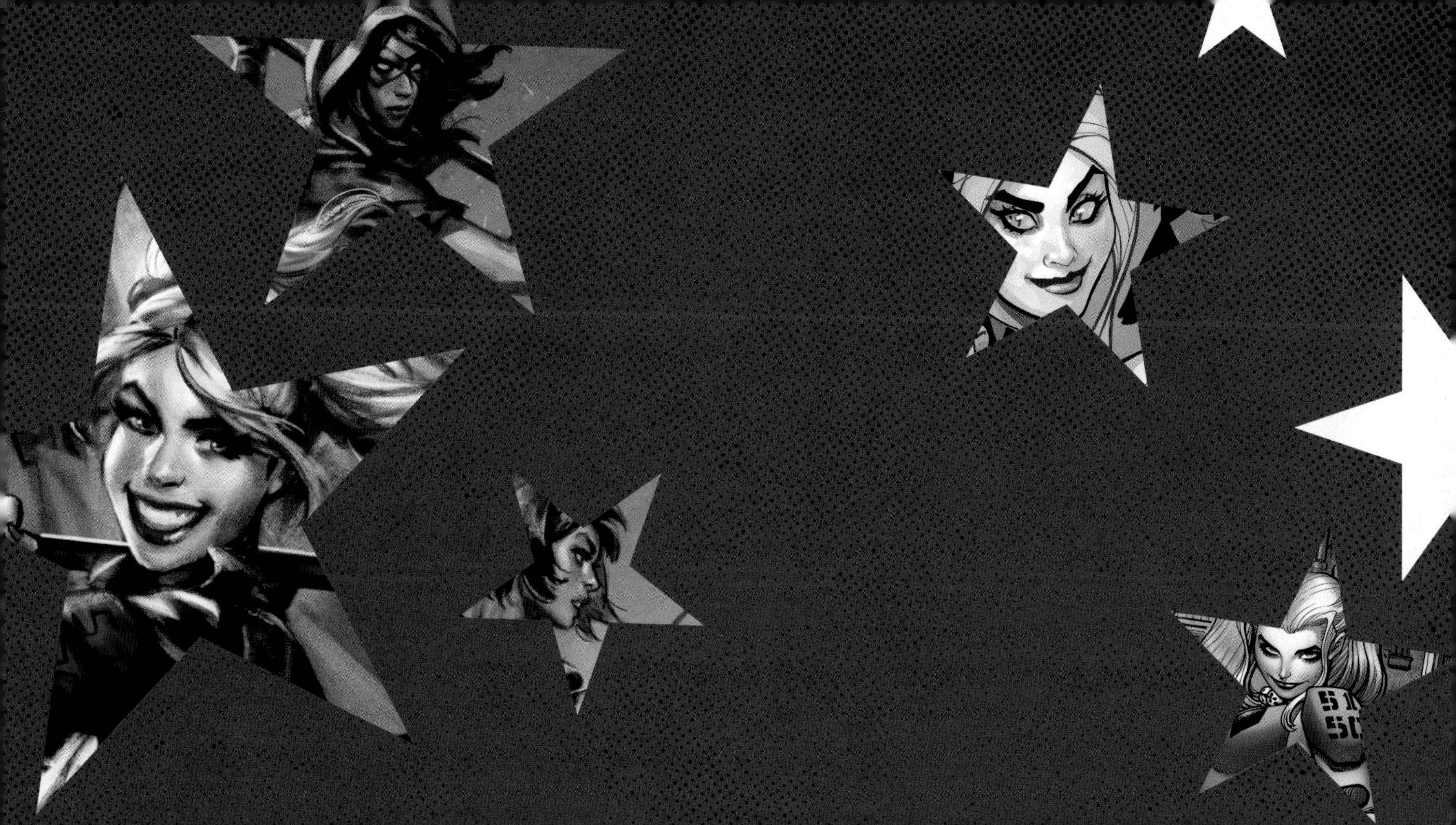

HARLEY QUiNN
and the BIRDS OF PREY

VARIANT COVER GALLERY

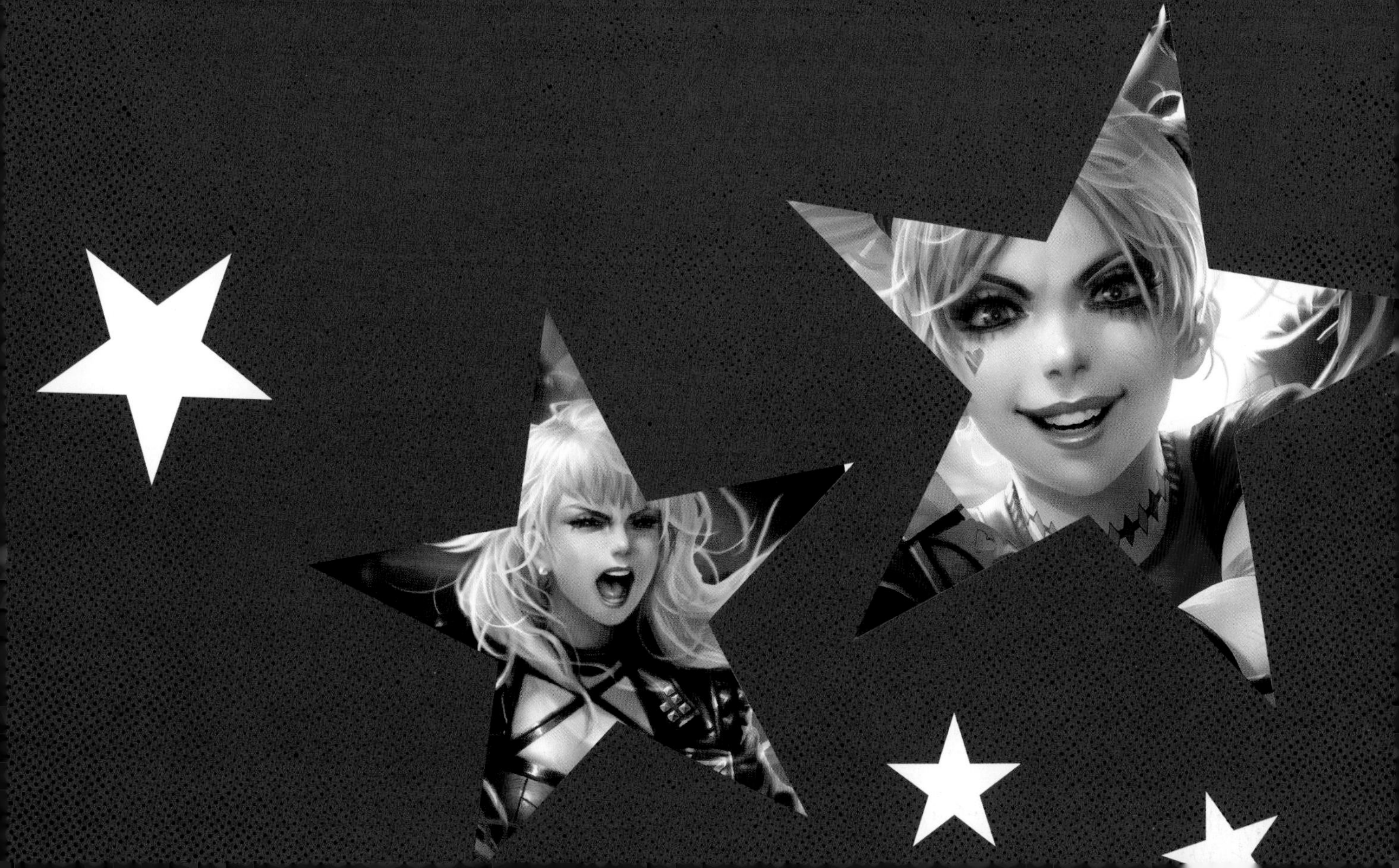

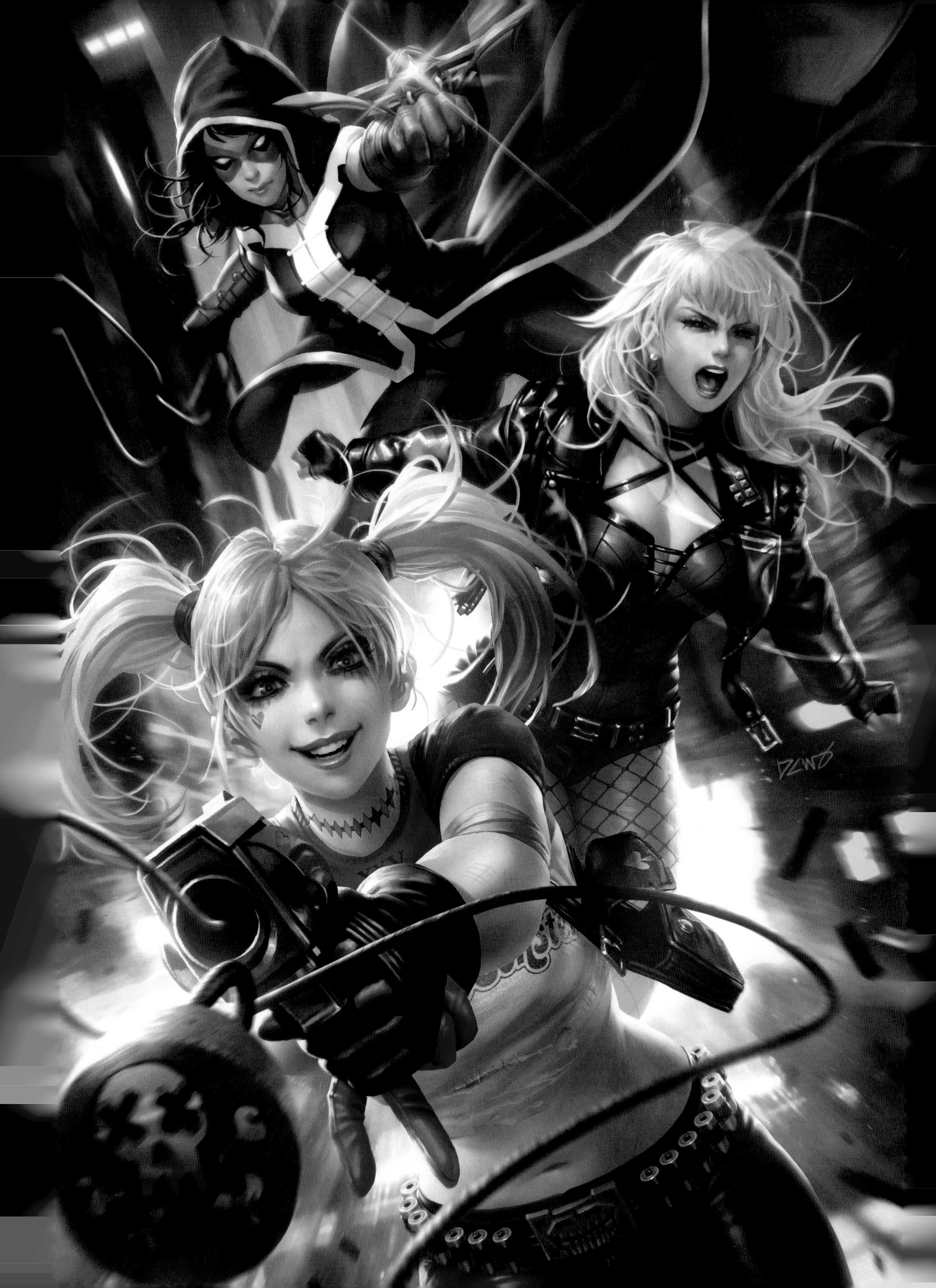

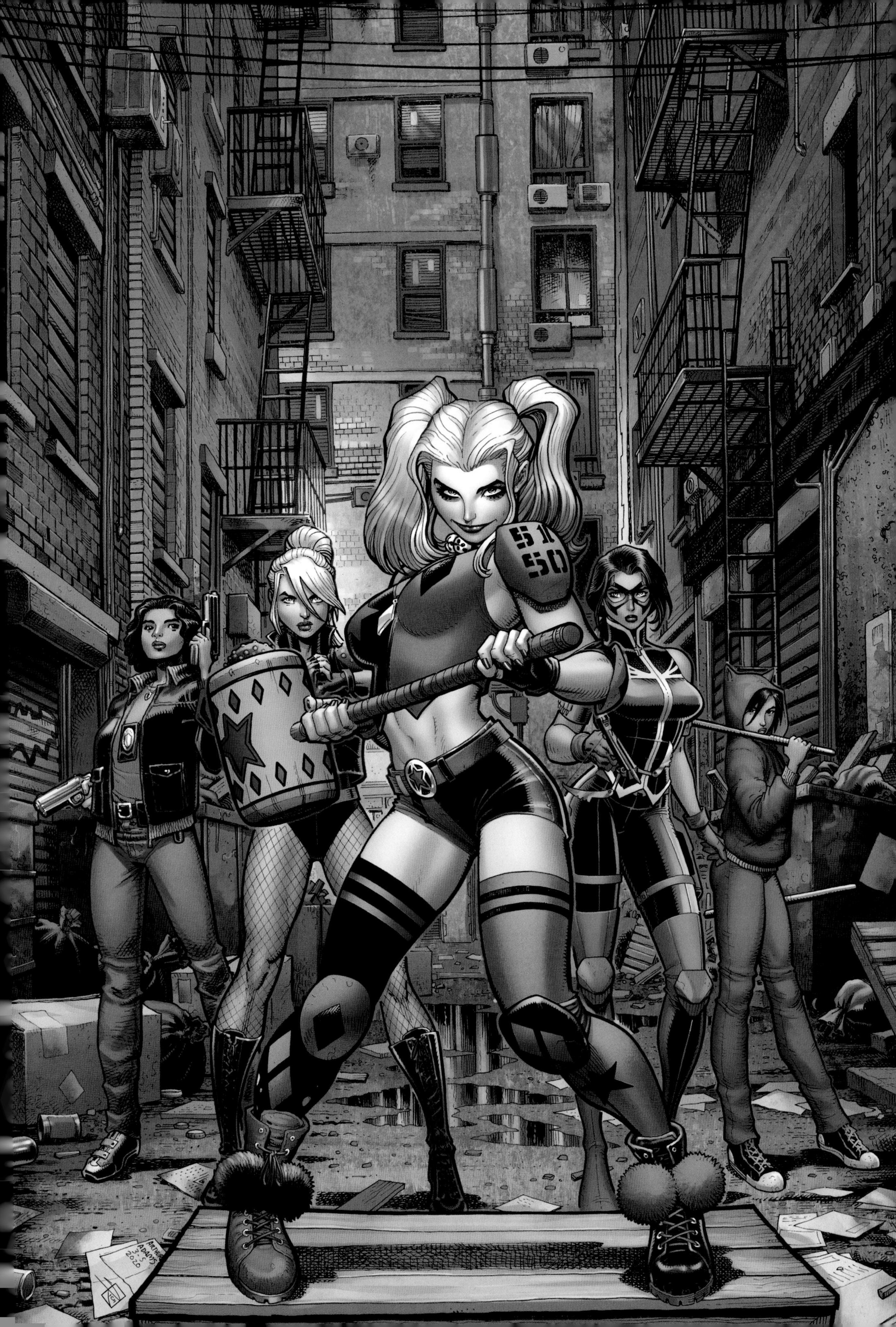
51
50

Issue #3 variant cover art by IAN MacDONALD

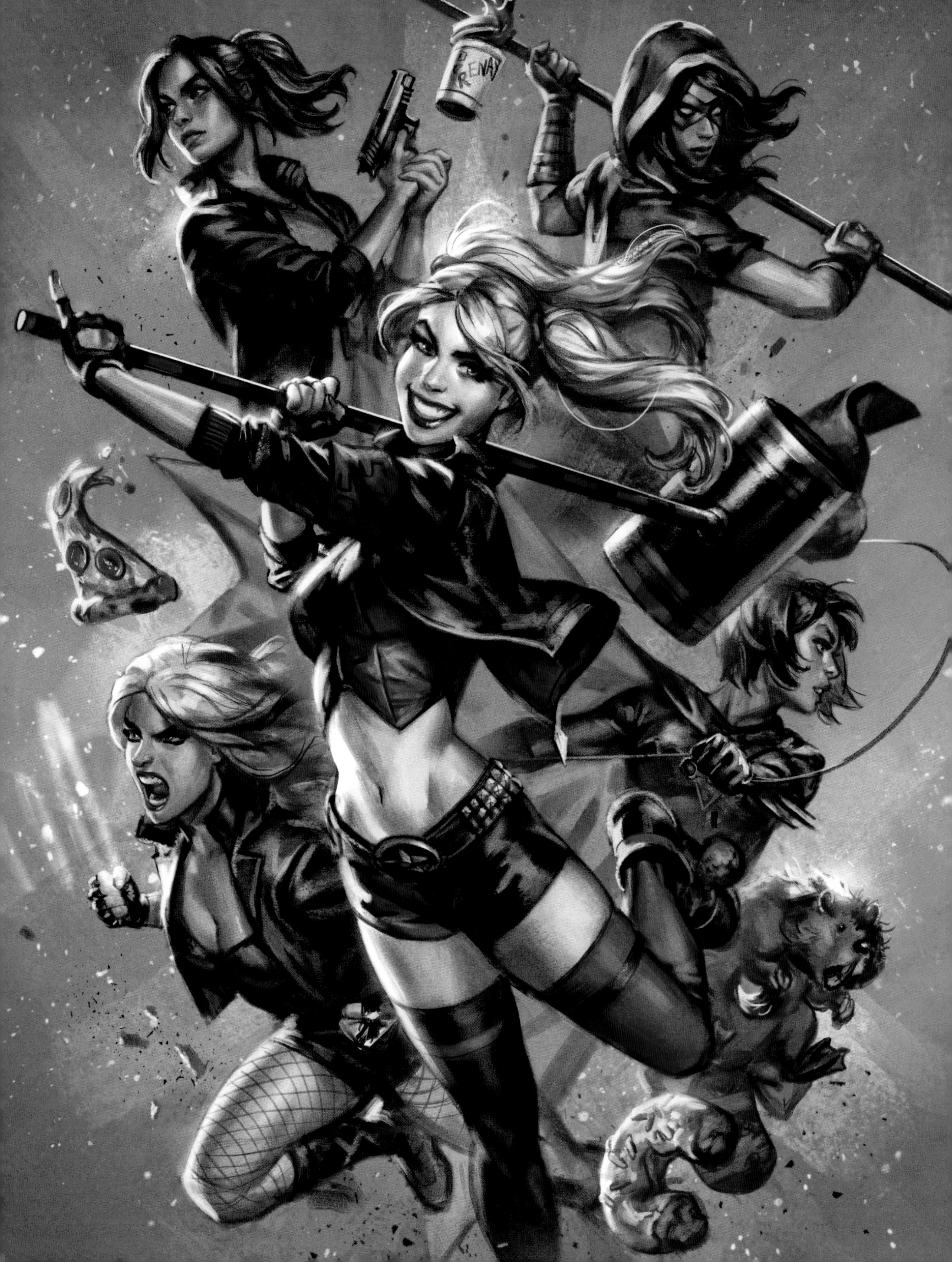

HARLEY QUINN

BLACK
and
WHITE
+
RED

CHAPTER
TWELVE

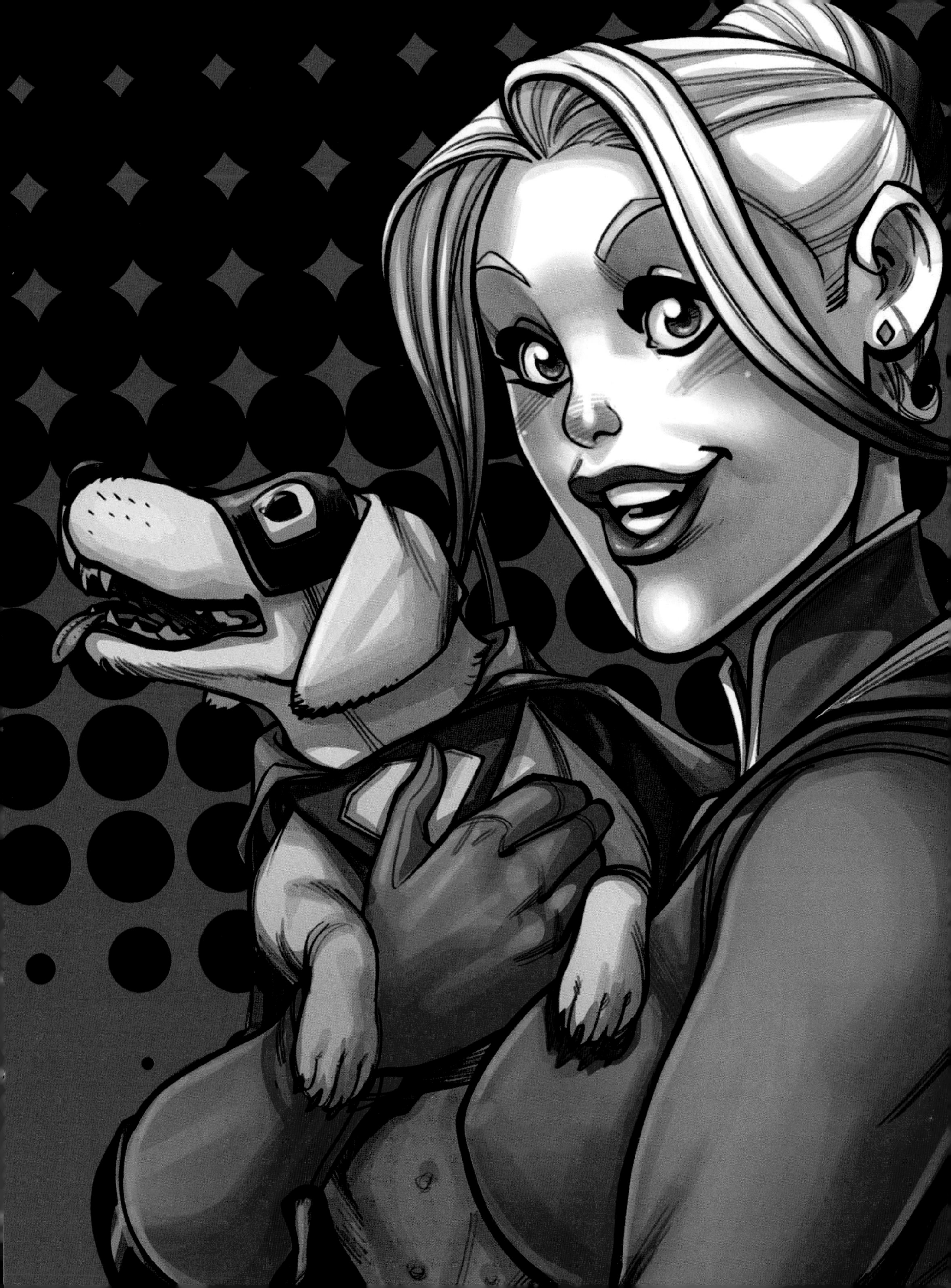

HARLEY QUINN BLACK + WHITE + RED

"HARLEY QUINN & THE ANNIHILATORS"

STORY
JIMMY PALMIOTTI
& AMANDA CONNER

ART
CHAD HARDIN

COLORS
ENRICA EREN ANGIOLINI

LETTERING
DAVE SHARPE

ASSOCIATE EDITOR
AMEDEO TURTURRO

EDITOR
CHRIS CONROY

HARLEY QUINN CREATED BY
PAUL DINI & BRUCE TIMM

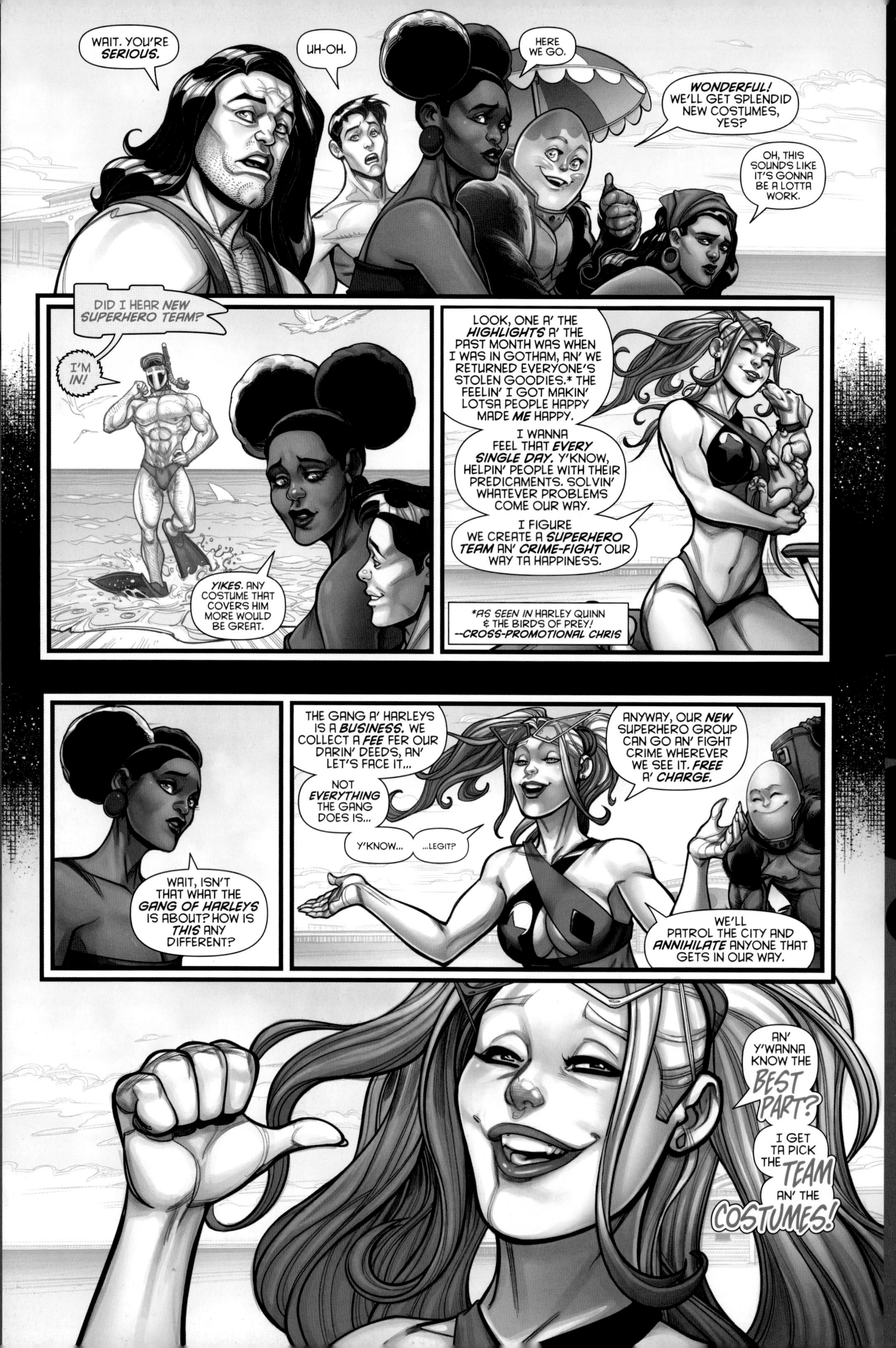
WAIT. YOU'RE SERIOUS.
UH-OH.
HERE WE GO.
WONDERFUL! WE'LL GET SPLENDID NEW COSTUMES, YES?
OH, THIS SOUNDS LIKE IT'S GONNA BE A LOTTA WORK.
DID I HEAR NEW SUPERHERO TEAM?
I'M IN!
YIKES. ANY COSTUME THAT COVERS HIM MORE WOULD BE GREAT.
LOOK, ONE A' THE HIGHLIGHTS A' THE PAST MONTH WAS WHEN I WAS IN GOTHAM, AN' WE RETURNED EVERYONE'S STOLEN GOODIES.* THE FEELIN' I GOT MAKIN' LOTSA PEOPLE HAPPY MADE ME HAPPY.
I WANNA FEEL THAT EVERY SINGLE DAY. Y'KNOW, HELPIN' PEOPLE WITH THEIR PREDICAMENTS. SOLVIN' WHATEVER PROBLEMS COME OUR WAY.
I FIGURE WE CREATE A SUPERHERO TEAM AN' CRIME-FIGHT OUR WAY TA HAPPINESS.
*AS SEEN IN HARLEY QUINN & THE BIRDS OF PREY! --CROSS-PROMOTIONAL CHRIS
WAIT, ISN'T THAT WHAT THE GANG OF HARLEYS IS ABOUT? HOW IS THIS ANY DIFFERENT?
THE GANG A' HARLEYS IS A BUSINESS. WE COLLECT A FEE FER OUR DARIN' DEEDS, AN' LET'S FACE IT...
NOT EVERYTHING THE GANG DOES IS...
Y'KNOW...
...LEGIT?
ANYWAY, OUR NEW SUPERHERO GROUP CAN GO AN' FIGHT CRIME WHEREVER WE SEE IT. FREE A' CHARGE.
WE'LL PATROL THE CITY AND ANNIHILATE ANYONE THAT GETS IN OUR WAY.
AN' Y'WANNA KNOW THE BEST PART?
I GET TA PICK THE TEAM AN' THE COSTUMES!

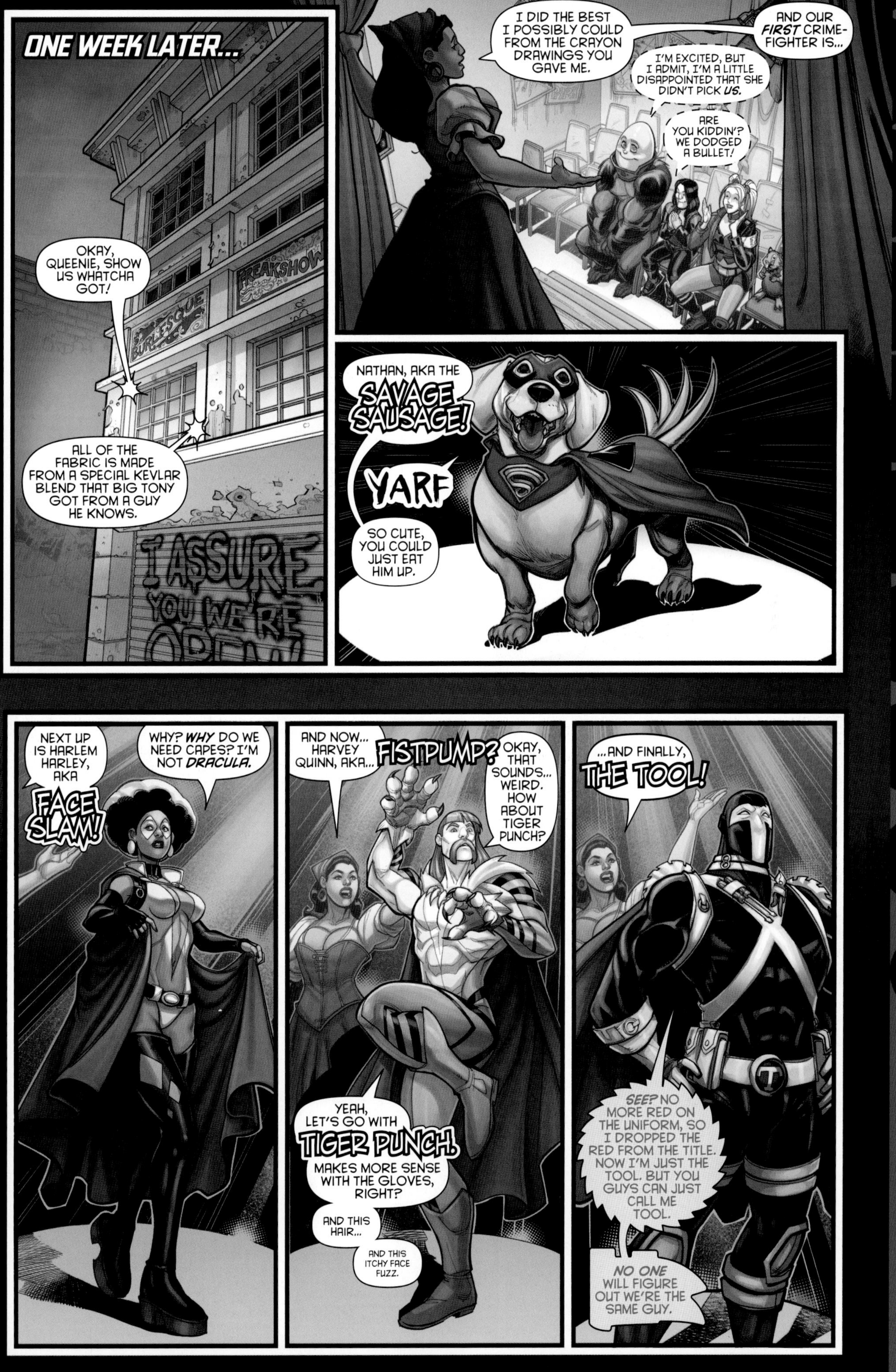
ONE WEEK LATER...
I DID THE BEST I POSSIBLY COULD FROM THE CRAYON DRAWINGS YOU GAVE ME.
AND OUR FIRST CRIME-FIGHTER IS...
I'M EXCITED, BUT I ADMIT, I'M A LITTLE DISAPPOINTED THAT SHE DIDN'T PICK US.
ARE YOU KIDDIN'? WE DODGED A BULLET!
OKAY, QUEENIE, SHOW US WHATCHA GOT!
FREAKSHOW
BURLESQUE
ALL OF THE FABRIC IS MADE FROM A SPECIAL KEVLAR BLEND THAT BIG TONY GOT FROM A GUY HE KNOWS.
I ASSURE YOU WE'RE
NATHAN, AKA THE
SAVAGE SAUSAGE!
YARF
SO CUTE, YOU COULD JUST EAT HIM UP.
NEXT UP IS HARLEM HARLEY, AKA
FACE SLAM!
WHY? WHY DO WE NEED CAPES? I'M NOT DRACULA.
AND NOW... HARVEY QUINN, AKA...
FISTPUMP?
OKAY, THAT SOUNDS... WEIRD. HOW ABOUT TIGER PUNCH?
YEAH, LET'S GO WITH
TIGER PUNCH.
MAKES MORE SENSE WITH THE GLOVES, RIGHT?
AND THIS HAIR...
AND THIS ITCHY FACE FUZZ.
...AND FINALLY,
THE TOOL!
SEE? NO MORE RED ON THE UNIFORM, SO I DROPPED THE RED FROM THE TITLE. NOW I'M JUST THE TOOL. BUT YOU GUYS CAN JUST CALL ME TOOL.
NO ONE WILL FIGURE OUT WE'RE THE SAME GUY.

OKAY, TEAM, JUST A FEW MORE MINUTES 'FORE THE SUN GOES DOWN AN' DARKNESS SETS IN. WE'LL ROAM THE CITY FIGHTIN' CRIME AS...

HARLEY QUINN AND THE ANNIHILATORS!

SO, ANY IDEAS ON WHERE TA FIND SOME *CRIME?*

THE WHITE HOUSE?

THERE'S AN ALLEYWAY IN DOWNTOWN MANHATTAN THAT'S PRETTY SKETCHY.

NOT ANYMORE. THEY PUT A FOOD TRUCK THERE. SELLS ONLY *RADISH-BASED DESSERTS*, WHICH IS A CRIME IN ITSELF.

RRR RR RAAAR RF

THE *SAVAGE SAUSAGE* CALLS IT!

THE SUBWAY IT IS! EVERYONE, TA THE **SCATAPULT!**

UUHHH... *WHAT?*

UNLESS ANY A' YOU CAN FLY, IT'S THE NEXT BEST THING.

THE Q TRAIN.

WOO-HOOOO!

HA! WE MADE IT.

~ulp~

~UHFF~

JEEZ...

NEVER... AGAIN...

UH...HEY... WHAT ABOUT TOOL...?

AAAAAAAH!

POOOM

HEY! YOU %$#@ TOOL!

Y'HEAR THAT? HE'S FAMOUS ALREADY!

YEAH, BUT WHAT DO WE DO ABOUT RED TOO--I MEAN THE TOOL?

WELL, TIGER, IT LOOKS LIKE FATE HAS DEALT HIM A CRUEL HAM.

HAND. IT'S CRUEL HAND.

I'M PRETTY SURE IT'S HAM. I'M HUNGRY. LET'S FIGHT SOME CRIME, THEN GO GET SOMETHIN' TA EAT.

NO CRIME TAKING PLACE HERE.

YOU AIN'T LOOKIN' HARD ENOUGH. I SEE A SUBWAY CAR FULLA INSOLENT EVIL-DOERS.

OR SHOULD I SAY, EVIL-DON'TERS.

SERIOUSLY, HARLEY. YOU SEEIN' SOMETHING DIFFERENT THAN I AM?

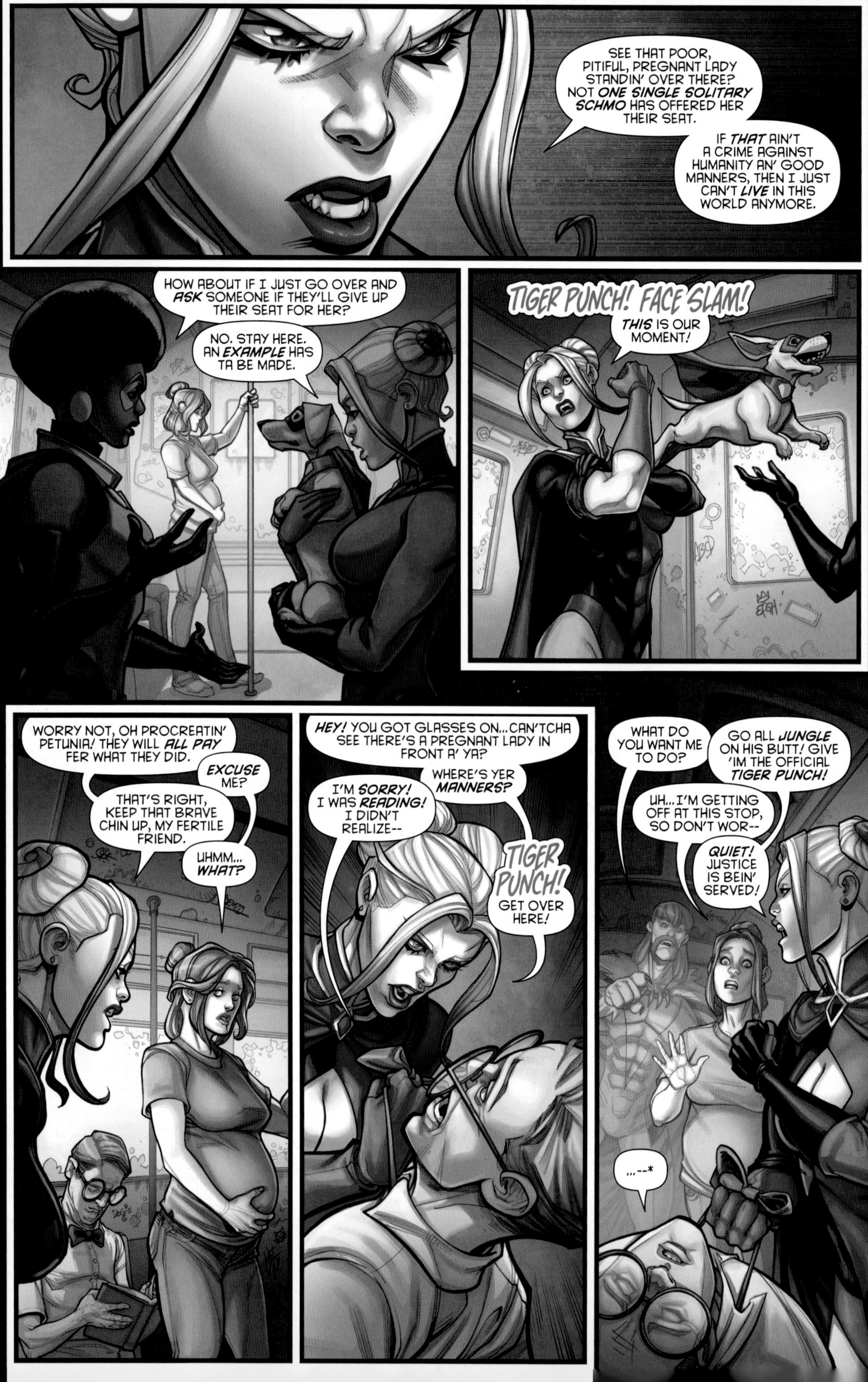

SEE THAT POOR, PITIFUL, PREGNANT LADY STANDIN' OVER THERE? NOT ONE SINGLE SOLITARY SCHMO HAS OFFERED HER THEIR SEAT.
IF THAT AIN'T A CRIME AGAINST HUMANITY AN' GOOD MANNERS, THEN I JUST CAN'T LIVE IN THIS WORLD ANYMORE.
HOW ABOUT IF I JUST GO OVER AND ASK SOMEONE IF THEY'LL GIVE UP THEIR SEAT FOR HER?
NO. STAY HERE. AN EXAMPLE HAS TA BE MADE.
TIGER PUNCH! FACE SLAM!
THIS IS OUR MOMENT!
WORRY NOT, OH PROCREATIN' PETUNIA! THEY WILL ALL PAY FER WHAT THEY DID.
EXCUSE ME?
THAT'S RIGHT, KEEP THAT BRAVE CHIN UP, MY FERTILE FRIEND.
UHMM... WHAT?
HEY! YOU GOT GLASSES ON...CAN'TCHA SEE THERE'S A PREGNANT LADY IN FRONT A' YA?
WHERE'S YER MANNERS?
I'M SORRY! I WAS READING! I DIDN'T REALIZE--
TIGER PUNCH!
GET OVER HERE!
WHAT DO YOU WANT ME TO DO?
GO ALL JUNGLE ON HIS BUTT! GIVE 'IM THE OFFICIAL TIGER PUNCH!
UH...I'M GETTING OFF AT THIS STOP, SO DON'T WOR--
QUIET! JUSTICE IS BEIN' SERVED!
...--*

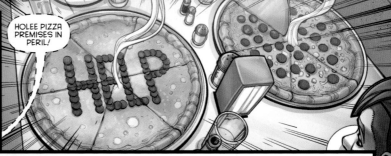

BLACK
LABEL

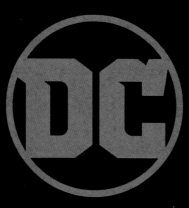